AF084543

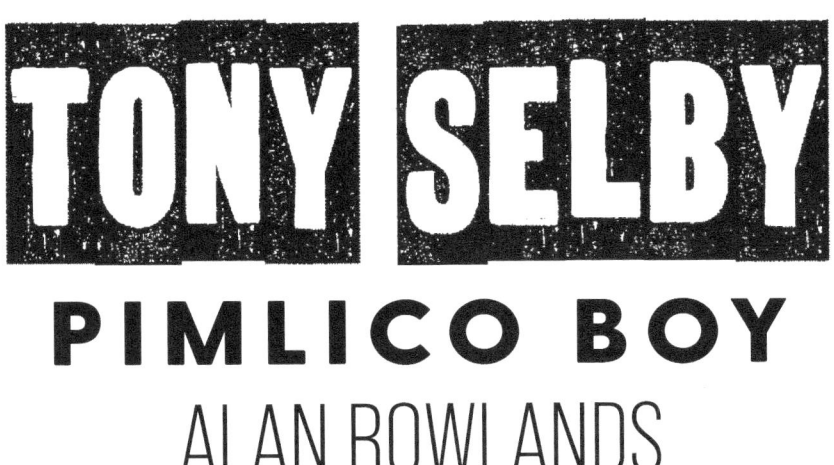

PIMLICO BOY
ALAN ROWLANDS

TONY SELBY
PIMLICO BOY

ALAN ROWLANDS

First published 2024 by DB Publishing, an imprint of JMD Media Ltd, Nottingham, United Kingdom.

Copyright 2024 © ALAN ROWLANDS

All Rights Reserved. No part of this publication may be reproduced, stored in a retrieval system, or transmitted in any form, or by any means, electronic, mechanical, photocopying, recording or otherwise without the prior permission in writing of the copyright holders, nor be otherwise circulated in any form or binding or cover other than in which it is published and without a similar condition being imposed on the subsequent publisher.

ISBN 978-1-78091-647-7

Printed in the UK

FROM THE AUTHOR

I first met Tony Selby in the 1980s at a party given by a mutual friend, Tony at that time was still enjoying a varied and successful acting career. He had an aura of confidence , he had charm, quick wit but also a genuine modesty.

We got on well, through our common interests, football, books and art. and of course theatre, then as we became close and firm friends lots of red wine, beer and lots of good food shared with our families and friends.

One afternoon we met up at another gathering when he arrived he strode over to me with a beaming smile.

"Hello mate, I want you to help me write my autobiography. what do you think?"

I had a couple of projects on the go but suggested we could have a more constructive conversation away from the madding crowd, thus began a regular journey over to Marble Arch clutching on to my iPad and note books.

Over a period of four years we delved into his life, laughed at his career anecdotes and stories or reflected earnestly on his family life. Although I knew Tony well, I was unaware of his enormous contribution to the ground breaking early work with Ken Loach and Tony Garnett, then his involvement with the Royal Court Theatre. He also had roles in some of the most surreal film and bizarre television productions.

It might seem four years is a long time to be working on a project but this period was punctuated by lengthy periods of ill health, both his then my own.

We finished the final draft of the book when Tony's health was deteriorating rapidly, we hoped to publish it while he would still be able to complete a busy schedule of interviews, it became increasingly obvious he would be unable to do so.

His family were having to deal with the constant demands of his medical care.

After Tony's death in 2021 the finished project was put aside.

Over time I was constantly asked about the story by some of his closest acting colleagues and friends, who all thought his life and career should be remembered.

I began to think they were right.

'Hello mate , I 've now written your biography"

Please enjoy Tony's legacy, Pimlico Boy.

Thanks to Jacqui Selby, Gina Selby, Sam Selby, Matt Selby, Sally and Tony Osoba, Johnny Wade, and Shirin Ghadialy.

More thanks to Isobel Harris. Jake Whittam. Joanne Cassidy.

Finally to Steve Caron, Michelle Grainger, Matthew Limbert and all at DB Publishing.

Cover Design by Paul Warrington.

FOR ALISTAIR AND BRUCE.

INTRODUCTION

Tony Selby was an admired and popular character actor who was born in Pimlico, London, in 1938.

He attended the Italia Conti Stage School, making his professional stage debut in *Peter Pan* when he was just 12 years old, then he went on to make his first television appearance in 1950.

In the 1960s he rose to stardom and national recognition through his collaboration with the director Ken Loach and producer Tony Garnett in the BBC Wednesday Play productions, *Three Clear Sundays* and *Up the Junction*, the former dealing with capital punishment and the latter abortion. Both films would have a profound and lasting social impact.

Following on from his work at the BBC, Selby was invited to join the English Stage Company at the Royal Court Theatre where in his debut play, *Saved* by Edward Bond, he became embroiled in controversy when the production was banned by the censors under the Theatre Act. Such was the furore from actors, writers, producers, and critics in protest against the act, the play was central in bringing an end to censorship in the theatre. Tony starred in the 1970s hit television series *Get Some In!* and the 1980s show Love Hurts, and also became a cult figure in *Doctor Who* through his character Sabalom Glitz.

He made over 500 television appearances in a career spanning eight decades during which time he co-starred in major films with Richard Burton, David Niven, and Vincent Price.

Tony was also an accomplished musical performer and appeared in many high-profile and successful musical theatre productions.

This is his full story, from his postwar childhood as the son of a firebrand London cab driver and a hard-working benevolent mother to his friendships with Peter O'Toole, Albert Finney and Richard Harris.

This is a story written with warmth, candour, and humour.

'Let us suppose we are confronted by a desperate thing – say Pimlico. If we feel what is really best for Pimlico, we shall find the thread of thought leads to the throne of the mystic and the arbitrary. It is not enough for a man to disapprove of Pimlico; in that case he will merely cut his throat or move to Chelsea. Nor, certainly, is it enough for a man to approve of Pimlico, for then it would remain Pimlico, which would be awful. The only way out of it seems to be for somebody to love Pimlico, to live with a transcendental tie and without any earthly reason. If there arose a man who loved Pimlico, then Pimlico would rise into ivory towers and gold pinnacles.'

Orthodoxy – G.K. Chesterton

1
PIMLICO

Thomas Farrier was a baker. King Charles II was his top customer.

After a hard day's work on 1 September 1666 he shuffled up to bed while his maid was dampening down the ovens. She was probably a bit tired herself. Her lack of attention resulted in the ovens not being dampened down properly which was not a good thing if your premises were mainly constructed from wood and straw.

Because the embers were not fully extinguished, sparks floated upwards to the dry timbered roof which caught fire. It spread quickly from the bakery in Pudding Lane and soon the entire city was ablaze; so started the Great Fire of London. It is not known if the poor maid survived the fire but if she did, she probably missed out on a Christmas bonus.

It wasn't all bad news though. The fire devastated the rat population, the cause of the bubonic plague pandemic the previous year, and destroyed hundreds of unsanitary homes and dwellings.

It was also good news for Mary Davies, a 12-year-old who had just inherited an area of land to the west of the city. The land was Crown Estate, leased out by James I to civil servants before he decided to flog it off. Mary's family bought most of the land, which became known as Ebury or the Five Fields, then later as Belgravia, Mayfair, and Knightsbridge. So not a bad deal then.

The West End of London was not particularly popular or fashionable at the time, but after the fire demand for land greatly increased as did the family wealth.

Unsurprisingly, Mary's guardians were fending off suitors and chancers constantly until eventually she was married off to Thomas Grosvenor who somehow materialised from a fairly obscure family in Cheshire.

Shortly after the marriage, Ebury became known as Pimlico.

The source of the name is a bit of a mystery; no one seems to be sure of its origin or derivation. It has been speculated that the area was named after a man called Ben Pimlico, a brewer of some repute, but his brewery and ale houses were in the East End around Hoxton. He did however deliver his beers and ales to other areas of London, while several customers would regularly walk through the park land along what was known as the Pimlico Path to imbibe in the pubs.

The name is certainly of foreign extraction. There are suggestions it came from pirates who were recruiting men and raising finance for adventures to the Spanish Main. They would hold court in the taverns drinking rum from Pimlico kegs.

Whatever the origin, Mary and Thomas began to develop the West End, and the Grosvenor family became very wealthy indeed. Their descendants commissioned the architect Thomas Cubitt to design and build what would become the heart of the area, the magnificent grid of streets with stunning townhouses.

At the beginning of the 20th century the area was attracting actors, artists and because of the proximity to the House of Commons, a powerhouse of politicians.

When Dolphin Square was built in 1938, residents included Winston Churchill and Oswald Mosley. Just up the road on Millbank the Labour Party and the trade union movement all had premises as headquarters.

At St Saviours Church where the Rev Gerald Olivier was the minister, he was often assisted by his son Laurence.

Just around the corner from Dolphin Square was a less-salubrious development built by the Westminster Trust – seven blocks of flats known as the Tachbrook Estate.

1938 was an interesting year. The theory of relativity had been finally accepted, which pleased Mr Einstein no end, the FA Cup Final and Test cricket were televised for the first time, and the ocean liner *Queen Elizabeth* was launched from its slipway in Clydebank. In Germany a smallish man with a distinctive moustache was becoming agitated and aggressive.

While all this excitement was taking place, Anthony Samuel Selby was born at St Thomas' Hospital. One other interesting fact about 1938: y-fronts were invented. If you were left-handed, it was suggested it might be advisable to wear the underpants inside out. Now one thing life would teach young Anthony, if nothing else, was that all men become ambidextrous if they need to get to their John Thomas in a hurry.

2
THE SELBYS AND THE WEAVERS

When the 19th century had handed the baton to the 20th and about the time Queen Victoria popped her clogs to join up with Albert at last, two men were criss-crossing their way over the bridges of the Thames, both east and west, on their horse-drawn vehicles. The one driving the Hackney carriage was Sam Selby. The Selbys were originally from Yorkshire but by the time Sam was born in 1878, the family had been living in south London for around 40 years.

The family business had started when they purchased a second-hand carriage from a private estate. They would have painted out the old markings with cheap black paint and then rented a horse from a local livery. Between them, and the horse, they earned a reasonable living, particularly as the carriage was the main form of private transport. Things moved on quickly. The Hackneys were aged contraptions, or disparately designed, and the newer and more uniform Hanson cabs began to displace them. The Selbys acquired a couple of the new vehicles and so began the family vocation as cabbies, or individually, a cabbie.

The term relates to the carriage design known as a cabriolet, then abbreviated to cab. Sam's cab was one of the first to be fitted with a clockwork device which measured fares. It was called a taximeter; the taxicab was created.

The other man driving his horse and cart across the bridges was Richard Weaver, who was originally from Kent before the family moved to Sydenham some time in the 1880s. As sole proprietor, Richard's business was haulage for local shops and factories. He had an unfortunate start as a haulage magnate. After paying £50 for his first horse, a significant amount of money, he found a stable. Folowing a good feed and water they set off on their first commercial venture and the business began well, with Richard and dobbin clip-clopping along the cobbled streets. Unfortunately after a few days the horse suddenly keeled over and snuffed it, thereafter turned into pots of glue. He was luckier with the next horse and began to earn a decent living. The Selbys and the Weavers eventually became near neighbours, their horses also neighing nearby. Both families were practising Catholics and they certainly did practice, finishing with a score draw of 12 kids each. In the house they all took turns to breathe.

Sam Selby was born on 27 February 1908, Anne Weaver in June of the following year. Despite the *coitus interruptus* programme not being an entire success within the families, the Weavers were probably the stauncher members of the Catholic Church. Anne and her family attended mass on a regular basis, while both she and Sam attended a school attached to Westminster Cathedral. Anne proved to be a keen and attentive pupil; Sam was untroubled by pedagogy. He preferred life and adventure away from scholastic confines, so he ducked and dived, ran errands for a few pennies, or helped to clean out his dad's cab and feed the horse.

Sam enjoyed exploring the riverside along the banks of the Thames. He liked to scramble through the ruins of the old Millbank Prison then on to the towpath, making his way towards the Lambeth or Waterloo bridges passing the old taverns, rickety wharves, rope makers and all manner of riparian activities.

He got to know the area well, finding shortcuts through secluded mews unchanged for a century or more, excited by the changes on the river. The water traffic was changing quickly, sailing barges replaced by steamboats while puffing tugboats headed towards the growing dock area to nudge and cajole the ships towards the estuary releasing them to the sea.

The Great War had just ended when Sam had begun his little adventures. When the Selby and Weaver families faced Christmas 1918, they had both lost sons, cousins, uncles, and friends. They had to regroup, take stock and with great fortitude continued their lives.

In 1919, Sam for some reason or another became an altar boy at Westminster Cathedral. The sole task of the altar boys was to hold the candles and assist with the paraphernalia during mass, while at the same time trying to keep out of the way during services to avoid tripping or causing a stumble from a passing bishop. In contrast the choir were from completely different backgrounds, coming from much wealthier families and having their own school within the cathedral grounds.

The more streetwise kids like to torment the posh boy choir, flicking ears as the choristers were passing or putting drawing pins on benches. The choir master would constantly give the altar boys a bollocking but new ways to annoy the choir boys had to be found. Clothing was hidden, socks had the ends cut off, shoe polish put on the inside of shoes.

Inevitably, a senior priest from the archbishop's office would be called, lining up the altar boys and asking who the culprits were. No one grassed. The miscreants just looked like young angels. If one of them had done, though, they might well have become an angel a lot quicker than they had expected.

It was at the cathedral that Sam had his first glimpse of privilege and class structure. He had not really thought about it before, not that it had bothered him much. To most families it was toffs and us, but at an early age Sam was looking at things through different eyes.

He was aware of the sumptuous meals being served and fine wines being quaffed by the priests and staff. Sam stayed at the cathedral for three years until he left school at the age of 14, without any qualifications or ambition but with a simmering anger.

Anne left school a year later, having passed her matriculation exams, then met Sam. They became childhood sweethearts.

During this early courtship, Anne encouraged Sam to read more, which he did with some enthusiasm and even joined the library.

His first job after leaving school was at Watney Brewery in Victoria. Sam Selby senior had given up the cab trade – horse-drawn vehicles were being replaced by motor vehicles; he had always worked with horses and among the few businesses that still used them were the breweries to pull the drays. Sam senior looked after the stables and grooming, and Sam junior's first job was shovelling shit into bags and changing straw.

Young Sam soon became bored at the brewery and took a job as a road sweeper with Westminster Council. He also joined the Transport and General Workers' Union (TGWU), soon becoming an activist and a shop steward.

Through the TGWU he attended sponsored workshops and, having immersed himself in socialist literature, by the time he was 21 he was awarded a Tolpuddle Marty award for his commitment to trade unionism.

In the meantime Anne had joined a leather goods retailer after leaving school and became busy designing and making bags and coats by hand. Although not mentally challenging, she had a flair for the well-paid work, while she was also making a significant contribution to the Weaver household. Anne was supportive of Sam's political stance and union commitments; he was gaining confidence and his intellect was sharpening.

They agreed that before they were to marry Sam needed a job that would bring in more money, so in the family tradition he decided to become a cabbie. While still working for the council, he bought himself a bicycle and, in the evenings and at the weekends, he began to learn the 'Knowledge' of London.

The 'Knowledge' is the process which all London taxi drivers then and now need to complete to qualify for a licence and badge. It is a formidable challenge, demanding physically and mentally, an endurance test set by the Public Carriage Office.

Each candidate is required to work their way from a six-mile radius of Charing Cross memorising all the main public buildings and railway stations. They also had to know all the side streets, the theatres sequentially up Shaftesbury Avenue and beyond, then the pubs, the clubs and the sports stadia. In just two years he earned his badge, he left the council job, bought his first cab, picked up his first fare, joined the Communist Party and married Anne.

As the 1930s progressed the political situation in Europe was becoming interesting, but politically and socially, the times were changing in Pimlico.

At the turn of the century the place still had a significant affluent population, However, when Laurence Olivier's dad moved in , a considerable part of his pastoral duties involved him working with the poorer families in the slum areas. Several charitable housing projects were started, mainly by Peabody Estates, who constructed social housing.

Unemployment was still a problem, and those with jobs were hardly on a high wage, so as a consequence the labour movement and the communist party became increasingly active. Sam was more active than most, helping to organise fundraising events and rallies. He was, however, reined in by Anne when in July 1932, they had a daughter called Kathy. The couple were living in a small flat just off Vauxhall Bridge Road and with the responsibility of a child, Sam had to put more energy into cabbing for a while.

Another Pimlico resident was also putting his energy into his own project. From Dolphin Square, Oswald Mosley had formed the British Union of Fascists. They were gaining support around the country, but at first, they were mainly causing problems in London's East End, then active in Battersea and Vauxhall.

As Mosley marched at the head of his 'black shirts', Sam and his mates began organising counter demonstrations or outright confrontation. To his wife's annoyance and great concern, he also became involved in several violent skirmishes. Fortunately he was never arrested by the police, many of whom were sympathetic to Mosley's politics.

Things seemed to have settled down a little in 1938 but Anne was about to experience her second parturition, just to shake their lives a little. When Anthony Samuel Selby was born, the man with the moustache in Germany had become a monstrous despot, and to celebrate the baby's first birthday, Hitler had signed a non-aggression pact with Joseph Stalin which really pissed off Sam. Then, six months later, the second world war started.

For the boy's second birthday, Adolf decided to celebrate by bombing London. Shortly afterwards, the evacuation of the city began.

Sam joined the Royal Air Force as a driver, no surprise there then, and was posted to an airbase at South Cerney which the RAF would eventually share with the USA Air Force.

Cirencester is a small town about 90 miles north-west of London, geographically in the heart of the Cotswolds, but was just a short distance from the airbase. Many London families were evacuated to the pretty town nestled in the banks of the River Churn. Anne, Kathy, and Anthony were placed with a family who lived in Chesterton Lane. It was to be their home for the next two years, although Sam was not around for most of the time; he was a visitor as often as he could be, in his blue grey uniform, always with gifts and goody parcels from the air base. These became more exotic when the Americans came – chocolates, toys and clothing.

Anthony started at Cirencester Infant School; the classes were larger than normal with the local kids being squeezed up to accommodate the incomers. His first memories would be of the cacophony of tin drums and triangles and high-pitched voices that could have cracked a Spitfire's cockpit windscreen as they danced and pranced around the classroom.

Kathy was attending the junior school just up the road, way ahead of her brother in her education, and in the evenings she would read him stories in their shared bedroom and encouraged him to read.

Just as the Selbys were getting used to life in the Cotswolds the war turned in the Allies' favour, Sam went to France to drive at the head of convoys while his family returned to Pimlico where they had been allocated a flat on the Tachbrook Estate, a development of seven five-storey blocks built by the Westminster Trust. They had become beneficiaries of Mary and Thomas Grosvenor's legacy some 300 years later. They moved into a two-bedroomed flat in Tuttle House where Sam joined them on his demobilisation in 1945.

While the family had experienced a fairly comfortable war away from London, the Selby and Weaver families as a whole had been devastated.

Their grandparents had stayed in their small, terraced home in Strutton Ground. One day the air raid sirens had wailed a warning of an attack, for some extraordinary reason, Anne's brother Dennis decided to drag his bike on a flat roof at the rear of the house to change a tyre. It was dusk, they had been through several false alarms and had become a little blasé about things, but their parents suggested he came down just in case, though he stayed put. Within minutes a bomb hit the row of terraces. All they found of Dennis was his 17-year-old head two streets away. Their parents were trapped under a large wooden beam for several hours, and when they were eventually released her mother's right leg was found to be badly crushed. The doctors wanted to amputate immediately but she refused them permission. Anne's father had been a little luckier – he had severe bruising and also suffered damage to his spinal vertebrae.

Anne's parents were eventually rehoused in a flat in one of the Tachbrook blocks, but her mother's leg became infected with gangrene. The family members would take turns to clean and dress her wound each day. Anthony Selby became haunted with the memory of his grandmother lying on her bed; she weighed next to nothing, she was gaunt and grey, and he would always remember the overwhelming stench from her rotting flesh. She died in 1945, and his grandad would walk with a pronounced limp for the remainder of his life.

On the Selby side of the family, his father's younger brother John had been captured when the British Expeditionary Force was annihilated by the German Army in France. He was sent to a prisoner of war camp from where he spent two years attempting to escape. In the best traditions of POW camps, escape committees were formed. John became involved as an escape coordinator and despite some daring and imaginative plans, they experienced failure after failure. It became obvious there was an informer in the camp, and he was eventually identified and found with his throat cut, a razor in his hand. John escaped shortly afterwards, then repatriated to the UK, but he was never the same or sane person after return, suffering from deep depression and mood swings.

He tried to take his own life by jumping out of a third-storey window, landing on a spiked railing. The impact ripped off his right arm as he then crashed down the casement stairs. John was eventually committed to the Hanwell Mental Institution where he died shortly after being admitted. He had slit his own throat. The family knew he could not bear the guilt of murdering a man.

Anthony's uncle, Wally Weaver, was a gregariously talented man. He had attended the Italia Conti School for child actors and entertainers in his younger years. When the war began, he could have become a member of ENSA, the armys' entertaining unit, but he chose to join a fighting regiment. He finished up in North Africa with the 8th Army. The fighting there was fierce, close-up and personal. During one skirmish a German hand grenade landed in the middle of Wally's unit, and instinctively he dived on top of it, taking the full force of the blast. Where's Wally indeed?

Just as in 1918, in 1945 the Selby and Weaver families faced peacetime depleted and saddened.

Anthony was seven on VE Day. There was a mission hall on Tachbrook Estate, festooned in bunting and flags, and as the day progressed tables and chairs were dragged from the hall. Alcoholic drinks materialised, more than had been available for years, then the music and the songs started. The young boy was captivated. The whole of the seven blocks of flats were involved; accordions, banjos, trumpets and even a couple of battered pianos appeared. The sound of hundreds of people singing the old musical songs seemed wonderful, and even a couple of ancient gramophones appeared blaring out scratchy jazz music.

As twilight came and the temperature dropped, fires were lit, as they dimmed with the wood stock diminishing, trestle tables were dragged from the hall and thrown on to the embers. This was followed by more raids on the table and chair stock until the fire was roaring again in orange and yellow glory. Nothing was to spoil this magnificent and raucous special day.

Young Anthony noticed a few couples in various doorways and slightly concealed stairwells going through an odd but enthusiastic dance routine. He learned later in life it was called the 'knee trembler'.

3
ITALIA CONTI

The Summer of 1945 was one of continuous celebrations. Servicemen and women were returning home in their thousands with demob parties taking place most of the time.

The whole of Pimlico was in a permanent party preparation but at the age of seven, Anthony was unaware of alliteration. The two families joined in the fun at every opportunity, contributing to the songs and music. Various aunts and uncles all seemed to have some musical or vocal talent to be able to knock out a song or tune.

Anthony was enthralled by it all. The children sat on up turned beer crates normally in pyjamas and dressing gowns. The old London songs would start as a communal, undisciplined wail until the more accomplished songsters would belt out a more modern ballad. The boy fell in love with the dramatic voice of Al Jolson and songs like 'Ragtime Cowboy Joe'.

In the morning he would wake up thinking he had dreamt it all, but he hadn't of course. Like all the other kids he had fallen asleep as tiredness closed in and they were carried off to bed. The words and music stayed in his head, ear worms burrowing and music buzzing inside his young brain. He remembered every note and syllable.

In the Autumn, life settled down a little, and Anthony resumed his schooling at Millbank Junior School, a two-storey, red-bricked Victorian building that squeezed in around 300 children and a few teachers. This was to be the beginning of his formal education.

At Cirencester Infant School it had been all about playing games, basic reading, and sums, all without any discernible discipline. It was also proved to be a strange experience, returning to his place of birth for which he had no real memory.

The fairly parochial and relatively peaceful atmosphere of Gloucestershire had now been replaced by this crowded, bustling energetic area of London. Anthony's transition was helped by the fact that because most of his new school mates had also been evacuees or had been displaced during the war years, they were able to assimilate and integrate into Millbank education fairly easily.

In the grown-up world things were moving. Another former resident of Pimlico had been kicked out of 10 Downing Street and Parliament with the rest of the Conservative Party. While Winston Churchill licked his wounds, the Labour Party swept into power.

Postwar Britain was austere. It was economically destitute. The infrastructure of the country had been run down and then abandoned by the privateers who had profited most from the conflict. Sam Selby caught up again with his communist party mates who had battled against Mosley, forming a sort of amalgamated grouping with the Jewish League and peripheral socialist groups. The flat was filled with boxes of pamphlets and manifesto literature such as Marx's Critique of the Gotha Programme and a host of other Marxist-Leninist propaganda. From the flat the stuff was taken to Hyde Park Corner, distributed among the crowds while Sam and his cohorts literally stood on soap boxes bellowing.

Sam was convinced he was being monitored by the British and American intelligence services. He probably was, on a very small scale, but he was never confronted or indeed questioned by the security people. He was probably very disappointed he had not been. While Sam continued with his agitprop activity, Anne, Kathy and Anthony looked ahead to their own future. Anne had long ago left her work with the leather wholesalers to bring up the family but now she had to design and make leather gear on her own. Working from a makeshift workshop in the corner of the living room she was knocking out leather goods for the ladies of the estate, most of whom carried a Selby designer handbag.

Kathy was a few years educationally and mentally ahead of her brother, but they were very close. A confident and intelligent girl, she had developed a keen interest in music and dancing. Kathy had started piano lessons and together with two cousins, Eileen and Dolly, she began regular dance lessons at a studio in Vauxhall.

At Christmas and family gatherings the girls went through the routines they had learned then Kathy decided to get her brother involved, first teaching him a few rudimentary dance steps then encouraging him to sing a couple of Al Jolson songs. Unfortunately he was 'blacked up' with some burnt cork. They progressed to become a troupe to play in local hospitals or old folks homes, their confidence growing as they expanded a more varied repertoire. Then they began to have some success in local talent competitions.

During the long summer school breaks, there were few families who could afford to have a holiday away. The council started holiday at home programmes for the school children, while their dad worked in his cab and mum stitched up cowhides, so Anthony and Kathy, together with Eileen and Dolly, were under the care of Westminster Council.

From nine in the morning they registered their name and address, put on a blue, red, green, or yellow ribbon, then were directed to a group wearing the same colour, then organised into teams for football, cricket or netball. Painting classes were held, then a puppet show suddenly appeared. On Friday, in the afternoon, a talent competition was held. Kathy and Anthony entered the first competition. She performed a tap and song routine, and he came on in full Al Jolson outfit to sing 'Mammy' and won. The following week he did the same act and won again. On the third week Anthony was all prepared to do it once more when another boy came on before him doing the same routine and won. He was devastated but not for long, as the following week he performed 'Ragtime Cowboy Joe' and won again.

Anne and Sam had a good chat, and with Kathy's encouragement, they concluded that Anthony might well benefit from some professional tuition. In 1948 they organised an audition at the Italia Conti School.

The school had been formed in 1910. Italia Conti had been a successful actress and had once worked in a production of a very successful musical play called *Where the Rainbow Ends*. The show had a huge cast, most of whom were children. During her involvement with the production, she became aware that child actors were receiving no form of education in that period. She began to provide them with basic lessons.

Teaching children training for theatre and entertainment became her vocation. With donations from her considerable connections and patrons, Italia set up a studio in Great Portland Street known grandly as the Italia Conti School of Theatre and Arts. Italia became the most influential figure in children's theatre, not only influencing legislation relating the ages of child actors but also the working conditions and tutoring.

In 1930 her niece Ruth arrived in London from Australia and became an integral member of the school organisation and future.

When the Luftwaffe blew the premises to nothingness in 1941, the school was moved to Bournemouth to start up again by the seaside. It ticked over, managing to keep solvent until they could move back to London and into new premises in Archer Street near the Windmill Theatre. Italia then rather sadly died. Anthony turned up for his audition when Ruth had taken charge. He arrived with his parents, took one look at the queue of other hopefuls and bottled it, scuttling home in utter humiliation.

The following year he moved to senior school at Buckingham Gate Secondary School where he settled in well, with enough friends from the Millbank and the estate starting at the same time. Buckingham Gate had a mixed London and Irish Catholic grouping and was also co-education. The school was perhaps somewhat rough but not too tough. When Anthony was given the role of King Herod in the school play he was not singled out in the playground as a 'poof'. His skill at football helped and his back was always going to be covered by the more pugilistic Tachbrook allies.

The year after fleeing from Archer Street, his mother in particular suggested he should try again for entry into the Italia Conti. His father offered to drive him over, but feeling a lot more confident, he jumped on to the number 2 bus to take him to the audition queue. This time he stayed.

There was a line of kids spilling from the entrance and along the street, most of them with bossy and arrogant parents. The entrance from Archer Street led up a flight of stairs leading to a sort of reception area and then various classrooms and studios spread over two floors.

Occasionally a staff member would come out to check what was going on, fuss a little, then quickly disappear back up the stairs. Anthony looked around at his fellow hopefuls; some had music arrangements clasped tight to their chests as if they were so unique that the world would be changed forever by their version of 'It's Magic' or 'Buttons and Bows'. They also clutched satchels containing dance pumps and tights.

Anthony had some arrangements Kathy had helped to choose; that was about it as he slowly ascended the stairs, smiling awkwardly at people he didn't know. At the top of the stairs he could hear the sounds of pianos and young voices in songs, until he passed through the studio doors to fill in a registration form. He then passed into a beautiful rectangular studio and when he walked on to the polished wooden floor it pushed up a minute cloud of dust and chalk, an odour that he would maintain lived in his nostrils for ever. Maybe it was just sweaty armpits and cheesy feet.

He was ushered into a group of around a dozen girls and boys. They were all lined up and asked to begin tap dancing so when the music started so did he. The girls had taught him well. Kathy had also taught him to jive, a variation on the jitterbug, a dance to become more popular over the next few years.

When the orchestrated tap concluded, Anthony started a spontaneous jive with one of the girls while most of the others looked on thinking he was a precocious arse. He then had to sing a short melody of songs; his choices were Billy Eckstein numbers learned from records Sam had picked up.

At the end of the late afternoon Anthony was offered a place at Italia Conti as a Saturday kid. In actual fact he would be attending on Wednesday evenings as well, but his group of part-timers were always known as the Saturday kids by the more precocious full-timers. After signing up the consent papers, Sam and Anne then had to pay the fees of 30 shillings a week then also had to fund trips to Charing Cross Road to buy sheet music.

Ruth Conti was a charming, attractive woman, but with a business hardness. Her main attention reasonably was with the full-time students, closeted away in hidden classrooms or parts of the studios not seen or explored by the part-timers. For young Anthony it didn't really matter – he was there to learn.

The person who became his mentor was the voice coach and main pianist, Helen Vokes, a kindly patrician woman. Helen always wore dark grey suits or the same dark grey suit, invariably covered with a shower of ash from the endless cigarettes planted between her ruby red lips. Helen had been at the school for many years. When Anthony had first been accepted, she had looked the new entrant over.

'You know, Anthony, you do so remind me of someone.' Anthony's uncle, Wally, had been a pupil at the school. Helen realised immediately.

'Walter Weaver. How is he?'

When Helen heard that Wally had been killed in North Africa, she nodded sadly, a tearful mist filling her kind eyes. It transpired her own son, a 20-year-old Spitfire pilot, had been shot down and perished during the Battle of Britain.

Helen, or Vokesy as she was known, was an absolutely committed teacher, and under her guidance Anthony's vocal range and timing improved each week. He became aware of song arrangements and the discipline of constant practice and rehearsal, although his full-time education was a little slower.

He was slowly plodding through his school syllabus. The 11-plus examination had been introduced just after the war and when the school leaving age extended to 15 years, Many people from a working-class background saw this as a hierarchical system, most particularly his dad, bellowing 'fucking class-driven streaming system'. Students who passed the 11-plus were awarded places in grammar schools, while those failing went into the secondary schools then later perhaps technical apprenticeships. Anthony flunked his 11-plus but was not necessarily concerned, as he was happy at Buckingham Gate.

His best friends at the time were John Slater and John Connor. As the decade was coming to its end, it was an exciting time for the trio, who were adventurous and intrepid. London was slowly being rebuilt, but there were still spectacular bomb sites or damaged buildings to explore. They met up with other lads from the area to play Brits versus the Nazis, running around with outstretched arms, the RAF against the Luftwaffe. Then it would be fighting on the ground, the staccato noises of machine guns, the boom of explosives. Then inevitably a brick would score a direct hit on an unsuspecting cranium, the pretend grenade provoking a proper rolling-about, fist-pummelling scrap.

They arrived home with split lips and bloody noses only to receive a severe scolding because their clothing was ripped, dusty and stinky. The boys were always on the cusp of minor crime, not exactly professional thieves, but certainly pilfering and petty theft, most of the time as a dare.

They progressed from nicking a handful of sweets from the pick and mix at Woolworths to full-scale larceny, in their eyes at least. Just to the rear of the Tachbrook was a group of lock-ups, garages, and sheds. Sam garaged his taxi there. The buildings were also rented by the stallholders from the Warwick Way Market, mainly the fruit and veg vendors.

At the end of each day's trading, the remaining stock was packed away, oranges, bananas, spuds and the rest. While Sam and other traders had enough locks and chains to discourage any chancer gaining access, the market boys just dumped in their stuff and locked the doors, which were so badly warped you could push a pregnant sow through.

The Tachbrook boys nicked fruit and vegetables, not huge amounts. They ate some, flogged some and brought some home. When Sam and the other dads found out, they were furious. The lads were messing with people's livelihoods; people were also still on rationing, so it had to stop. A few orders went in for Brazil nuts at Christmas though.

Football was becoming the main sport for Anthony and his mates, in the school playground and after school on some wasteland which had been concreted over. Eventually this became the home of the Tachbrook League. Each block of flats had a team, playing each other on a regular basis, the footballers a mixture of ages wearing a rag, tag and bobtail array of colours.

Sam turned out for Kent House; he was the goalkeeper. He made himself thick pads from old newspapers which were tied to his knees and elbows allowing him to dive around without incurring too much damage.

During the winter, games were actually played under floodlights as an enterprising bunch, the players with the connivance of the estate manager, managed to rig up extra streetlights and 'borrowed' theatre lights to the council main supplies.

The estate manager was a very popular man. He also lived in Kent House so did not have far to go to get to work. His wife worked as one of the clerks in the estate office. They liaised with the council on applications for housing. The office was always full of gifts at Christmas or ad-hoc presents during the year. Most of the families therefore had relations or close friends housed around them. The estate office was certainly of help to the Selby family over the years.

On alternate Saturdays during the season, Sam would stop work at lunchtime so he could get to Stamford Bridge to support his team, Chelsea. One Saturday in November 1949, he picked up Anthony from the stage school, something he often did if he was in the area, and ordered him to throw his clobber in the corner of the taxi. Anthony was going to see the Blues for the first time. They parked up near the White Horse pub (later to become known as 'the Sloaney Pony') then walked to the stadium. It was that time of the year when the fog and mist was always wet, sinister, and threatening, a sky that was always going to become darker. Like every youngster, the smells, the sights and sounds when attending his first match stayed with Anthony.

They went through the turnstile; Sam the great socialist pushed them both through, paid for one, and then they were in, ascending the steep stairway to the top of the concrete mass of terrace. In collusion with other dads, the young ones were ushered behind the goal with the Shed just to the left. Anthony looked down at the greyhound track around the perimeter of the stadium, then at the pitch – not a magnificent great green, more a brownish mud bath.

Chelsea, feeling the effects of the heavy ground a little more than their opponents, lost 4-1. At least Portsmouth went on to become champions that season. Chelsea finished in the top half of the table in 11th place. Anthony attended a few more games that season, but that first experience would always be special. There were always going to be first-time experiences of other things as well although he didn't realise that at the time. One strange incident happened just before Christmas in 1949 when he opened the front door to two nuns, both of them with a countenance resembling a crushed walnut. The duo pushed past him and walked into the sitting room where Anne was at the table making patterns, Sam counting out his takings for the day while Kathy was reading her book in the corner.

The nuns marched up to the parents demanding to know why the children had not been to Mass for as long ago as they did not know when. On one of the walls was a photograph. The nun who was not nagging slowly pointed towards it. It was a framed photograph of Lenin. She quickly walked over to turn the frame inwards to the wall, and on the reverse side was a picture of Joseph Stalin. They quickly left in a swirl of habits through the open front door. Anne nodded towards the door, Anthony closed it after the departing visitors and the family resumed what they were doing without discussion or comment.

Strangely, the Selby family were invited to Christmas Mass at Westminster Cathedral. They had seats at the back. Anthony would always remember the choral works of such beauty and pitch; they really were one heavenly choir. Sam would have had his eye on the altar boys, hoping the drawing pin and shoe polish pranks were still going on. That was the last Mass the family would attend together, as only Anne continued to attend. The other Selbys fell by the wayside to the probable dismay of the Pope, Archbishops and certainly two startled nuns.

4
PETER PAN

On 21 January 1950, George Orwell died. Anthony had never heard of him although his father certainly would have done. It would be a few more years before the boy knew that Orwell's real name was Eric Blair or that his works would have any significance or influence on him.

George Bernard Shaw snuffed it later that year, but it would be a while before Anthony would act in one of his plays. Instead, for him it was the publication of the *Eagle* comic, far more exciting than *Pygmalion* and *Saint Joan*.

As the 1940s shook hands with the new decade, wishing it luck and prosperity, the country as a whole had voted in an intrepid and radical government making immense social and economic changes: the National Health Service, nationalisation, more social housing. The unions were becoming more powerful, negotiating better pay and conditions. At least three of the Selby family drifted along in a fairly relaxed and orderly manner, allowing and welcoming this new order. The exception was Sam who raved and ranted, not that the rest of the family could really understand. Anne just let him get on with things; she had an understanding of his politics and did not obstruct his activism. She was however the fulcrum of the family.

Sam's occupation gave him the freedom to work his own hours, some selfishly to fit in his political activity and football, sometimes selflessly to work long hours to bring in an income to provide a good family lifestyle. There were, however, dark secrets for Sam to hide.

Anne organised the children with a disciplined approach, while Sam had his unconventional working hours. Anne had to organise the children's schooling and most of their other activities. Kathy by this time was attending the Grey Coat Hospital school for girls, a school with a considerable academic reputation. She was a very good student, excelling in English literature and language, and had read most of the works of Charles Dickens and several of Shakespeare's plays by the age of 14. In between her schoolwork and piano lessons which both Kathy and Anthony were taking from a retired music teacher who lived in the flats, she was also dancing on a regular basis at the local youth club. Kathy was also building up an impressive collection of records. She was developing into a precocious teenager and neither of her parents put up any objection or argument when she and her friends went into town after school or at the weekend where they obtained a few MGM yellow label records.

American service personnel who would be returning home would sell their collections for next to nothing to fund a last few nights in London. Kathy and her friends in the

Grey Coat uniform were attracting a less than healthy attention but they always remained secretive about their activities. The Selby flat however, was always filled with the sound of jazz and contemporary American records.

When they were evacuated to Cirencester during the war, the family got to know the Hulls who had been evacuated from Eastbourne because it was feared the town could be a likely landing point as part of a German invasion. The two families became good friends. Anthony had a best friend in Patrick Hull, he was the same age, and they were in the infant school together. The Hulls invited the Selbys down to Sussex for a holiday.

The two boys had vague memories of their first meeting but when they met again, they really bonded. They were also left to their own devices for most of the day and it helped that Patrick knew the area.

Anthony would remember that the air was so fresh and clear, he could taste the ozone from the sea breeze – it blew up his nostrils and cleared his ears of wax. The greenery and beauty of the Sussex Downs proved to be breathtaking.

One of the first attractions they visited was to the funicular railway. They were ushered into the carriage then carried up in a steep trajectory to the top of the South Downs, and once there they walked for miles, consuming the packed lunches well before lunchtime all the while glugging bottled dandelion and burdock which made them belch like a Tudor monarch. They trekked through woodlands and fields, filled the empty pop bottles with water from streams and scrumped apples and pears. Patrick would always be pointing out the birdlife – skylarks, swallows, martins, or kestrels – while the gulls would squawk and swoop out to sea. This was exotic for a south London boy used to pigeons and sparrows or the occasional robin or blackbird.

Around five in the evening they would arrive back at the house, stomachs rumbling like a blocked drain. Both mums were great bakers and each day there were batches of cakes, pies, and rolls. This was still a time of rationing, so it was like walking into a H.E. Bates novel with the Larkin family. In the evening they would all pile into the taxi for a drive up to Beachy Head and Seven Sisters where they would park up at the Beachy Head pub high above the beach.

The two boys walked over to the cliff edge, but not too close, then peered over at the sea below. As they gripped on to the rickety safety rail they were well aware about the tales of lovers' leap where couples for whatever reason had thrown themselves over the precipice on to the jagged rocks below, or the sad desperate suicides of lonely people leaping to oblivion. Others had gone over in cars, motorcycles or even pushbikes. They gaped in fascinated horror.

Back at the pub garden the grown-ups had secured a table filled with pints of bitter and glasses of port and lemon. The boys returned to glasses of lemonade and packets of greasy crisps with a screw paper of salt which was sprinkled enthusiastically over the sliced fried spuds. The lemonade made them burp again and they were told off for being rude though the volley of farts from the dads as they visited the lavatories went without comment. After the dads had finished expelling wind, Mr Hull told them the pub had been a lookout post during the war; indeed, all along the cliff tops one could see lookout posts and pill boxes. Most nights on the pub visits the two boys wandered among the old military buildings, looking for souvenirs, bits of military detritus or even just interesting pebbles.

Towards the end of the holiday a unique yet scary phenomenon happened.

Anthony remembered the early evening sun slowly descending, the sky a brief but stunning amalgam of blue, purple, red and oranges, then suddenly it became full of towering, rumbling thunder clouds, a Tolkienesque Mordor vision. The storm was rushing towards them, the rain thumping and splattering along the clifftop. It chased the boys all the way back to the pub, and just before they reached the garden a tremendous down-draft with an icy feel to their collars hit them, then a volume of rain of such velocity soaked them to the skin as they gulped for air.

The garden was completely deserted, the families beckoning the boys from the pub's entrance. The publican found some towels and they were dried off. The storm and its clouds disappeared, while the sun continued its descent the summer evening smelled sweetly of newly drenched fauna and boys. Anthony learned later that the storm and the clouds were known as cumulonimbus; it took him a long time to pronounce it correctly. The whole experience had given him a jolt of excitement and he felt as if he was part of a huge show put on by nature. More importantly, he was a part of it and loved the attention.

The last night of the holiday included a visit to the Hippodrome Theatre to see a variety show. There were the usual tired old acts – jugglers, dancers, singers, and comics – but Anthony's eyes blazed with joy as he loved every minute of the show. When the family returned to London, he couldn't wait to return to school and Italia Conti.

The Italia Conti had its own agency for child actors, and at one time producers were casting for the part of the Artful Dodger in the film version of *Oliver Twist*. The film's casting agent was sitting around in the office with the school's agent when one of the students came in with the teas and coffees and gave the elders a bit of cheek as he served them. They didn't see anyone else, and immediately cast Anthony Newley in the role.

Shortly afterwards, Anthony Selby auditioned for a part as one of the lost boys in a production of *Peter Pan*, due to open for a seven-week Christmas run at the Scala Theatre. Six students from the Italia Conti arrived at the theatre together with another 20 from other acting schools. He got the job and became a professional actor, but before that there was a lot of paperwork to get through to enable him to work, not least permission from his headteacher at Buckingham Gate. Once that had been organised, he attended rehearsals for his professional debut. The two principal actors were Margaret Lockwood, playing Peter Pan, and Stanley Holloway, playing Mr Darling and Captain Hook, the traditional roles for the leading male actor.

The rehearsals went well, and both stars were warm and encouraging, but the most important person in the fledgling actors' life was Mrs Watson, the wardrobe mistress, mentor, disciplinarian, and chaperone. On the first day she sat the young actors down in a semi-circle on the stage and stared at them one by one, her words ringing out like a Cromarty gale, 'You may be children in stature and mind, but when you report to theatre you will act and behave as adults. You may address me as Mrs Watson or "Watty", which I prefer.' Her severe manner faded away to be replaced by a beaming smile as she continued, 'We will also be having lots of fun.' She also told them this was to be the most disciplined time of their lives so far, and that discipline had to be meticulously maintained. They were now all professional actors so there would be less tolerance for mistakes, inconsistency, or temperament. Watty ensured they were signed in at the stage door, up to the dressing rooms, into costumes and makeup, then making enough time for last-minute visits to the lavatory.

Various calls were drilled into their heads, such as '35 minutes to curtain'. This was called the half, at 30 minutes plus an extra five. Then it was '15 minutes to curtain' and 'five minutes to curtain, beginners please'.

The theatre still had a page boy who made the calls as tannoy systems were slowly being installed in theatres then. The Scala was certainly a battered old trout of a theatre and needed modernising urgently.

Watty soothed nerves, made little jokes, fussed and tidied them up, then they were on. Sam would drop his boy off on most nights, otherwise Anthony travelled by bus over to Tottenham Court Road. He was always picked up by his dad after the show; perhaps some of the cast were envious he had his own personal transport.

On the opening night, the cab dropped him off at the stage door. Stanley Holloway was outside smoking a cigarette and signing a few autographs, and he looked on in curiosity as the curly headed cast member clambered out. Sam lent over from the driver's seat and nodded, 'Evening, Mr Holloway.'

As Holloway nodded back with a half-smile, Sam called out to his son, 'Good luck, Sir Henry.' Holloway chuckled then led a slightly mystified boy through the stage door. Anthony asked why his dad had called him Sir Henry.

'Well young man, Sir Henry Irving was the first actor to receive a knighthood. Your father obviously has great ambition for you,' Holloway replied.

Stanley Holloway was a relaxed avuncular man. He had recently starred in a great Ealing comedy called *Passport to Pimlico*, which involved the residents of Pimlico declaring itself as a republic and becoming a separate country. Anthony told him he could not remember it being filmed in Pimlico.

'No, it was filmed around Hanwell and a bomb site in Brentford,' said the star.

Watty adored Holloway and knew his repertoire by heart; by all accounts he was capable of mimicking 60 different accents. He was also very accomplished at monologues. His two most famous were 'Sam, Sam pick up thy musket' delivered in a flat Yorkshire dialect, and 'My word you do look queer'. Remember that was an innocent time and it did have a happy ending.

As the show progressed Sam and Holloway developed a bit of a repartee and banter.

'Good evening, Mr Holloway.'

'And to you, Mr Selby.'

'How is the show going?'

'Well, Mr Selby, and the cab trade?'

'Fine, Mr Holloway. How do you think young Henry here is doing?'

'He's doing fine, Mr Selby.' Sam had obviously decided to strip his son of a knighthood. Holloway told Anthony that Bram Stoker had based Count Dracula on Henry Irving. Stoker was the manager of the Lyceum Theatre and also Irving's business manager. When he was picked up after the performance, Anthony couldn't wait to tell his dad. Sam said it was possible his grandad could have carried Stoker in the Hansom cab through the thickest of fogs from the Lyceum to his home.

'Do you know where that is, son?' Sam asked.

'No, Dad.'

'St George's Square, just opposite the cab rank.'

Anthony caught the bus to the theatre one night, arriving just as Holloway was coming outside for his pre-show smoke. Holloway nodded to his arriving fellow actor, removed a silver cigarette case from his jacket pocket, took out a cigarette, tapped the end of the case then lit it with an exquisite gold lighter. Anthony was fascinated by it all; by the very class of the moment, most people lit their fags with matches. He vowed to smoke like that when he eventually started.

Holloway asked, 'No chauffeur tonight, young Anthony?'

'No, Mr Holloway, he is picking me up though later.'

'Hippocampus.'

'Hippocampus, Mr Holloway?'

'Hippocampus, that part of the brain controlling spatial awareness and memory. Your father has a well-developed one, spatial awareness for his memory and driving skills and his geographical knowledge, and you know, most actors, good actors, have a well-developed Hippocampus.'

The apprentice was then ushered through the stage door by the master.

Later in the run Holloway took Anthony to one side before a show and told him,

'Now young man, for the opening nights and then once a week, Mrs Holloway sits in the Gods to monitor my voice projection. She has mentioned to me that of all the younger cast members, yours is the one with strength and clarity. Thought you would like to know.'

Anthony's cheeks turned pink in embarrassed gratitude.

The other star of the production, Margaret Lockwood, was a huge film and stage actor who proved gracious and kind to all the cast; she was yet another graduate from Italia Conti and had made her own stage debut at the age of 12. She had just finished a run in Noël Coward's *Private Lives* before joining *Peter Pan*. Lockwood had recently divorced her husband, Rupert Lean, which possibly explained why her daughter Julia was at the theatre for most performances although neither of them seemed particularly melancholy.

Julie was known as Toots by everyone. Most of the boys had a bit of a crush on her. She was a polite girl but very confident as she had been around theatre and film fold long enough to handle most things. Toots's mother used to organise the most lavish tea parties in her dressing room, so between matinees and evening performances the whole cast would troop into the large space and demolish the mounds of cakes and sandwiches piled on tables.

Watty made sure her charges didn't overindulge though, 'I don't want my charges being sick over Mr Holloway.'

Indeed, Captain Hook would be most displeased.

Anthony would always position himself as close to Toots at every opportunity. She once confided to him that one day, when it could be arranged, she would play Wendy to her mother's role as Peter Pan, which eventually happened not long after. Like her mother, Toots had a beautiful, velvet English accent. There was no harshness; it was posh but soft and lilting accompanied by a smile that could melt a glacier. The show had been a resounding success with the theatre full, the reviews good and the experience priceless. When the run finished, after fond and tearful goodbyes to everyone, Anthony was back at school.

His school mates and friends on the estate were very envious that he had been off school for seven weeks until he told them he had to complete six hours of schoolwork every day. His parents or Kathy had to pick up a school week's worth of lessons from the headmaster, then from ten until four he worked through the textbooks with his completed papers returned to school at the end of the week. When the unorthodox schooling finished, he was back in his classroom again looking over the river at the South Bank where a lot of activity and building work was taking place. Suddenly the Festival of Britain appeared.

That side of the river towards Southwark Cathedral had always been a mass of rubble and derelict buildings from war damage or just neglect.

The new Labour government decided the whole country would benefit from a festival to celebrate the arts, so cultural events were planned to take place around major British cities.

London was to have a permanent site, however, one which would symbolise modernism, technology, and science.

Pimlico watched on with interest as the site across the river took shape. The whole area became an impressive architectural development: the Dome of Discovery was over 100ft tall, the Royal Festival Hall was built for music, theatre and dance and the most exciting of all for the schoolboys, the Skylon Tower, a metal cigar-shaped structure resembling a rocket ship, like those depicted in the *Eagle* comic. The Skylon Tower was held upright by thin metal cables, so from a distance it seemed to be balanced on nothing but a slender base. 'It doesn't have any visible means of support, rather like a bloody economy,' came one refrain from a Tory detractor.

The Festival of Britain opened at the end of the football season. Father and son Selby attended Stamford Bridge for the last game of the season, which Chelsea needed to win by a large score, if they didn't, they would be relegated to the Second Division. Although all three of the bottom teams did win, Chelsea's 4-0 victory meant they finished safely in 20th position to stay up by the slenderest of goal difference.

On their way home, Sam stopped off at Bob White's seafood stall just over Vauxhall Bridge near the Oval cricket ground. He loaded up a couple of pints of winkles and whelks then drove up to the festival site and parked up, watching the crowds of people thronging around the South Bank as the early evening sun prepared to dip down over Waterloo station. They sat back in the cab and speared winkles. Later someone would write a song about the sunset and someone else would design a shoe.

Sam always had two newspapers tucked down near his driving seat, the *Daily Worker* and the *Daily Telegraph*. 'One to keep an eye on what the brothers are up to, one to monitor what the capitalist bastards are up to,' he explained.

The Selby family didn't visit the Festival Grounds because just up the road in Battersea Park was the most fantastic funfair, which they went to on a regular basis. The fair lasted a lot longer than most of the festival site.

Politically things were changing again.

The Labour Party were really struggling. Ernest Bevin had died just before the Festival of Britain had opened and Clement Attlee's government, despite reforms in welfare, the introduction of the National Health Service and grand-scale nationalisation, was under great pressure, the economy groaning with the cost of it all – 'no visible means of support'.

Sam tried to explain to Anthony, from a communist and socialist point of view, what it all meant but he didn't understand a word.

Winston Churchill was suddenly back in power and the limelight. The first thing he did in a fit of pique was to destroy the Festival of Britain site, with the exception of the Royal Festival Hall, the whole area was bulldozed and destroyed within weeks.

Anthony would always remember as he watched with his school mates the tugs on the river, huge ropes attached to their stern then on to the base of the Skylon Tower; the tugs pulled away, the structure brittle and vulnerable, twisted and groaned as it collapsed into the river.

Sam's mood was only lifted by the fact that Churchill was more pissed off than him when two spies, who used to bugger about in Dolphin Square, literally in their case, defected to mother Russia. He raised a glass to Mr Burgess and Mr McLean.

Anthony was now looking more at his development at the Italia Conti rather than his scholastic future. His time in the *Peter Pan* production was now pushing his ambition. He was hoping for more opportunities to come along quickly.

They did.

5
WHERE THE RAINBOW ENDS

Lime Grove had been a film studio for many years. The BBC bought the property in Shepherd's Bush to convert it for television use as they were planning to use the space as a main studio until the new Television Centre was built around the corner in Wood Lane.

The Corporation had just started to develop children's programming, producing short films and plays specifically for youngsters.

They had started initially with puppet programmes such as the hugely popular *Andy Pandy* and *Muffin the Mule*, but for the newer shows they needed child actors.

Producers descended on the Italia Conti and organised auditions for one of the very first live broadcasts, *Mencius Was a Bad Boy*. Anthony Valentine was hired to play Mencius, while Anthony Selby secured the role of Porky; not only were they to make their first television appearances, it would also be shown live.

Television was so new and exciting; TV sets were mainly rented then from Rediffusion or Radio Rental. When Selby told his parents he had secured the part they rushed out to rent one.

When the two new actors arrived at Lime Grove, slightly apprehensive and nervous, they became more at ease when they entered the studio. It was less intimidating than the theatre, there was no live audience to contend with, and everything about this new environment was different, an intangible smell of modernity, metal and machines.

The producer and director showed them around, explaining how the crews worked, the ways camera operators were directed, how the sound technicians collaborated. When the rehearsals began, the studio had marks similar to a theatre stage, however there was a camera script to become familiar with, then they had to consider close-ups, fades and points of view. The show went out live early on a Saturday evening.

Back on the Tachbrook, the family and a few neighbours waited as the television warmed up, that was, for the valve to fully function – a wonder and great novelty for most of them.

The two boys were comfortable in the studio. They had learned the disciplines of TV acting quickly, the nerves had gone, and they were off.

The half-hour passed quickly, and despite small mistakes, muffled lines, or stutters, it was considered a success. Back in Pimlico the assembled group were impressed and complimentary to Anthony's mum and dad about the show and performance. When Anthony returned to his school on the Monday, there were few accolades or congratulations, because none of his school mates or most of the teachers had access to a television set.

Anne and Sam opened an account at the Post Office for their son, with his earnings now amounting to over £100. As another Christmas approached he was offered a part in the Italia Conti production of *Where the Rainbow Ends* at the Stoll Theatre.

The play had become synonymous with the stage school; performances had been held every year since it was first written by Clifford Mills and John Ramsey with Roger Quilter adding and arranging the music.

The first producer was Charles Hawtrey, and by coincidence an actor called Charles Hawtrey attended the school in the 1930s who said he was the nephew of Charles senior. It proved to be untrue. The man who would achieve fame in the *Carry On* films, renowned for his role as Private Widdle, was in fact born Charles Hawtree in Hounslow, the son of a bus driver.

The story of *Where the Rainbow Ends* is a fantasy set in Rainbow Land, featuring witches, strange talking animals, plus lots of mythical creatures. It was then essentially a Christmas show and competed with *Peter Pan* and pantomimes. Unlike *Peter Pan*, though, in the story it is the parents who disappear and not the children, rather unkindly leaving their two boys, two girls and the normal family pet, a lion cub, to find them. The children, together with the lion, travel on a magic carpet accompanied by St George of England all armoured up, his trusty sword in his hand ready to fight and defeat dragons, ghouls, and very nasty people before rescuing mum and dad.

In reality it was all pomp and circumstance, nationalistic certainly, Britain the land of hope and glory ruling the lands and the seas. It was also about the kids, though – fun–living and adventuresome, then lots of fear and emotion.

The production had gone through various changes over the decades while the music score often varied in content. The original five acts were often reduced to four, then the fourth act called the Lake Scene was sometimes left out for reasons of length. The cast was huge: over 50 child actors, a dozen adults, dancers, acrobats, and a full orchestra. When it was finally decided how this production would take shape, Anthony's role was that of Willian the Page Boy, part of the Dramatist Personae as a mortal. Such was his versatility by then, he also played the non-speaking part of Slitherslime.

The part of St George was played by Anton Dolin, a choreographer who worked at Italia Conti as a dance teacher in between his other West End work and the buttocks of his more flamboyant colleagues. Anton carried the sword of the knight with a swagger and a leer and the campness of a row of tents.

The success of the show depended almost entirely on the children, who were all exclusively from Italia Conti. Their concentration had to be immense, particularly in the vastness of the theatre.

The Stoll Theatre on Kingsway had formerly been the London Opera House; its auditorium held over 3,000 people. The backstage areas were also unusually large. The rehearsals lasted for several weeks but the cast were all ready to go by opening night. Unfortunately, so was Anton.

A whole troupe of children were lined up behind the curtain waiting for the opening line, 'Now, whosoever shall read this book, whose faith is strong and heart pure, will find when they close its pages, the way to the land where the Rainbow Ends. Here are where all loved ones are found.'

A whole row of kids about to go on stage jumped involuntarily as one by one, their bottoms were goosed by St George's sword. For the next eight weeks Anton's sword continued its pre-curtain activity without stricture or complaint. Despite that, Anthony was rather sad when the run finished and his school life resumed, the anti-climax after the excitement and glamour.

Life at home seemed to go on as normal; he and Sam would go off to watch Chelsea or the odd game at Fulham while the games on the estate were still being played with enthusiasm. A change was happening though, as on most evenings as the light began to fade and the makeshift floodlights were eventually dimmed, a strange social practice had developed of parents whistling from the balconies which meant it would be time to come in. Each whistle was unique for an individual child, they would recognise it, a shrill three-tone blast for one, a long shrill note for another. It would have certainly confused an ornithologist, a peewit here, a blue tit there. It was remarkable.

The NHS put a stop to it unintentionally, as parents gradually benefited from free dental treatment. Teeth were being pulled and removed by the millions to be replaced by dentures, in many cases whether they were needed or not. Slowly but surely the avian calls of Pimlico diminished, as without their own teeth or stumps the whistling stopped. The Selbys witnessed the sad end when a neighbour, 'Shorty' Williams, came out on to his balcony to whistle for his son, 'Short Arse Pete', to come in. Shorty could be seen, a disembodied head moving along the balcony parapet, where he put his little fingers to the corner of his lips and blew from his lungs at full blast. His top set of teeth flew out of his mouth, revolving gracefully towards the tarmac below while everyone watched in fascination as 16 bits of white plastic attached to pink plastic gums crashed down to the ground and shattered into shards, spread out like a fairy's vomit.

Shattered dentures notwithstanding, it was now becoming a crucial time for Anthonly, puberty and an identity crisis. On the estate he was called Tony, Tone, or Selbs, at the schools he was known as Anthony by the teachers, in the theatre he was billed as Anthony Selby, while his father called him Henry.

From a puberty point of view, every morning was a full morning glory, so he and his mates now had a new activity to discuss at school.

Kathy Selby had developed into a very attractive young woman, and although she was underage to work in clubs, she was a regular visitor to Soho, worming her way into a job as a girl of all trades at the Seven Club in Irving Street, owned by Johnny Dankworth and his wife Cleo Laine. Kathy would take the entrance money, run the cloakroom, and push away randy drunks trying to get a leg over. Neither Anne nor Sam disapproved of her lifestyle. As a family they certainly did a lot together. There were always trips to the West End to see the latest shows, big band nights at the London Palladium for shows with Ted Heath and his orchestra, then tickets for the Chelsea Palace or Essoldo. Sam was as ever involved with the Communist Party or Socialist Worker and Trotskyite splinter groups.

There was, though, something of a mystery about Sam who seemed to exist on two hours of sleep a day or night. A lot of the time Sam was often gone by the time Anthony was up and ready for school, regularly not home by the time he was off to bed, but the son treasured the time they had together, reasoning his dad worked hard but always around when he was needed, supportive of his acting, scrambling about in goal for the team, visits to Stamford Bridge, looking after the family. His mum was always there, doting and fussing and encouraging him and Kathy. Anne had decided to cut down on the leather business and was now part-time, taking the odd commission here or there, then Christmas presents to order. Anne developed a great fondness for whist and was a regular at whist drives and competitions around the area while she still attended church regularly. It was probably that Anne felt she needed some divine intervention in other matters. The wind had started to sough, that sighing sound heralding a dramatic change in the lives of the family.

6
BIG CHANGES

Anthony used to wake up most morning in a good frame of mind, feeling cheerful and optimistic, looking forward to the day if not necessarily to some of his school lessons. One particular day he had to walk to school, not much of a hardship. His bike had a puncture, and he was going to fix it with his dad at some point after school, he returned to the flats just as a removal van was leaving his block. The door to the flat was open and his mum was sitting on a suitcase; the flat echoed, nothing was left in but the linoleum. He looked at Anne, whose eyes were filled with tears. She hugged Anthony to her, picked up the suitcase and left. A few neighbours shuffled about, mainly female, looking on sadly but without saying a word.

They arrived at his uncle John's flat in the adjoining block, Abbotts House, where more suitcases and some personal items were stacked in the entrance hall. Anne then told him that his father had left the family, Sam would not be coming back. Anthony was bewildered. Hesitantly Anne tried to explain that she and Sam had not been getting on to well for some time and the nights that Anthony assumed his dad was working, he had not come home at all. Then the bombshell: Sam had met someone else. Her name was Maude Brown, and he was now living in a flat in Fulham with her.

So many questions for a boy to ask. How could his dad do that to them? What was going to happen? Why hadn't his mum or Kathy explained what was going on? Sam had dropped him off at school the previous day, when they arranged for the bike repair, and he had not said a word about what was going on. Kathy and Anne were in retrospect quieter than normal but gave no hint of the awful circumstances.

Now his mother was explaining to him that they would be staying with John for a time, then the three of them would be starting a new life together. Anthony was angry with Sam, the absolute betrayal and the hurt he was causing, and vowed not to speak or contact him again. He attended school again the following day accompanied by Anne; she had a word with the headmaster who kept a benign eye on him for a few days.

It was so different in the 1950s. Couples seemed to stay together regardless of misdemeanours, it was a social stigma for marriages to fail, unless you were film stars or aristocrats. They were allowed to divorce without stricture.

Sam kept well out of the way for a while, until Anthony came across him on the cab rank in St George's Square. His dad shouted over, 'Hello, Henry, let's have a chat.' Anthony blanked him and walked on.

After a few weeks in the crowded flat, a new flat had been allocated in the adjoining Malcolmson House. The furniture was carted back from the lock-up and the trio settled in quickly; there were no pictures of Russian leaders or left-wing literature. The flat was devoid of Sam.

Kathy had started work for Betty Farmer, a theatrical agent with an office in Dean Street, while she still worked weekends at the Seven Club. When she found the time she also attended the dances at the Lyceum or Battersea Town Hall. In the meantime Anne organised their flat. She loved the balcony, which was filled with geraniums, tomato plants then more exotic ferns and palms.

Anthony still ignored his father. Sam's fellow cabbies asked Anthony to talk to his dad but he was stubborn, adamant he would not contact him. In truth he was really missing Sam. He missed the football, the outings, the fun, even Sam's rantings about the government, politicians and the system.

Despite the turmoil, Anthony was concentrating on his studies while developing his acting skills and career. His voice was breaking although it still had a lightness to it, and his range was also improving as were his accents: Scouse and Manc, Geordie even, then posh and American. He was offered another chance to appear in *Peter Pan* at the Scala Theatre, schoolwork had to be completed during the run and it was more intense this time ready for his final examinations the following Spring.

At the Scala he had a fond reunion with Mrs Watson, Watty, and was comfortable as she ran through the usual briefing. The two main actors were Pat Kirkwood and Donald Wolfit. According to salacious gossip, Kirkwood was rumoured to have had a passionate affair with Prince Philip, something that she always denied.

Kirkwood did have an air of mystery about her. She had come a long way from a humble background in Manchester to her status as a leading film and theatre celebrity. The lingering though not necessarily true notoriety of her love life was always going to sell tickets. Anthony was too young to know that then but discovered much more about her in later life from older actors who seemed to be well informed.

Kirkwood proved to be kind and patient throughout the run, and was the source of sweets and chocolates for all; more importantly she was patient and encouraging.

Donald Wolfit didn't seem to radiate much warmth or charm to Anthony. He was always polite and well mannered but came across as a distant man. On the stage however, he was magical. His normal taciturn countenance transformed the minute he made his entrance, joy in his Mr Darling, a playful menace as he pranced through his role as Captain Hook.

The other figure of note for Anthony was Russell Thorndike, who played Mr Smee. He was as pissed as a newt most of the time but sobered up almost immediately when he had to perform, although the fumes from his breath made the company's eye water.

The show finished and was a success. No longer the innocent, Anthony was now a reasonably experienced actor. He was told that the production was to go on tour, he eagerly agreed to a contract to go with it. His final examination was due in May, while the tour would not be finishing until the end of April, but fortunately his headmaster thought his schoolwork was up to standard and trusted him to be diligent in his studies while on the road.

Anthony was about to leave home for the first time.

The whole company met up at the station for the train call. The producers booked a whole train carriage for the actors and technical crew, then a freight carriage for the scenery and props. The train pulled away to Nottingham and arrived around lunchtime, when everyone was then herded to the theatre carrying suitcases followed by the props and scenery vans. It was a wonderful chaos. The theatre manager fussed and flapped, then after picking up the call and rehearsal times there was really only one important thing for Anthony to do, find a place to stay for the week. The stage doorman had a list of places that looked after 'theatricals'. The more experienced of the group had booked ahead. One young actor who thought he was experienced sucked at his thumb and stared at the list, but fortunately one of the others called from the 'pay' phone and booked them both into a nearby bed and breakfast.

They arrived at a four-storey Victorian house where one of them rang the bell. When the door opened a deep voice told them, rather than invited them, to enter. They were led to a room at the top of the house, where the voice ordered them to push the suitcases under the two single beds, told them that the bathroom and toilet were on the floor below and that breakfast was at eight sharp. A hand opened up to receive the 30 shillings for the week and then vanished with its body.

The room was really small, with an odour of unwashed bodies and stale, lingering farts. The tiny window would not open. The sheets and pillows at least looked clean and fresh and there was a small sink in the corner. Anthony and his companion decided to look around; the bathroom contained an incredibly deep bath and a marble sink, but there were no towels or soap. Fortunately they had both packed their own, or rather in Anthony's case, Anne had.

The toilet next to the bathroom had a huge cast-iron cistern below which sat the ceramic lavatory with a wooden seat, and hanging just to the right was a rusty chain attached to a wooden grip handle.

After discovering where they could bathe and defecate, they wandered downwards and found the dining room because it said that on the plaque above the door, but before they could explore further the hand that had taken their 30 bob each appeared in front of them this time with a head and shoulders in full view.

'If you want some supper it's half a crown but you have to order it the day before.'

The body disappeared.

They worked out that they had not been there the day before. His companion decided to return to the room to rest. Anthony was feeling hungry so decided to go for a walk and get his bearings. The theatre was a ten-minute walk away so he set off towards it, passing a few closed cafes but finding a fish and chip shop. In the chippy he asked if they had any saveloys. The proprietor looked mystified, so Anthony tried to explain that it was like a sausage but didn't tell him it was normally stuffed with sawdust, entrails and a small amount of undefinable meat.

'No son, but we've got pickled eggs,' came the reply.

The man pointed to a large jar on the counter, which contained some grey-looking spheres floating about like severed testicles. Anthony left the shop with his newspaper wrapping of hake and chips.

After wandering around for a couple of hours, he headed back to the digs where he and his fellow cellmate decided to have an early night. They were ready for breakfast the next morning and arrived on time so they sat at a table awaiting their fried food when they were joined by a tall, unshaven figure who nodded to them, sat down, then grabbed all the salt, pepper, and condiments with a bewildering flurry with his hand. The items suddenly vanished then re-appeared from his trouser pockets, his jacket, and then from behind the two transfixed table-mates' heads. The man roared with laughter and lit a cigarette. His name was Tommy Cooper.

Most large cities had at least two theatres, one for touring variety acts and the other for conventional theatre and drama, and all the actors and show business professionals would mix together in the available accommodation.

After breakfast it was off to the theatre for rehearsals, arriving as one crew was moving out of the previous week's scenery and props while theirs was set up.

A hugely important part of the *Peter Pan* production was Kirby's Flying Ballet. The technicians were responsible for all the aerial manoeuvres as Peter et al whizzed and soared into the air during the performance. Each stage was different in size and depth, so angles and height had to be worked out in meticulous, mathematical detail. The scenery blocks had gaps or shutters where the harnesses were rapidly clipped on to the wires hoisting the cast up and away. The Kirbys were brilliant professionals and never messed up.

Peter Pan opened on a Monday night. It was performed every night with matinees on Wednesday and Saturday, then the digs were vacated early on Sunday morning. They were off to Newcastle by nine, and by the time they hit Glasgow the following week Anthony had settled into a regular routine for an actor on the road.

Once board and lodging had been sorted out, he would walk about the place, then find the best and cheap places for food or the local Woolworths to buy toothpaste, soap, and shampoo. They were things he had always taken for granted at home, where Anne had always done everything for him: a holed sock was darned, a frayed collar was turned while his underwear was always fresh and skidmark-free. Life was very different on the road: underpants were washed in the basin in your room if you had one, or in the bathroom then hung to dry on a chair or bedhead. Anthony's worst experience was once entering a bathroom to wash out his smalls to discover some vile bastard had left a turd the size of a yule log in the sink.

He was lucky that Watty, the wardrobe mistress extraordinaire, was also on the tour. She arranged for some of the younger actors to have everyday clothing to be included in the company wash but did however insist they would have to press shirts or trousers themselves, so he learned the skill of ironing. On the rare occasion Watty's workload was too heavy, she always knew of a laundry she used who would normally provide a discounted service.

The tour continued on to Liverpool, Manchester and then Sheffield. Anthony was missing home a little, but because the schedule was so intense, there was little time to be homesick, he was needed at the theatre at one o'clock for matinees, then schoolwork before an evening show then back to the bed and breakfast or hotel.

There was little opportunity to get to know or connect with the locals; any action or fun or incident happened at the digs. Sometimes it was a lucky chance to have a single room. It might well have been an unventilated coffin but at least there was some form of privacy to make up for the lack of oxygen. Most of the time performers had to share accommodation that had two, three or even four beds to a room, many times with complete strangers. He was no longer under the protection of Italia Conti.

In Liverpool Anthony arrived back from the theatre and entered his room to find he had inherited a room-mate. A suitcase on the opposite bed was covered in stickers advertising the *Billy Cotton Band Show*. He undressed and drifted off to sleep only to be woken and he was not alone; a sweaty naked man stinking of booze was licking his face and had a hand over his meat and two veg. Anthony reacted very quickly and Billy Cotton's trombonist was quickly elbowed to the floor where he curled up into an embryo position and passed out. Fortunately he was not around in the morning.

It was also in Liverpool that Anthony met a man whose chin came around the corner several seconds before the rest of him. He was staying in the same digs. He nodded to everyone in the dining room then went off into the front parlour where he sat down on a stool in front of a battered piano which he played beautifully although his singing voice was a bit suspect. It was Bruce Forsyth; he was probably only in his 50s then! Someone rather unkindly named him Bruised Foreskin.

The final leg of the tour was Sheffield, where for the first time most of the company were housed together in a large grange house.

Anthony shared a cavernous room with two of the Flying Kirbys and one of the Lost Boys called Patrick. The others discovered that Patrick was shit scared of ghosts; he claimed to have seen a ghost in every theatre and lodging they had been to. The Kirby boys exchanged glances and a snigger.

On the final night of the tour the four of them returned to the house and bedded down for the night, from across the room came cheery good nights, then suddenly there was a loud whoosh and a banshee wail as a figure floated above Patrick's bed. He screamed, 'Aw Jesus, Mother of God.'

The figure continued to whirr and swerve about until it crashed to the floor. Gales of laughter came from his three companions; Paddy realised the Kirbys had rigged it all up.

'Yer feckin' eejits,' cried a voice from beneath a grey eiderdown.

The company arrived back in London late on Sunday evening. Farewells and hugs had taken place after the final performance, then at the station the train emptied quickly, everyone anxious to get home to family and loved ones. Anthony bid a fond farewell to Watty. Sadly it was the last time he saw her.

He arrived back in Pimlico to a fussing mum, each week he had been away he had sent home a £1 postal order to help with the household budget. The first thing Anne did was show him his new bed she had bought with the money. Then it was back to school for his last few weeks as a student. He did well in his examinations, and he left school life for good. Shortly afterwards he passed the cab rank in St George's Square, where Sam was parked. His dad bellowed, 'Hello Henry, how are you doing?' It had been a while since that last bitter snub by his son. Anthony knew Sam arranged to see Anne each week because he used to hand over money for maintenance payments, and although they had some formal separation, Anne was adamant she would not go through divorce proceedings.

The only other form of contact from Sam with his two children was when he sent them birthday and Christmas gifts. Anthony looked over at the taxi, then walked over; his dad nodded to the back seat, and Anthony climbed in. They sat in silence for a while, then Sam clambered into the back with him. He said he was really sorry about everything that had happened, that he missed Anthony and Kathy, he was still fond of Anne but unfortunately life does change, there was now another person in his life and things could not go back to the way they had been.

Anthony listened, his bottom lip trembled, and his eyes watered. He tried to suppress the tears but looked like Stan Laurel being told off by Ollie. This really was grown-up stuff he needed to understand so after a while he climbed out of the cab, blew his nose loudly and scared a few pigeons.

He talked to Anne about the meeting, and she thought for a while, picked at the bobbly bits on her cardigan then agreed she would allow him to see Sam again. Anthony was however never to visit his father in Fulham and the new woman in Sam's life. When Kathy heard the news about the reconciliation, she was more than a little circumspect. She had a bohemian approach to life and a relaxed social attitude generally. Her parents had allowed her to develop as a woman without a puritanical streak. Kathy was also a woman with a keen insight and instinct and knew her dad was capable of much duplicity, so she would keep her own counsel for the immediate future.

Anthony's final term at school finished as the country as a whole was preparing for a momentous event – and it was not his examination results.

King George VI had died the previous year, so protocol dictated there had to be a period of mourning before the royal successor was officially crowned. Elizabeth II was to have her coronation on 2 June 1953.

For weeks beforehand central London had been tarted up, buildings cleaned, bomb sites hidden by hoardings, everything freshly painted. The rest of the country prepared for the coronation as well; street parties were being organised as were marches and flotillas on the rivers and at the coast.

Anthony also wanted some of the action, not out of loyalty to the new monarch but because he wanted to meet up with girls. By this time he'd had a few snogs on tour, he'd had a few gropes, fondles and dry humps, now there would be thousands of girls in town on the streets of London at the same time, all in a party mood. It was irresistible for him and the two Johns, Salter and Connor, the morning glory boys. The previous week they had hatched a plan as they sat by the river, the sun baking down on them at a luscious 75º Fahrenheit.

They would go up to St James's Park on the Monday, 12 June, sleep under the tarpaulin covering the deckchairs, creep out in the morning and then be at the heart of the action; the crumpet would be dazzled by this trio of young bucks and be dragged away, possibly as far as Kew. All the parents consented, well to the sleeping in the park bit, so the boys arrived with fish paste sandwiches, lemonade, and towels to lie on in case it became a little bit chilly. Chilly was an understatement.

The area all around was covered with tents and makeshift shelters, and a few friendly caped-up coppers looked on benignly, sharing crafty fags and nips of scotch. They boys dropped off to sleep as the rain pitter-pattered on their shelter, then when they woke again after an hour or so the water was still falling but more splattering than pattering. They ate the sandwiches, drank their pop and were grateful when the grey light of early morning appeared.

They queued to use the park lavatories, and washed their faces from the cold water taps. They found a place to watch the procession. The weather proved to be kind; the downpour had turned into a light drizzle. When the event began, nobody seemed to recognise most of the dignitaries. One coach passed containing a startling large figure smiling and waving.

'That's the Queen of Tonga,' someone bellowed.

'Sure it ain't the fucking King,' someone bellowed back.

Ah, the informed and generous wit of the British. By the time Liz and Phil went by, the boys were bored and wet as hell, but when the rain eased off a little more they found a tea stall that also sold bacon sandwiches. They found themselves next to three girls about the same age, who were from Stepney. One had a front tooth missing, one had a chipped front row while the third had a splendid set of teeth and hare lip. The boys persuaded them it was much drier under the covered deckchairs, so the sextet scrambled underneath and were ready for a snogfest. Anthony's choice, the girl with the front tooth missing, told him his breath stank so she gave him some of the beech nut she was chewing then they got down to business where he immediately copped a left breast. Connor apparently copped a right breast while Salter was so fascinated by his partner's unusual *labium superius oris* that he did not cop anything.

Then there was a sudden great rustling and flapping as the canopy covers were rolled back. A head wearing a peak cap bellowed at them, 'Right you lot, fuck off.' Everyone ran, and in the confusion the girls ran one way while the three priapic boys ran in the opposite direction, regrouping near the lavatories. The deckchair attendant could have still hung his hat on any one of them.

    They eventually made their way back to Tachbrook. Street parties were still going on, fireworks lighting up the Victoria Embankment. The three virgins made their way back to their parents. Anthony stood on the balcony with Kathy and Anne looking down at the lights, candles and listening to the music rising up towards them. The two women in his life sniffed the air then sent him for a bath.

7
LITTLEWOOD, BEHAN, AND HARRIS

When Anthony Selby left Buckingham Gate school he continued to attend Italia Conti, which still acted as his agent. He was sent for a few television jobs, and when he did get work it was as an extra or a role with maybe a couple of lines, most of which were uncredited.

Another problem became apparent when he turned up for roles for characters who were 12 or 13 years old – the bum fluff and slightly spotty skin was the giveaway. He was no longer innocent or angelic.

His connection with Italia Conti finished after he appeared in another production of *Where the Rainbow Ends* at the Royal Festival Hall. This show was to include the Lake Scene which stretched the run time for further 25 minutes. The choreographer was once again the St George of wandering sword, Anton Dolan. The role of the Spirit of the Lake was to be performed by Alicia Markova who together with Dolan had founded the English Ballet Company. Dolan had been born in Finsbury Park; Alicia's family were Jewish immigrants called Marks.

Alicia had been a talented and precious dancer from an early age, training with a Russian ballet troupe when she adopted her stage name. She was in her early 40s and still one of the world's prime ballerinas when she accepted the role, ensuring the run would be a sell-out.

Working at the Royal Festival Hall was to be quite different from a conventional theatre as it was built and designed as a concert hall, mainly for orchestras. When Anthony first arrived there, he thought as he stared out to the auditorium with its walnut panels and parquet floors that he would be performing inside a giant radiogram.

The stage direction had to be adjusted somewhat to allow for a more flexible layout, but the unique stage geography helped in mustering up the huge cast, orchestra and the dancers because of the generous space off-stage. They reached the dress rehearsal and were ready to go. Anthony had a pleasant reunion with Kirby's Flying Ballet, who were considering giving Dolin an unscheduled flight during one performance, but their absolute professionalism ruled.

Alicia and Dolin were superb in their performances, and the show was a great success once again, but from a personal perspective Anthony didn't really enjoy it. He was maturing quickly and needed to move on. After the last performance on the South Bank he caught the number 24 bus home as an out-of-work actor with no agent.

One of the problems was solved by Kathy who was still working at the Betty Farmer Agency, so through a contact she helped her brother get taken on by a theatrical agency called Fraser and Dunlop. Anthony went over to the offices in Soho and met up with two of the campest people he had yet to meet, certainly Jimmy Fraser was the tallest, most camp Scotsman ever.

Jimmy agreed to take Anthony on as a client, but nothing much happened, there was no work for him. It was fortunate that his savings account was still relatively healthy. He also began to see more of his dad. Sam was still a rabid left-winger politically, although no longer a member of the Communist Party. He thought the Labour Party was too liberal. There was certainly a lot going on in the world though: the Suez Crisis, the Cold War and the nuclear weapon threat.Sam started to influence Anthony, who began to see the world through his eyes.

Anthony began to read newspapers from cover to cover rather than just the sports pages and he also read books voraciously, not necessarily just the political tomes his dad recommended. He was a fan of Ian Fleming's James Bond novels and particularly *The Quiet American* by Graham Greene. While Anthony was enjoying his reading, Winston Churchill resigned with Anthony Eden succeeding the cigar-chopper.

Sam's view was that it was another privileged toff following another but interestingly he was now showing some admiration for the new Labour leader Hugh Gaitskill. As the political situation ebbed and flowed, man and son became close again, which meant they were able to attend more games at Stamford Bridge.

It seemed it would just be another average season as just before Christmas in 1954 Chelsea were in their familiar position of mid-table, not performing as an exciting or ambitious team, then they spectacularly began a winning streak to be neck-and-neck with Wolverhampton Wanderers in the race for the First Division title. Wolves were the dominant team of the 1950s and favourites to win the league once again. A crowd of 75,000 turned up at the stadium to watch the two contenders.

Sam and Anthony stood in an area known as Pimlico Corner because most of the spectators were from the Tachbrook. They were on the opposite side to the Shed stand, or the Monkey House as they called it. They all celebrated together as Chelsea won 1-0. If their team could beat Sheffield Wednesday in the next home game, they would become champions. They did, and 50 years after their foundation Chelsea had won their very first trophy. Unfortunately it would be another 50 years before they won their next title.

Anthony's own football participation had been somewhat curtailed since school matches and the estate games, which were becoming less frequent as the family units were evolving or moving on, so while Sam was no longer diving around on the concrete pitches with his makeshift padding, at the age of 40 he was still diving around of more forgiving grass pitches.

Sometime during the 1920s a cabbie had a little think, because of the antisocial work patterns it meant they were missing out on leisure and sporting activities the rest of the world was enjoying. He thought about it some more and decided to set up the Motor Cab Trade sports and social club. It was known as the MoCaTra.

By the early 1950s there were darts, snooker, and angling sections but by far the most popular section was the football group.

The west London-based drivers formed a team which played in the midweek South West League with matches playing each Wednesday afternoon, against other teams made up from other groups working irregular hours or shifts: police officers, fire brigades, public sector, or airline staff. The drawback for a self-employed group of players was that it was always feast or famine in terms of availability; sometimes they could field two teams and others they could barely scrape together a starting 11. Sam gave Anthony the call and he began playing for MoCaTra on a regular basis.

MoCaTra was to become a big influence on Kathy's life, although she didn't know it then. In the meantime she was to come to her brother's aid again. The television industry had gone through a significant shake up and the Independent Television Channel had been formed as a commercial enterprise to directly challenge the BBC monopoly. The first advertisements had started to appear; Gibbs toothpaste and Pepsident had everyone rushing to achieve that pearly white smile. More importantly for the acting profession, greater opportunities would be opening up in the dramas and serials the ITV companies were to create.

Over a few months Anthony would appear in a few television productions including *An Alligator Named Daisy*' as boy with stick, a series called *John and Julie*, and then a few uncredited walk-ons. He was earning a living of sorts, confident with the medium of television still limited as an actor, so he really needed a good stage role for him to develop.

Kathy had enjoyed her work at the Betty Farmer Agency but she was badly underpaid. She was an accomplished secretary and a good organiser, so when an opportunity arose to move to where her skills would be more appreciated, her wages considerably better, she became a PA to the boss of a large office equipment firm, Ofrex. She asked her boss if he had any vacancies that might suit Anthony; he did and soon they had a new clerk earning a fiver a week. Anthony was also allowed to take calls from his agent, generally telling him there was no work. He had actually attended some auditions during lunch hours but they had come to nothing.

One day Anthony was told by the agency to be at the Comedy Theatre, he was to audition for a play being produced by Joan Littlewood. It was called *The Quare Fellow* by Brendan Behan.

There was a problem, however: he had to be at the theatre at three o'clock, his lunch hour had already been taken and he was not confident enough to ask permission to attend. He decided it would only take an hour or so to get to the theatre, go through the paces then return to the office without anyone there noticing.

He went down to the toilets on the ground floor, climbed out of a window and legged it to Penton Street where he joined a group of actors hanging about the entrance to the theatre. A coach pulled up and the group were told that Joan Littlewood was in Brighton where the audition would take place, which put Anthony in a bit of an awkward position. He nevertheless climbed on to the transport and headed down to the seaside.

He was given the script to read on the journey down, went straight in to the audition, and by eight that night he got the part. The cast then broke off for some food then rehearsed overnight before pausing for breath at breakfast time, dossing down in the theatre for a few hours then rehearsing again for the rest of the day.

Anthony had managed to phone his mum to let her know what was going on but he was now entrapped in the mad and chaotic world that was Joan Littlewood and Brendan Behan. Littlewood was legendary though not for all the right reasons. She was brusque, rude, and hypercritical with a vile tongue and equally vile temper. She possessed no humour or grace, but other than those character defects she proved to be exciting to work with. She was an active member of the Communist Party at the same time as Sam although there is no record of them being active together. Joan was married to the folk singer and fellow activist, Ewan MacColl.

Littlewood was under an exclusion order issued by the BBC because of her political stance and more than probably her extreme personality. She had also been a force among left wing theatre groups, mainly in the north-west, where she had met MacColl. Then she formed a professional bond, followed by a sexual one, with Gerry Raffles, another experimental actor, producer, writer and lunatic. Joan divorced MacColl, who went on to write several songs including 'The First Time Ever I Saw Your Face' and 'Dirty Old Town', and was the father of Kirsty MacColl.

Littlewood and Raffles set up the Theatre Workshop, secured a lease on a dilapidated crumbling Theatre Royal in Stratford not on Avon, where they organised a massive clean-up and repaint, organisation for them being a fairly loose term: the work was carried out by the actors and stage managers they had recruited, most of whom lived in the theatre itself. Joan didn't live there though, as she liked to return to her home in Blackheath. Her standing and reputation as a champion of working-class writers, actors and plays had now brought her into mainstream as a pioneering innovative producer, and it became more so after a tatty, beer-stained script was pushed through the letterbox at the theatre. She read it and became intrigued then convinced it was a work of brilliance. She invited the writer to come to Stratford where a man as tatty and beer-stained as his script arrived. Her extraordinary collaboration with Brendan Behan began.

Behan came from a well-connected Republican family in Dublin and in his younger days he had been a member of the IRA, though not particularly successful because on his first operation he was arrested attempting to smuggle explosives into Liverpool docks. He served some time in a borstal in Lancashire before he was shipped back to Ireland. He was arrested immediately on his return after being implicated in the attempted murder of two police officers and was incarcerated in Mountjoy Prison. He got lucky at the end of the war when he was released under a general amnesty when he began his career as a writer and author.

The Quare Fellow was written as a direct result of his experiences in Mountjoy Prison. The plot revolved around the lives of the prisoners, staff, and the warden on the day a new prisoner arrived. It would only be a rather brief stay because he was going to be executed by hanging the following day. The prisoner was not seen or heard and was just referred to as the Quare Fellow, a name given to the poor souls who were to die from the gallows. There was no literal interpretation of the term queer, or homosexual; in that context it meant strange or odd.

Confusingly there is a gay character in the play, called the Other Fellow. How queer or odd is that? In précis, the plot is that the Quare Fellow is to be executed for the undisputed crime of chopping a friend into several pieces with a very sharp axe. The dialogue reflects the despair of the prisoners, the reactions and attitude of the prison officers and how they coped and reacted to daily life. So far so good and jolly.

The central theme though is the general reaction towards the condemned man. The other inmates feel little towards him as an individual and have not even heard or seen him; their concern and horror is about the punishment. They even react more in anger and prejudice towards the Other Fellow while they bicker and argue among themselves about their trivial and meaningless lives.

Brendan Behan, as Anthony soon discovered, was a world-class piss-artist, the first of many he was to meet, befriend or take care of over the years.

One of the first stories the cast had heard about Behan, or from him, was that he first started consuming alcohol when he was eight years old, actively encouraged by his alcoholic grandmother.

One day they were found staggering about and trying to support each other in the street. A woman passing by had commented it was a shame to see such a fine-looking boy so deformed. Granny looked her in the eye, and responded,

'He's not feckin' deformed, he's feckin' drunk.'

Joan had managed to rein his drinking a little, but she had to re-write a lot of the text and she also added the music, most memorably 'The Auld Triangle' written by Behan or his brother or the both of them depending on who you believed. Either way, it became one of the most well-known and recorded Irish songs.

The Quare Fellow was about to open in the West End after its successful run at Stratford, so the new cast arrived back from Brighton late on Sunday. Anthony returned home to the flat wearing the same clothing he had put on three days before, two females sniffed the air again and off he went for a lengthy clean-up.

The cast had to be at the theatre by noon ready for the afternoon run-through so before that he made his way to the Ofrex offices to explain his sudden disappearance to the boss. The man roared with laughter, gave the surprised absconder his last week's pay then two weeks' holiday money in lieu of notice. The boss in return would receive two free tickets for the show.

When Anthony arrived at the Comedy Theatre, the stage manager told him that the rest of the cast, the writer and the director were in the Hand and Racquet pub next door.

Joan and Behan had decided because of the frantic process of casting and the pummelling schedule of rehearsals it would be an idea for all of them to have a lunchtime sandwich and drink to get to know each other a little better, all 23 actors.

They were right though, they really didn't know each other at all, and for most of the group, Anthony included, it would be their West End debuts. On entering the pub the first thing Anthony did was to bump into an actor playing one of the main characters, but could not remember his name so called him by his character's name.

'Sorry, er, Misker,' Anthony said. Misker held out his hand,

'Richard, Richard Harris.'

Richard led Anthony to the bar and bought him a pint. They began to talk, Richard telling his new colleague that he was in his first year at LAMDA when he first went for the part at Stratford but he was told the role had already been cast. He insisted on talking to Joan, who told him in no uncertain terms that the character was written for a middle-aged man, not one for someone in their early 20s. Richard told her he had been living on scraps and the drink for years, dossing in shitty lodging, the life of a pauper.

'And this face of mine, Miss Littlewood, it looks like firewood has been chopped upon it.'

Joan agreed, the axe fell on the other actor and Richard came in.

Anthony talked to Richard about the dialogue and characters generally; he valued the older man's opinion and advice. He asked Richard why the Odd Fellow was such a prominent character.

'Well you see, Brendan likes a bit of bum?'

'Eh?'

'He's bisexual, he won't be interested in us though.

He likes a bit of rough!'

'Eh?'

'Never mind, I'll explain when you are a bit wiser'

'Eh?'

They were all then ushered back to the theatre, had a full dress rehearsal, and two hours rest before curtain up at eight. Anthony played one of the two young prisoners and was to sing 'The Auld Triangle' but he hadn't realised it was a duet on the opening night. As he started the song, another voice, raucous, loud, and crude, exploded from stage right. It was the author, hammered from Guinness and Sherry, bellowing away.

They were to see less of Behan as the run continued. Joan suppressed his unscheduled guest appearances, but by then the esteemed writer had found comfort with his fellow exiled community in the pubs of north London.

One Saturday night the cast met up in the Hand and Racquet for after work drinks, Brendan was already in the pub when they clattered through the door and he had a serious look on his face but insisted on buying them all a drink. Once all were served, he pulled out a telegram from his pocket, waved it around then handed it to Richard Harris who read it, rubbed his chin and passed it to Anthony who raised his eyes, passed it to the publican who whistled, passed it back to Richard who passed it to another actor who scratched his balls, his own, not Richards's, then passed the telegram back to Behan. It read,

'In your absence, the Irish Republican Army has sentenced you to death as a traitor to the Irish People.'

Richard Harris looked around at everyone, realised he was the Spokesman for them all and asked Brendan what he was going to do.

His sad face suddenly lit up into a broad grin.

'You know what fellas, I'm going to sendem a reply,'

'In my feckin absence you can feckin shoot me.'

The Quare Fellow ended its run in the autumn and had been a critical and personal success for everyone involved. During the run, Richard and Joan convinced Anthony to change his stage name to Tony because he was now a mature, promising actor.

The IRA never did attempt to carry out the assassination threat, but Brendan probably helped them to relax about it, he later died at the age of 41 from diabetes and alcoholism.

Richard didn't finish his course at LAMDA as the director Lee Strasbourg dragged him off to Hollywood after seeing him in *The Quare Fellow*. Tony and Richard met up briefly over the years but did not appear together again.

One other interesting thing happened during the run at the Comedy Theatre: Tony gave two tickets to his mum and to his surprise, when Anne turned up, she was on his Dad's arm.

8
A WEDDING, CONSCRIPTION, AND FRANKIE HOWERD

Tony was being optimistic about his parents getting back together again. Anne still loved Sam and she persistently refused to go through divorce proceedings; now they were seeing each other on a fairly regular basis. Anne's side of the family, the partying side, were also still in touch with Sam, while her two brothers Ted and Billy worked on the cab rank alongside him. Eve, Anne's sister, had the party flat, and besides birthdays, engagements, and Christmas, she held an open house at least once a month. Sam was always invited, telling his jokes, and sharing cab stories with Ted and Billy.

Unbeknown to Tony and certainly not Maude Brown, Sam was, as he explained a few years later,

'havin' a bit of how's yer father with yer mother'.

Kathy knew what was going on, and she also confided later in life that she suspected that Sam was having a bit of how's your father with a few other mothers. She was always a little cold and distant towards Sam since he had left home, which was about to become a little more uncomfortable as her father was about to introduce her to her husband to be.

The MoCaTra football team had formed an association with their opposite numbers in Edinburgh, after a few London cabbies met up with some Scottish cabbies at an England v Scotland game. They decided to play each other on the morning before each annual fixture then attend the international match in the afternoon. A convoy of cabs would leave London on Friday, play the match at Hibernian's Easter Road ground on Saturday morning, then would drive to Hampden Park for the international before going back to the capital for an evening of Scottish hospitality. The following year Scots travelled down to London where the MoCaTra game was played at Craven Cottage, then they saw the match at Wembley Stadium and in the evening attended a dinner-dance at Battersea Town Hall. The Selby family were sitting at their table when a young, good-looking man came over and asked Kathy if she would like to dance. Sam said jokingly,

'Don't, Kathy, he put two goals past me this morning.'

His name was Jimmy, an unusual name for a Scot, although his full name was James Keegan. The couple spent the rest of the evening dancing or at the bar talking, then went outside for some 'fresh air'. Intrigued, Tony crept out after them and caught them snogging, their lips stuck together like barnacles to a barge.

A WEDDING, CONSCRIPTION, AND FRANKIE HOWERD

The following day the London crowd waved the Scots off for their long drive back. Jimmy had obviously made a big impression on Kathy as she dabbed her eyes, her bottom lip flapping in a far-from-elegant quiver.

Jimmy was not a taxi driver; he was a skilled coach builder working for the main company in Scotland which built cabs. The two lovebirds wrote and telephoned incessantly; Jimmy visited London as often as he could then eventually moved down permanently which meant that Tony was to have a room-mate. Jimmy was immediately taken on by the London Cab Company as a coach builder, but he now wanted to drive the things, not just build them. Sam provided him with all the relevant books and tips to prepare for 'the Knowledge' and his soon-to-be son-in-law became a licensed taxi driver. Then, when the young couple did get married, they asked Tony to give Kathy away rather than Sam and to make matters slightly worse, Sam wasn't even invited to the wedding. He wanted to bring along Maude, which was a typical selfish and insensitive decision, particularly as he was still horizontally involved with Anne. Kathy thought this would be humiliating for her mother and for Maude who was probably unaware of the deceit.

The marriage was Tony's debut at Caxton Hall, a venue he would get to know well, and it was also good news for him as the happy couple moved into their own flat and he had his room to himself again. However this life was far too comfortable with the home comforts, home cooking with no real responsibilities. God knows how his parents fitted in their tryst, or where, but he was blissfully unaware.

Socially life was beginning to change for Tony's generation. The Wootston Youth Club had been a good part of his life and he developed his passion for table tennis eventually becoming the west London champion. He was still dropping in from time to time, but most of his friends and acquaintances had moved on, preferring the pub and the West End clubs.

The other significant reason life was changing for his age group was National Service where all fit young men between the ages of eighteen and twenty one were called up to undergo compulsory Military Service for two years. The reason for peacetime conscription was to have a permanent force of reservists to be called up in the event of future wars or conflicts, many of which were being fought in British colonies.

Many of the men from the Tachbrook and Pimlico area had been conscripted, to fight in the Korean War, then over the years became involved in the fighting in Malaysia, Aden, Cyprus and Kenya. Some returned home hardened by their experiences, some broken, some disfigured and some as amputees.

There was a deal. If you were a student about to enter university or about to begin an apprenticeship, conscription would be deferred until the completion of the degree course or apprentice training but both options were not available to Tony. There were differing opinions. Some conscripts thought it had changed their lives and direction, while others told of the bullying and unpleasantness, particularly in the army which took most of the intake. It also caused resentfulness because of the disruption to lives and families.

Every two weeks a few thousand youths were called up. Tony's name was on the list one particularly fateful fortnight.

He turned up at the army drill hall in Lambeth, and rather ruefully he approached an anteroom where 30 or so other miserable-looking sods were told to strip to their vests and underwear and waited to be seen by the medical officer. It was interesting for Tony to observe who was wearing their Y-front inside out. He remembered the place stank of sweat and smelly pumps, the ones they had to slip on to their feet or the ones squeaking out of nervous arses.

When he was eventually called into the medic's office, he was checked over, a few notes were made, then he was sent to the room next door to be assessed by an army psychologist. Tony was told to sit, he was stared at for a while, he looked on as the assessor stroked his chin, asked the potential recruit a few questions then told Tony to get dressed and go home, which he did, bemused and apprehensive?

A few days later a letter arrived from the Ministry of Defence which Anne brought to him while he was eating his boiled eggs and rather ironically soldiers. It informed Anthony Samuel Selby that because he was psychologically unfit, he would be unable to meet the standards required for army training as he was not fit or able. It was Sam's influence of course; he had a contact at the drill hall who told him about a possible escape clause.

When Tony was about six or seven, he used to piss the bed on a regular basis. He also learned how to swim at the same time. His parents arranged an appointment at All Saints Hospital where he was examined by a bladder and kidney specialist. Fortunately the specialist did not find any renal damage or complications and after a long discussion with Anne and Sam, they concluded it was probably the effects of the war and the injuries suffered by his grandparents that had traumatised him; it was a mental issue.

Tony showed the letter to Sam, who read it slowly then smiled. He admitted he had written to the War Office to point out that his son still suffered from severe incontinence which would put him in danger of serious abuse and humiliation if he was to be placed in a barrack room environment.

Sam looked Tony in the eyes and told him in no uncertain terms – both families had suffered so much from the two world wars.

'They've had too many of us son, they are not taking any fucking more.' It was around this time Sam finally left the Communist Party. The Hungarian uprising, then the full truth of the Stalin gulags and death camps being revealed, finally extinguishing his fervour, but there was also another reason.

After the success of *The Quare Fellow*, the production transferred to Broadway, and at the time Equity had an agreement which allowed a quota of British or American actors to transfer with their shows between the two countries. Tony's name was on the list of actors submitted to the Americans but had been vetoed. When Sam heard this, he was convinced that the rejection was solely down to his political allegiances and activism. The veto also scuppered any chance of Tony appearing in any American stage production, film, or television show.

Sam, by now approaching his 50s, was still working long hours while juggling his complicated and rather selfish love life. He never discussed his relationship with Maude Brown nor ever mentioned her existence; it was as if that part of his life did not exist. Tony had no interest in the separate relationship, and neither Anne nor Kathy would ever bring up the subject.

As they say, life has to move on. Tony attended an audition for a farce called *Hotel Paradiso* which was to be produced by Billy Chappell, and had already been on a well-received run in the West End with Alec Guinness and Kenneth Williams as the principal actors.

Hotel Paradiso, written by Maurice Desvallières and Georges Feydeau has a typically convoluted French farce plot. Tony was offered the job to start a UK tour opening at the Theatre Royal, Plymouth. The star was Frankie Howerd.

When the cast met up for the first rehearsal, Tony was surprised by how tall and thick-set Howerd was. The second surprise was that Howerd clearly fancied him from the off, constantly pouting and blowing kisses in his direction then doing an Anton Dolin by touching him up at every opportunity. He told Howerd to pack it in but Frankie was nothing if not persistent.

For some reason Howerd was staying out of town, well away from the rest of the cast which they found a little odd. The stage manager, with some glee and satisfaction, told them why. On a previous engagement in Plymouth, Howerd had been caught in one of the naval barracks in a rather compromising position with a few eager matelots. In the stage manager's exact words, 'He was in the middle of a a fellatio competition.' Once the cast confirmed that fellatio meant blowjobs, the stage manager eagerly continued the story. Howerd had been escorted off the naval base and taken to the police station, but no charges were made against him. The relevant authorities had to suppress the story on the orders of the Admiralty and Howerd was banned from entering the area within six miles of any naval base, hence his banishment to the far side of Plymouth.

He was fortunate; if the newspapers had been given the story, his career, waning at the time, would have been finished, not to mention the probability of a prison sentence. The problem for Tony was that Howerd still persisted in trying to take him up the tradesman's entrance, after one show he arrived at his dressing room and tried it on again, Tony had to physically fight him off. Howerd was strong, and the younger man had real fear of being raped. His south London toughness took over and he eventually evicted his attacker through the door.

First a Billy Cotton Band musician, now a famous comedian, where would it all end? Tony had had enough and called Billy Chappell who promised to have a word. The following night things came to head.

The plot of *Hotel Paradiso* revolves around the henpecked owner of the hotel and his domineering wife. A hotel inspector arrives accompanied by his beautiful wife. The inspector is investigating complaints and rumours about ghosts and supernatural noises which are in fact the result of dodgy plumbing and rain gutters. The beautiful wife begins an affair with the hotel owner while his nephew, played by Tony, begins an affair with one of the maids. Cue lots of running around, door-slamming and misunderstanding until eventually the police arrive to arrest everyone, or nearly everyone. The set for this production had two rooms, a hallway and a sweeping staircase with a rostrum on either side, and at one point during the performance Tony had to run up the staircase together with Howerd who gave a little push. Selby would then do a prat fall, get up and continue upwards after him.

Howerd shoved Tony as hard as he could, his fellow actor crashed on to the stairs and cracked two ribs. Tony continued through the rest of the performance, took the curtain call then collapsed in severe pain as the rest of the cast fussed and tried to help him.

Howerd, in his own unique stuttering way, offered an insincere apology but they all knew he had caused the injury out of spite and fury. Thankfully the unwanted advances ceased after the unpleasant incident.

A few nights later they were in the middle of a scene when Patrick Newell, playing a police officer, entered the stage to arrest Howerd's character. Howerd was then to scramble through the legs of the rest of the cast and hide under the table. Unfortunately, or more fortuitously for the others, as he scrambled between Tony's leg, his wig became detached and stuck to Selby's crotch like a merkin before it fell to the stage floor. The table was covered with a large cloth reaching down to the floor, and from his viewpoint beneath the table Howerd could see the syrup of fig through the gap at the bottom, so his hand stretched out in a furtive attempt to retrieve the now popular Irish jig. Tony's deft inside flick left Howerd watching as the hairpiece reached Patrick who kicked it further away. They awaited a reaction; suddenly Howerd scrambled from under the table, picked up his hair and walked over to the prompt corner ordering the stage crew to go and fetch his wig glue. His fellow thespians looked down at the floor, hands clasped in front of them, shoulders heaving with suppressed laughter. Howerd's head then the rest of him appeared from stage right as he shouted out at the audience.

'Oh, er, accidents do happen, won't be a jiff.' A minute or so later he returned on stage.

'Now, where were we, oh, yes.' He slid under the table, and they all carried on.

9
COMING OF AGE

The *Hotel Paradiso* tour, despite Frankie Howerd, had been a good professional experience. Tony had matured more as an actor but unfortunately television and stage work was proving to be startlingly consistent: irregular or nothing at all. He had started to fill in with temporary clerical work. Sam also decided it was time for his son to learn how to drive, not, however, in a normal motor car but in his taxi. They began in the quieter parts of Battersea and Vauxhall, Sam squatting in the luggage well bellowing instructions as Tony sat in rigid concentration, tongue between his lips, hands in a tense grip around the steering wheel. Eventually he relaxed and after a few weeks he borrowed his uncle's car then passed the driving test at his first attempt.

Tony soon found a few temporary driving jobs, at a small laundry in Knightsbridge, then a few other ad-hoc roles around the West End. Parking in London was far easier then and the driving work meant he could attend auditions easily as well, so eventually he saved up enough to buy an old banger of a car for £50. The old Austin gave him mobility, no more reliance on the last bus or tube, or the lucky chance Sam or one of his dad's mates would be passing to pick him up. He also hoped the car would impress the girls and with that salacious thought, he bought a nice blanket for the back seat, just in case. It would have been practical to learn how the combustion engine worked but he could not be arsed. A few of the boys on the Tachbrook had trained as mechanics and were always up for fixing stuff on the side for a few bob.

Tony's main interest outside of acting was music, particularly jazz. One of his close friends was David Orchard and between them they had a decent collection of records and pottered around the music shops; attending live performances though was a different matter. The problem was venues as very few pubs or clubs had a live music licence. Live music was concentrated in the coffee bars around Soho, the Three I's, or the Flamingo Club in Wardour Street, and as these venues did not serve alcohol, they didn't have to worry about strict opening hours and consequently they could stay open late, and even later at weekends.

The British jazz scene grew from the basement clubs of Soho, and as a result Tony and David were around to see the emergence of the early pioneers, Chris Barber, Dick Charlesworth, and Kenny Ball among them. The only downside was the jazz scene was also attracting many earnest humourless beats or beatniks a basement of beards, existentialists reading copies of *The Age of Reason*, smoking Gitanes while tapping their cheesy, sandal-clad feet to the music, heads nodding in time with the endless double bass solo. The males in the audience were just as bad.

There were also a few among them who were considerably more knowledgeable, the ones who had been over to Paris where the jazz scene was more cosmopolitan and the Gitanes considerably cheaper. In the clubs there was also much lively discussion about jazz forms, the traditional jazz fans against the increasingly influential modern jazz movement, the Dixielanders against jazz blues, but all of them united when it came to country and western. It was all good fun and utterly pretentious, but fun was becoming more important, and for Tony and David the new venues alternated between jazz, blues, folk and skiffle, exciting times. The car blanket had some use as well.

In the meantime Tony needed some work. Early in 1958 Billy Chappell was casting for a new show called *Living for Pleasure*, a two-act revue written by Arthur Macrae and Richard Addinsell. The stars were Dora Bryan, Daniel Massey, George Rose and Janie Marden. They wanted him to understudy Massey and Rose then also work as part of the company. He thought it over for a few seconds then a few days later arrived in Manchester where the show was to preview for six weeks at the Opera House Theatre – which seated over 2,000 people in a stunning auditorium – before opening at the Garrick Theatre for a London season. Just opposite the theatre, Selby checked into his digs at the less stunning but certainly interesting New Theatre Pub. The landlord, Arthur Gosling, showed him to his room. Arthur, who was only in his early 30s, looked twice his age, probably because he stank of booze, chip fat, and cigarette smoke. On the other hand the whole pub did. Out of interest, Tony asked Arthur why the pub was named the New Theatre.

'Because t'Opera House was called the New Theatre before t'Opera House so really t'New Theatre is really t'old theatre, intit?'

Tony supposed it was. Arthur showed him to his room which was clean, bright, and importantly, near the bathroom. Arthur staggered off and after offloading his things, Tony made his way over the road to the theatre where he met up with the cast. He warmed to Dora Bryan immediately, finding her endearing, attentive and extremely funny. She was a local girl, born in Oldham, and married to the Lancashire cricketer Bill Lawton. Everyone gelled straight away; they rehearsed long and hard and were ready to go very quickly. They opened the first week in February and the opening night went well, about a full house then good reviews the following day.

The writers and the director were still fine tuning though, they needed the whole company to have a full day in rehearsal before the show on the Wednesday night. They were all pretty knackered when they finished work that night. The good thing about staying in a pub hotel was the landlord could keep the bar open after official closing time, that's if he was still conscious, if he wasn't; the guests would help themselves to drinks and leave the money in a pint glass by the till.

Tony was looking forward to a couple of welcome beers after finishing work. As he was leaving he had a quick chat with Johnny, the stage doorman, who was a Manchester United supporter. Johnny was in a strange mood because although his team had just drawn 3-3 in Belgrade against Red Star meaning they would progress to the next round on aggregate. He wasn't happy.

'They were fuckin' free-nil up as well the bastards.'

It really was a horrible, grey misty night, the dampness pervaded hair and clothing from a constant drizzle. Arthur had told him the reason it was so damp in the city.

'It's t'fuckin' clouds bouncing off the fuckin' Pennines.'

Relieved to get in from the depressing weather, Tony headed to the main bar for a nightcap. The New Theatre had a metal staircase leading up to the rooms, not a spiral shape but upright leading off to a landing on each of the upper floors. As Tony made his way to the bar a body suddenly flew down the stairwell gap from the third floor, landing with a splendid thud at his feet. It was Arthur. He eventually picked himself up, staggered a while then looked at his guest.

'Fuckin' 'ell.'

Arthur wobbled off into the bar. Two of the cast were already in there and had served themselves a couple of pints, then one of them pulled a pint for Tony and the three of them looked over to the prostrate Arthur lying in an alcove with a lump on his forehead the size of a snooker ball. The drinkers were debating if they should call an ambulance, but it proved to be a two-pint decision, so they pulled themselves another one. Suddenly Arthur woke up, looked around, lifted himself off the bench and staggered off toward the stairs.

'See you in't morning, lads.'

In the morning he did indeed see them again, and as they gathered for breakfast Arthur was mooching around carrying a clutch of paperwork. The snooker ball had subsided more to the size of a gobstopper, and he seemed to be showing few side-effects of his sudden plummet.

Tony was needed in the theatre again early because of some re-writes. The reason he was needed was twofold: as a member of the company he had to be aware of any new dialogue or musical arrangement changes, but also as understudy for Rose and Massey he needed to know any script changes. They finished in the late afternoon, so he decided to have a quick sandwich then go across to the pub for a brief rest before the performance. When he reached the stage door area Johnny was hunched over the big brown Bakelite radio squatting on his desk. Tony asked him what was wrong.

The distressed reply was, 'It's fuckin' United. Fuckin' plane crashed.' Tony patted him on the shoulder, consoling him and saying he was sure the team were fine, then went next door to buy a sandwich in the milk bar, but the news of the accident was spreading around the city and people had concerned, anxious expressions.

The pubs had just opened when Tony arrived back, and Arthur had set up a radio and a television set. The news was getting worse: the death toll was rising, and it was becoming obvious that many of the players would have been killed, but there was no official casualty list.

When Tony returned to the theatre the streets and the areas around were empty of people and traffic. Johnny, who was still listening to the radio, ticked his name off the list. The producer, director and the cast were gathered around the stage to decide if the performance would be cancelled. It was decided to prepare for the show then await the audience turnout; in the event it proved to be a near full house they needed something to take their minds off that freezing chunk of metal in the Munich snow.

Johnny was still at his desk as the cast left the theatre. Tony put his arm around him as Johnny shed a salty tear. 'You're not United son,' he said. 'No, but I'm a football supporter, Johnny.'

The following day brought the worst of news: seven players were dead, more were severely or critically injured, and the United manager Matt Busby was in intensive care. The effect the disaster had on the community was something that Tony would never forget. He and his friends had a job to do, to cheer people up.

The revue continued with a healthy box office and he had played both Massey and Rose's roles a few times then towards the end of the run, Billy Chappell confirmed to the cast that *Living for Pleasure* was going to open at the Garrick Theatre for a lengthy run of nine months. After the last show in Manchester, Tony said goodbye to Johnny who was a little more buoyant with the news Busby was out of intensive care and on his way home. He then made his way back to the New Theatre, where before going upstairs he checked carefully for any publicans in freefall. The following day he boarded the train at London Road Station and headed back to Pimlico.

It was the start of spring when Tony arrived back; the balcony at the flat was bright and cheerful from the fragrance and colours of the daffodils and tulips Anne had planted in the containers. He was thinking about the run at the Garrick when he was brought back to reality by his mum telling him off for flicking fag ash over the balcony, 'The postman will think he's got dandruff.' Tony looked down at the postie, who wasn't brushing his shoulders, so he was in the clear.

It was going to be three months before rehearsals began for *Living for Pleasure*'s London run so Tony had a few weeks to fill in, and his thoughts turned to some extra work or a cameo role or two. The best place to find out about new productions or film projects was the Buckstone Club, an actors' watering hole in the basement of a building next to the stage door at the Haymarket Theatre.

The club was owned by the actor Gerald Campion who had opened it shortly after the war. He became very famous in the 1950s in the role of Billy Bunter, the fat owl of Greyfriars School in the eponymous television series. Billy was a greedy, corpulent schoolboy everyone bullied. It was a strange part to play because Gerald and the rest of the actors were well into their 30s when the series was made. Gerald was not particularly fat, so the costume department had to pad him out. The content of the show, besides bullying and fat shaming, also included racial stereotyping and corporal punishment.

Gerald, possibly as a result of his regular humiliation was a miserable and rude man. He was also the slowest and impolite mine host in town. He was tolerated because people made and treasured some wonderful friendships at the Buckstone, then later at Gerry's Bar which Campion opened over the road in Shaftesbury Avenue.

One evening Tony heard that a casting director from Danziger Productions was in the club. The production company had been founded by two American brothers, Eddie and Harry Danziger. They made cheap cops and robbers B-films that would normally precede the main attraction in cinemas, or even cheaper television productions. They famously could turn around a low-budget film in less than two weeks or a telly show in about four days, and their reputation was built on their featurettes. Helen Parker was the casting director, and her colleague was a man called Ronny Curtis who had a glass eye and a lisp. Tony introduced himself, then after a short conversation they hired him immediately, got his agent's details and told him to turn up at Merton Park Studios for a few days' work at £15 a day. A few other actors were still hanging around after the Danziger people left, and one of them nodded towards Tony and asked him how he had got on. Tony liked him right away; there was a confidence about him and genuine friendliness. He was a RADA graduate who had just finished a stint with the Royal Shakespeare Company. He was from Salford, and although RADA had not quite smoothed out his flat vowels, Albert Finney's voice and mannerisms were self-assured.

Finney was slightly older than Tony, but they fell into conversation easily. They talked of the difference between stage and film acting, their ambitions, and how television was now opening up all manner of opportunities for working-class actors. As they spoke another group of actors came into the club, one of whom stood out like a beacon, blond with azure blue eyes.

He came over to them and hugged Finney who introduced him to Tony and said, 'This is Peter, we were at RADA together.' Finney's friend shook Tony's hand. 'Peter O'Toole, now what are you having, Tony?' He ordered the drinks which were poured and served by Gerald Campion after which O'Toole remarked in his not particularly sotto voice, 'You know he does possess a countenance as if he has just been handed a bag of wet farts.'

It was by all accounts a very enthusiastic piss-up.

As Tony was enjoying the company of new friends, he was catching up with old ones, particularly David Orchard; they were still going to jazz clubs amid the still sordid and seedy Soho. Paul Raymond was expanding his strip club and sex shop empire while the Maltese mobsters were muscling in on some of the action. There was that frisson of danger and excitement around.

The pubs were also becoming well-known and trendy: the York Minster which later became the French was frequented by film and television people; the Coach and Horses in Greek Street attracted mainly artists, writers and actors, where the publican, Norman Balon who was more rude, certainly more creatively rude than Campion. Tony was once in the pub with a couple of actors and regulars when someone approached the bar and asked for his normal. Balon looked at him and asked if he was a regular customer, which he was, Norman just didn't like him.

'No your're not' Norman said pointing to Selby and his group.

'Those cunts are fucking regulars, bunch of arse holes.'

David Orchard was going steady with a girl named Carol, and he suggested that Tony meet up with them and one of her friends. He was introduced to a tall, brown-haired elegant girl called Jacqui Milburn. They got on well and flirted and laughed a lot, but what he did know was she should not have been in the pub as she had only just turned 16. They arranged to meet up again the following weekend for a drive in the country. David had a relative who ran a hotel near Tonbridge Wells, and its great attraction was the outside swimming pool. On a lovely sunny morning the four of them drove down to Kent, the car coughing and spluttering on its first longish run for a while, then the men quickly changed into their trunks and awaited the girls to arrive at the sun beds. As they appeared several whistles rang out across the pool when they came out of the changing rooms, mainly for Jacqui. Tony gasped as she approached; she looked stunning in her swimsuit as she glided along on her long shapely legs.

When Tony had regained his composure, he found out more about Jacqui. She told him her hope was to become a professional dancer in the West End, then to travel to Las Vegas to work there; she was certainly confident and ambitious. Jacqui told Tony she had been more artistic than academic at school. Most of her weekends had been spent on dance and speech training, and she managed to gain a place at Sutton Art College but had not taken it up. Her reasoning was that because of her working-class background, three years at art college was not a realistic option. Her family would need her to bring money into the household so she had ended up working in an office typing pool which she hated immediately.

Jacqui had seen an advert seeking dancers at the Windmill Theatre so had auditioned and was successful, but unfortunately her age was a problem. She needed to be 18 to appear in the shows, although her parents would have most likely objected anyway. Tony and Jacqui quickly became a couple, and he eventually met her parents. Mrs Milburn was called Nora, but she was known as Nonnie, and had started her working life as a waitress then became a reservation clerk with British European Airways. Jim Milburn came from Cumbria where he had worked as a farm labourer when he first left school, then he thought he would try something a little easier, he became a coal miner. Jim was a cousin of the Milburn and Charlton football families; he was a promising prospect himself until he suffered a serious leg injury. He decided to move south, became a school keeper then a caretaker in Tooting which was where he met Nonnie.

Jim was an avid socialist, and when he met up with Sam they gelled immediately and became firm friends. Although Jacqui was disappointed that she was unable to work at the Windmill, her figure and good looks enabled her to become a model for most of the main fashion houses in London. She also received a good discount and dresses from which the females in both families had a good benefit. In the meantime, Tony was still in the revue at the Garrick. On Thursday, 26 February Princess Alexandra, the Duchess of Fife, died, which was a pity because it meant she was unable to attend Tony's 21st birthday party, not that he knew one was being planned.

At the end of the performance that night, Dora Bryan had stepped forward to inform the audience it was his coming-of-age party, and she got them to sing 'Happy Birthday' which they did, gave him a mini ovation then rushed out. The cast would normally be hurrying off as well, eager to get home, but they were all gathering in the wings conspiratorially. Dora led Tony back on to the stage in front of the safety curtain. They stood looking at the empty theatre with some odd noises coming from behind them, then the curtain suddenly ascended quickly and on the set were his parents, along with Jacqui, Kathy and Jimmy, all the cast and orchestra. A large table was groaning under the volume of drinks and stuff and there was another chorus of 'Happy Birthday'. A few of the orchestra became an impromptu backing band and Tony sang some jazz numbers with Janie Marden.

It was around one in the morning before the party wound down and it was noticed Kathy was missing. She had been necking down the booze quite happily most of the night, and after a brief search she was found passed out in Janie's dressing room.

When the birthday boy came into work the following day, the company manager called him into the office and told him, 'Miss Marden informs me, and I quote, "someone has been fucking sick in my hat box and it wasn't fucking me" unquote.' It cost Tony half a week's pay to replace the rather unpleasantly soiled head gear and box.

As much as he loved the show at the Garrick, he was feeling a little restless; it had been a very successful revue but for him it felt a little dated. The West End was beginning to change and more new plays by young playwrights were being produced while exciting young actors were beginning to shine. During the *Living for Pleasure* run Tony was approached to take a part in a new show to open at the Saville Theatre, directed by Billy Chappell. The producers had seen his work and thought Tony would be a good fit for one of the characters. It was called *Expresso Bongo*, a satire about the pop industry. The two principal actors were Paul Schofield and Millicent Martin, and Tony hoped to become the third, playing Herbert (Bert) Rudge, a budding pop star managed by Schofield's unscrupulous manager. Bert has a name change and becomes Bongo Herbert. All sorts of nastiness, duplicity and downright unpleasantness happens, and the denouement was that everyone got stitched up.

There was a big problem though. When Tony was offered the part, he could not get out of the contract for *Living for Pleasure* despite Billy Chappell pleading with the producers to release him. They wouldn't budge and the part went to James Kenny. A year or so after *Expresso Bongo* had opened on stage, a sanitised film version was made starring Laurence Harvey and Sylvia Sims. The part of Rudge went to Cliff Richard.

10
THE RADAS

When Tony Selby woke up on 1 January 1960 the prime minister, Harold Macmillan, went to Africa for six weeks to get away from the cold but to also make his wind of change speech directly challenging the apartheid system in South Africa.

In the United States of America, John F. Kennedy was practising his inaugural speech still stuck on the 'think what you can do for country' passage.

The wind of change was also starting to flow through Britain, socially, within the arts and popular music, and while the rock and pop revolution was still in its infancy, it was the film and theatre industry which first kicked off with what was to become a notable decade.

It was to see the emergence of the exciting new actors. In addition to Albert Finney, Peter O'Toole and Richard Harris, other up-and-coming talents included Ronald Fraser, Robert Shaw and Bryan Pringle. Through O'Toole and Finney, Tony had met the other three, and he in turn introduced them to two of his actor mates, James Villiers and Patrick Newell. Most of them had studied their craft at the Royal Academy of Dramatic Art – RADA. They were the RADAS as Ronnie Fraser liked to call the group. Other than RADA, they all had something else in common: they could not decide what drink they preferred, champagne, beer, whisky, vodka or gin, so they drank the lot in no particular order.

James Villiers came from a very posh and aristocratic background; he was the great grandson of the fourth Earl of Clarendon. He would often bellow after a few drinks, 'I am 48rh in line to the throne of Great Britain, don't you know.' Which nobody did know, of course, or indeed cared about. It was also Villiers who introduced the term 'luvvie' into the language to describe members of the acting profession, although he called everyone 'luvvie' anyway. Villiers and Tony had done a brief repertory together and despite their differing backgrounds, they became firm friends.

Tony knew Newell from the *Hotel Paradiso* tour. Newell was a large man, weighing in at 18 stones. He was always cast as a fat villain or the sinister boss in series like *The Avengers* or *Danger Man* over the years. He would complain to one and all, 'You know chaps, every time I try to lose weight the less work I get.' Villiers looked at him scornfully and replied, 'You know what luvvie, that's just your bloody excuse to remain circumferentially fucking enormous.'

When *Hotel Paradiso* was touring, Newell had picked Tony up at Brighton station to take them to their digs along the coast road towards Roedean Girls School, but unfortunately his mode of transport was a Vespa 125cc scooter. They started the journey hardly inconspicuous, a fat man, a reasonably thin man and two large suitcases, when the scooter broke down halfway there. They dismounted; Tony sat on the suitcases while Newell farted around with the engine. A police car pulled up beside them. In law a person could ride a scooter if they had a provisional licence but was not allowed to carry a passenger without a full licence, particularly a passenger holding two large suitcases. Patrick had no intention of taking the test. The police asked for his documents, then looked them both up and down.

'Ah, this gentleman kindly stopped to help me, officers,' Newell said, referencing Tony.

They looked at Tony.

'Did he indeed, where are you heading then?' Tony mumbled the name of the place they were staying. They looked up and down the stretch of road they were on, the sea behind them, rocks, and trees on the other side. The scooter engine suddenly burst into a tinny splutter, so Newell clambered back on and said to Tony, 'Well thanks for stopping, old chap.'

Taking off, Newell left Tony with the two suitcases. The police officers stared at Tony as he picked up the luggage and began a forlorn walk along the mile or so towards the hotel. The police car disappeared in the other direction so there was a faint hope that Newell would be waiting around the bend for him. He was gone. Tony found him propping up the bar but at least he had a pint and a scotch waiting for him.

Of all the RADAS, Ronnie Fraser was the most prodigious imbiber, although only marginally. Ronnie was born in England but had been brought up in Scotland; he said he went to RADA in order to speak English again, then all the parts offered to him were to play Scotsmen. His drink of choice though was not whisky but vodka, although he was always willing to finish a bottle of Bell's. In the pubs and clubs, Ronnie would offer a cheery smile and wave to the bar staff, asking,

'A Fraser water if you please.'

The drink would start as a small vodka and tonic, progressing to a double with slightly less tonic to a treble with even less tonic. One evening he was with Tony when someone bought them both a schnapps, so Fraser poured it straight into his own drink.

'To a new Fraser water, Tony, vodka and teutonic.'

Fraser, Pringle and O'Toole together with Robert Shaw had been working in a play by Willis Hall called The Long and the Short and the Tall. The play had opened at the Royal Court and directed by Lindsay Anderson which then transferred to the Cambridge Theatre.

O'Toole had spoken to Tony about his character – he was playing a Cockney soldier, part of a group of British troops holding a Japanese soldier captive in the jungle in the Far East towards the end of the war. O'Toole felt he needed some voice coaching and advice on his accent, so Tony agreed to help him but said that in his opinion there was no such thing as a Cockney accent. The London accent was generic, the Pearly Kings and Queens cor blimey luv a duck, apples and pears was a load of bollocks. They met up with Sam Selby who more or less confirmed Tony's synopsis. They argued that the East End of London to the south of the city was less than six miles, and accents did not vary that much in such a relatively small area. Tony's own accent had flattened out and was now slightly more refined, while Sam's still retained the rawness. O'Toole listened and practised, working hard on the vowels and cadence, and when the play opened at the Cambridge he was perfect.

Tony and Jacqui were invited as guests but before the show they were told to meet the boys in a pub near to the theatre for a drink. They were taking the show calls via the pub phone with an anxious assistant stage manager acting as a chaperone. It was all slightly weirder because they were all in full costume and makeup. Tony and Jacqui took their seats five minutes before the curtain came up, just as the cast were strolling through the stage door.

The actors were stunning and gave a faultless performance, and after a few curtain calls they scurried back to the dressing rooms, changed into their civvies, and wiped off the grease paint in no particular order. Tony and Jacqui had arranged to catch up with them at the Buckstone Club, and remarkably they were already there by the time the couple arrived, sort of swaying in a rictus grinning row. They were gracious, courteous, and flirtatious towards Jacqui, who had already fallen in love with them all. Tony fell in with their banter and anecdotes and life was grand.

Jacqui had developed into a stunning head-turner; her work as a model was still ongoing but she finally made her career choice happen when she was 18 and became a dancer at the Windmill Theatre.

The Windmill had gained a somewhat exaggerated reputation for its perceived gauche shows, with nudity and supposedly erotic connotations. It presented non-stop revenues from around midday to 11 at night, and to meet the schedules the performances needed fitness and stamina. Jacqui could more than meet the physical demands, but more importantly for her further career, she gained an Equity Card. Vivian van Damm was still producing the shows when Jacqui joined the company. He kept a watchful, protective eye on the girls, having personally interviewed and hired all of them, and had a strict moral code. Unfortunately, shortly afterwards he fell seriously ill and his daughter Sheila took over his role, where she continued his disciplined, watchful approach.

The Windmill Theatre had a capacity of around 400. The performance format would be an opening dance by the Revue de Belles, then a boy and girl song and dance routine followed by a spot from the resident comedian for the week, Peter Sellers, Bob Monkhouse and Jimmy Edwards among them. It was then time for the climax of the show – although it was probable a few of the audience had already reached theirs – the Tableaux Vivants, the famous nude living statues. This was performed under strict censorious conditions.

It was the censor's decision that it was unlawful for any movement on stage which could cause titillation or lascivious thinking. Nudity could be seen if it was in paintings in galleries or statues in museums, but if nudity moved then it was rude. The performers' discipline had to be absolute.

Jacqui and her colleagues had the benefit of two superb choreographers – Keith Lester, who had trained and worked with the Russian ballet companies, and John Law, a musical theatre veteran. They had to have flawless routines, perfection in every show.

The two men were also clever and innovative stage designers. The first performer had to enter the stage already naked behind the closed curtain. Law and Lester arranged for the backdrops and scenery to be easily manoeuvred across the performer's body so that when the curtain was raised the moving props only revealed tantalising glimpses. There was also an elaborate fan 'dance' in perfect synchronisation. The dancers, each holding a large fan, would sway and pass the fans over the nude girl, covering the most intimate parts; the audience, despite strained necks, did not even catch a peek. The fans were then withdrawn for the big reveal, in which the nude would hold the pose for ten seconds then the curtain would drop. The model did not even blink.

It was always known by the theatre staff when censors would be sending a spy over, mainly because the censors' office would telephone ahead and let them know. After the surprise expected visit the officer would always avail himself of a drink or two and a quick peek behind the scenes after the show.

Jacqui had found the more experienced dancers to be really helpful. The very nature of the job meant they had to bond quickly, so they gave her advice and careful warnings about some of the shadier patrons. The Windmill's female company were accommodated in dressing rooms in the basement, with the male performers and musicians on the top floors, as the van Damms did not want any hanky-panky going on. Unfortunately Jacqui and Tony were not getting much opportunity for it either.

Their working lives and anti-social hours meant it was all rather hasty, and then as luck would have it that changed when she moved into a flat in Westminster with two of the girls from work. She had her own room which proved to be another bonus.

Tony's career was not moving much. He had a couple of short-lived stage revues, then some uncredited film and television parts but nothing of note. By contrast Albert Finney was going from strength to strength; he was just about to open as the lead in *Billy Liar*, so he invited Tony to the show but asked him if he would do him a favour. Finney was married to Jane Welham whom Tony had not met but understood from his mate that the marriage was not happy, probably because Finney was having a passionate affair with the beautiful and talented actress Samantha Eggar. Finney wanted her to come to the show, but her attendance had to be cloak and dagger so he asked Tony to escort her to the theatre then have dinner afterwards. When Tony told Jacqui the plan, she thought it might be interesting if he and Samantha were photographed by the newspapers.

He picked up the tickets from the box office and met Samantha in the bar. He recognised her and she knew him by sight which proved helpful; they made small talk about the biz, work or lack of it, then took their seats in the stalls. Finney was exceptional as Billy Liar, magnetic almost to the point of showing off, which he may well have been doing to impress his secret guest. Part of his performance required him to carry a cane which was used as a prop, first as an umbrella, a cricket bat then as a gun. During the show a woman sitting to the front of the stage was proving to be somewhat disruptive, talking to companions and chomping loudly on confectionery, as Finney recalled later,

'Sounding like a camel chewing a bag of unshelled Brazil nuts.' On the stage Billy Liar stopped in front of her, aimed the cane as it became a Tommy Gun and fired a volley of imaginary bullets towards her. Billy gave her an intense stare; there were no further distractions.

Tony and Samantha went around to Albert's dressing room straight after the show where they had a couple of drinks as the star wiped the performance from his face and put Billy away. Albert asked Tony to arrange for a taxi to take them to the White Elephant over on Curzon Street in Mayfair. When he found that the driver was an old mate of his dad's and one of the football boys, they waited around for a few minutes chatting about Chelsea and the weather. Presumably the happy couple were having a quickie.

The White Elephant was part-owned by Leslie Linder, a producer and agent who looked after Sean Connery. The restaurant was also registered as a club therefore it attracted a large number of show business people. It was a rather grand, imposing place; it was Tony's first visit and certainly Samantha's. When they arrived, Albert was taken aside by the maître d. Albert nodded, said he needed a pee and went off to the land of Armitage and Shanks, while the maître d led the other two to their table where they sat looking around the ornate dining room at the elephant motifs and figures. A few of the diners were staring at the beautiful woman and her slightly awkward escort, even if he was smartly dressed.

They both hid behind their menus, and while they were doing so there was a discernible change in the restaurant chatter. It went quiet, not even a slurp from a spoonful of soup. When they looked over the menus all eyes were on Albert as he joined them at the table. He kissed Samantha's hand and shook Tony's, an impish smirk upon his face, and for the first time Tony realised how famous his friend had become.

After Albert's first film role in *The Entertainer*, alongside Laurence Olivier no less, his second was as the lead in *Saturday Night and Sunday Morning*, and as he sat down the other diners continued to stare and murmur.

Albert explained to Tony and Samantha that on arrival, it was discreetly pointed out he needed to be wearing a tie, so he had wandered off to the toilet to put on one handed to him. They stared at the elegant silk necktie and nodded their approval.

Albert had been going through a heavy work schedule for a year or two, so he was keen to catch up with the news and antics of his fell RADAS. They enjoyed catching up and made Samantha laugh out loud at their stories. They left after a couple of hours, the two lovers anxious to continue their Ugandan discussions. Albert nodded graciously to the other tables as he made his way through. Tony was dropped off by their taxi at Jacqui's flat, and when he entered there were three Windmill girls wearing curlers, dressing gowns and slippers sipping mugs of Ovaltine. In the corner were several pairs of freshly washed nylon stockings hanging from the clothes dryer. The glamour of show business. He was rather anxious to have an enthusiastic snog of his own, but three pairs of eyes were fixed in his direction and he had to deliver the hot gossip.

It was around that time the Windmill dancers were getting offers of better-paid work from other venues. Their theatre had become a little old-fashioned while it was also losing audiences to other theatres copying the show. Private members' clubs were also opening up around Soho and the West End, most of which were rather seedy clip joints or places like Murrays which employed hostesses to entertain customers. Two of the girls from Murrays went on to achieve fame and notoriety.

Al Burnett, yet another former actor, established an American-style nightclub scene in London, modelled on those in Las Vegas and New York, in particular New York's Stork Club. He opened his first club called The Stork Club in Swallow Street; he obviously liked birds. Burnett then opened the Pigalle club in Piccadilly, presumably because he liked sculptors.

The two venues had the same entertainment formula: a resident band, show girls and cabaret, then a big-name singer or comedian. They would offer a limited but expensive food menu with an extortionate drinks bill and that was it.

Jacqui had enjoyed her time at the Windmill but really wanted to progress her career in musical theatre. She talked with Tony about this at length, and he understood her frustrations particularly because she had attended a few auditions with little luck. Jacqui needed to gain some stage experience and Tony assured her it would happen eventually, but in the meantime she accepted an offer from Burnett. It was for considerably more money, a shorter working day albeit with later finishes and routines with a less static and rigid repertoire. The other attraction was the clientele, rather than a more or less exclusive attentive male audience. Burnett's clubs also attracted big stars, as performers and customers; Frank Sinatra, Doris Day and Judy Garland were regular visitors when they were in town. More interestingly, politicians frequented the club, notably Harold Macmillan when he wasn't touring Africa, and more interestingly John Profumo. Jacqui started work at the Stork Club, quickly learning and adapting to the new disciplines, and within weeks she became an important dancer.

One Monday, Jacqui had to go into work early to tighten up a new routine for the appearance of one of Tony's great heroes: Al Burnett had engaged Sammy Davis Jr. for a week. Tony dropped her off at the club, and as they were early she suggested they had a coffee before she started rehearsals. As they entered the main club area, sat on the stage with his legs dangling over the edge was Davis, alone with his bongo drums. The couple glided slowly and silently to the table at the side just as he began tapping out a rhythm to his own percussion accompaniment. He sang a mesmerising version of 'Summertime', when he finished they were both tearful. Davis was magical and they had experienced their own brief, private show. Sammy waved over to them, although the magic was broken when the backing musicians clattered on to the stage.

Jacqui was now working harder and frequently switching between the Stork Club and the Pigalle. She was sleeping late then she and Tony would have the afternoon or early evenings together. He had become more involved in the jazz scene as a regular visitor to venues then to a limited extent as a performer.

Ronnie Scott had opened up a club in a basement on Gerrard Street along with his saxophone-playing friend, Pete King. They obtained an alcohol and late-night opening licence, a world away from the old coffee bars. Importantly, more and more American musicians were granted performance permits so Ronnie's became the place to go.

One of Tony's good friends was an actor, Sean Lynch, whose girlfriend was Annie Ross. A gifted and accomplished jazz performer, Annie had a gig at the club, so Sean invited Tony to her show and when they arrived, Dean Martin met them at the entrance. It wasn't really Dean of course, but a dead ringer, his real name was rather more prosaic, Tom, but everyone called him Dean. As he became a regular at the club, Tony got to know Dean well and with each visit he was discovering such great performers as Zoot Sims, Sonny Rollins, Cleo Lane and Lena Horne. He even put up with Ronnie's jokes.

'Did you hear about the jazz hating Kamikaze pilot who bombed Pearly Bailey?'

Outside Soho, other places were opening up, among them the Half Moon in Putney and the Bull's Head in Barnes. The Half Moon had firstly introduced jazz, then progressed to blues and rock bands. The embryonic musicians and groups from the London area all cut their teeth there, mainly with the British blues pioneer Alexis Korner, but Tony would remember the early years of the Rolling Stones and Manfred Mann.

The Bull's Head – more commonly known as the Bull – situated on the river at Lonsdale Road became his favourite jazz venue after Ronnie's. The music room then crammed in around 100 people but was worth the scrum to see Acker Bilk or George Melly. It was also the place that Tony performed at with a good friend of his dad's, George Heywood, another cabbie and a gifted piano player. They had first met at a MoCaTra social evening. George was fiddling about with the piano so Tony went over for a listen and together they began to knock out a few numbers. One night they turned up at the Bull on what was an open evening so they wandered over to the stage, performed a few songs that were fairly well received and became regulars.

One night a couple of years later, they were performing the song 'Goody Goody' when during the middle eight break a large bloke sidled up to the side of the stage while Tony was awaiting the intro. The man beckoned Tony over to the side of the stage. Tony bent down and a large upright palm cupped around his ear.

'A word in your shell like, Mrs Goody would appreciate it if you didn't take the proverbial.'

'Hey?'

'Mrs Goody.'

He nodded towards a table where an elderly lady with a blue rinse sat with some dodgy-looking geezers. The penny dropped.

Gordon Goody was the professional criminal from the Great Train Robbery gang and had just been given a 30-year sentence. The elderly lady was his mum. Tony looked at George, wandered over and whispered into his shell like, then George looked over at the large bloke, then at Mrs Goody and went straight into 'Mac the Knife', perhaps not the best choice but Goody's mum seemed to like it.

Sam Selby liked to get over to Barnes when the boys were performing, as did Kathy and Jimmy and a few friends, so they always had support. They gained a bit of a following and picked up a few dates in other pubs around town.

Tony and Sam were now meeting up two or three times a week. He would go down to the Buckstone from time to time and meet up with the RADAS who rather liked his cabbie anecdotes and left-wing views.

'Makes Stalin seem like a liberal luvvie,' opined James Villiers.

Sam had purchased a new cab. The Austin had given up wanting to progress much further as a partnership, so it was sold for 30 shillings, and Selby Junior inherited the retired taxi. It was stripped of the meter and the Hackney cab licence plate, and given a general tidy-up making it legal to drive as a private vehicle. The first time Anthony drove it he was hailed a dozen times.

One evening in the Buckstone Anthony and Sam were having a drink with Ronnie Fraser and a couple of other actors when Peter O'Toole arrived with his very attractive girlfriend, and immediately bought a round of drinks. Sam was just drinking a half of bitter because he was off to work.

'Good man Sam, did you know the first person arrested for drinking and driving was a London cabbie?' said O'Toole.

Sam smiled, 'Yes I did, if you get in a cab and it smells of oranges and peppermints, your driver has been on the lash.' Sam then told them a cabbie story that had passed into folklore. In Victorian times, cabs were used as Sam put it by the 'ladies of the night'.

'Ah, *belles de nuit*,' O'Toole added.

After being entertained, the customer would have to pay her and then the cabbie. One night a customer refused to pay and was taken to court. The court ruled that the contract between the passenger and the cabbie, whether written, oral, or implied, was in fact invalid because it was tainted by sexual immorality. O'Toole suddenly had that look on his face of mischief and adventure; he knew of Tony's vehicular inheritance and knew it was parked up the road. O'Toole had a whispered conference with his girlfriend who giggled conspiratorially.

'Selby dear boy, shall we go for a drive?' he asked Tony.

So they did.

It was important they journeyed along the original route, and as the cab entered Hyde Park, Tony kept his eyes firmly ahead as O'Toole entered his own area. They eventually finished up at the wedding cake, the Victoria memorial outside Buckingham Palace. O'Toole and partner, having completed their frolic, both shouted for their driver to stop, which he did, illegally near to where O'Toole was pointing, one of the statues. O'Toole clambered on to the roof of the vehicle and covered the statue's head with his underpants and his companion's knickers.

'Something warm and fragrant for a cold night, well reasonably fragrant.' They then drove up the Mall and returned to the Buckstone where they met up with Villiers and Fraser who were delighted to hear of the adventure.

'Ex dolo malo non oritar actio,' murmured Villiers, mysteriously.

Tony's 'second customer' was Albert Finney, who had decided he was not being fair to his wife, and they had separated when she told him to fuck off. Finney asked Tony to help him move to his new address. His affair with Samantha Eggar had ended by the time he rented a new flat in West Hampstead. They did three round trips from Swiss Cottage to the new place before Finney took Tony out for a meal before he was dropped off again at the flat. He asked Tony how much he owed him, but the offer was declined.

'I knew you would say that,' said Finney.

He gave Tony a box containing a magnificent camel cashmere coat with a fur collar.

'Thanks for being such a good friend, Tony,' Finney said.

Tony wore the coat with pride for years.

Over their meal earlier, Albert had told Tony that he had been offered a part in a big budget film about T.E. Lawrence to be directed by David Lean and produced by Sam Spiegel. Alec Guinness, Jack Hawkins, and Omar Sharif had already signed up.

Tony asked him when he was going to start. 'I'm not,' Finney replied. 'I've told them to offer it to O'Toole.' They did.

11
MILITANTS, BLUEBELLS, POLITICS AND SCANDAL

Many years ago the only means of sustenance or warmth for cabbies would be in the pubs or ale houses, but they had a problem – it was illegal to leave a cab and a horse unattended. They got around this by employing young lads as minders, so instead of sitting in their boxes in the wind, snow, or rain they rushed off to the nearest hostelry leaving the boys and the horses to freeze their arses off instead.

One cold winter's night a gentleman called Captain Armstrong, the editor of *The Globe*, a London newspaper, sent out one of his staff to hail a cab. The man returned to tell him all the drivers were in the pubs, inebriated and unfit to work; whether he told the captain about the frostbitten children and horses was not recorded.

Armstrong, being a reasonable man, thought about things, then came up with the idea of providing shelters for the cab men to rest and also provide food and drink, temperance only. He spoke to a few of his contemporaries who thought it was a splendid idea and they agreed to sponsor the shelters through the Cab Shelter Fund.

The structures, resembling cricket pavilions or very posh sheds, were painted a distinctive olive-green colour and became an immediate success.

They accommodated up to 14 people, and each had a kitchen which was run as a business by the cooks and was open for 20 hours a day. As the system evolved the taxi drivers each had a carnet or food ticket. The name and cab number was recorded each time it was used and the Jack and Jill, as they called it, was settled at the end of each week. The public were allowed in to buy food and drink but only the drivers were allowed to use the seats and tables.

Tony used to meet Sam in the shelter at St George's Square for a cuppa and bacon sandwich, but they would also meet up at other shelters around town so the staff got to know him. If he ever went in one on his own, he would give his dad's details then repay him at a later date.

One night he was at a party in South Kensington with Ronnie Fraser, John Villiers, Robert Shaw, and another actor with them had been the understudy to Peter O'Toole in *The Long and the Short and the Tall*. His name was Michael Caine. Tony had seen him around, at auditions or the usual hangouts, but they had not socialised much, and Caine seemed to be on the periphery of everything, not too friendly but not too cold.

The party was held in one of the mansion blocks near the Victoria and Albert Museum. There was a good amount of booze but very little food, probably crisps and nuts and sausages on sticks. They were all starving hungry when they left, it was late and there was little hope in finding a cafe or restaurant open, and they were all pissed.

Tony suddenly remembered the Bull and Horn, and there was a cab shelter just across the road from the pub. He went in first and there were just a couple of drivers and the lady who was cooking the food. They all recognised him and said it was fine for him to bring in his friends. Ten minutes later they were all scoffing pie and chips. Michael Caine confessed he was struggling to get parts but like the others, he was hoping to land a good telly part and then a film.

Michael liked to tell the story of how he came by his working name. He was born Maurice Micklewhite but when he became an actor, he changed it to Michael Scott. He called his agent from a box in Leicester Square about attending some auditions but was told by his agent that he had just discovered another actor in Equity who was also called Michael Scott, so Michael would have to change his name, there and then. He looked out of the phone box and saw that *The Caine Mutiny* was on at the cinema. It was fortunate he had not looked immediately to his right or he might have been known as Michael Gentleman.

Fully replete, Tony signed for the food against Sam's badge number and decided to call it a night. The others were debating whether to wrap up as well but decided to return to the party, leaving just Tony and Caine. Tony asked one of the cabbies if he wanted a fair, then asked Caine if he wanted dropping off anywhere. It seemed he didn't have anywhere permanent to stay.

He had his wife and daughter living in Suffolk while he had been crashing on a sofa for a while and hoping that someone at the party might put him up for the night – or, as Tony suspected, to get his leg over for a few nights with an obliging partner. That's how Anne found Michael Caine sleeping on the couch when she got up the following morning. Tony didn't meet up with him for a while afterwards, and when he did, the former very nearly Michael Gentleman was about to become a huge box office success.

Peter O'Toole by this time was also about to become one. He had started filming *Lawrence of Arabia* and was constantly on the move between Morocco, Jordan and Spain on location then back to London when he could where he would invariably call up the RADAS and Tony. He invited Tony for lunch, just the two of them, and said he just wanted a quiet day. He told Tony that the film had been beset by problems, the script had been re-written several times, there were difficulties with some of the locations and also the hundreds of extras, and while they were being resolved he had come back to London for some tranquillity.

O'Toole then told him of a technical problem he had to deal with, 'I was having a problem with the camel saddle. My gonads, perineum and arse crack were chafing, bloody, blistered and sore. I tried smearing Vaseline everywhere but then I began sliding around and finished up with an erection, so I went to the market and bought some sponges, stuck them up the dish-dash and it fucking worked. So all the Arab chaps the camel riders did the same, I'm surprised they hadn't thought of it before.

They called me
"Abal Ishfanjah"
Know what that means Tony?'
Er, he of the smooth and comfortable bollocks?'
'No, nothing so poetic and beautiful. It means "Father of the Sponge", rather disappointingly.' O'Toole hung around for a few days catching up with everyone, then

was hurried back to one of his locations where there was some semblance of calm and order. When O'Toole finished the film and was back in London, Tony was out of work for a while and sniffing around the West End to see if anything was coming up. He stopped off at a pub in St Martin's Lane, slipping a few pennies over the bar and settling in the corner with his newspaper and half a bitter. Suddenly O'Toole blundered in with Ronnie Fraser and a couple of others, he immediately saw Tony and beckoned for him to join them. Tony knew straight away he couldn't afford to buy a round of drinks so told O'Toole it was great to see him, but he had an urgent appointment and was just leaving. As he did, Fraser whispered into O'Toole's ear, telling him that Tony was on his uppers at that moment. Tony finished his drink and told O'Toole he would catch up soon. O'Toole called over for Tony to wait outside for a minute or two, which he did, then O'Toole came out of the pub and pushed something into Tony's top pocket. O'Toole tapped it and told him it was a little gift. Tony pulled out the gift, a cheque made out to him for a sum of £50.

While Tony was going through a tough time, Jacqui had been enjoying her work at the Stork and Pigalle, but she was feeling it had started to become a little more salacious. Al Burnett had 'hostesses' working at his clubs, but even so, he now wanted the dancers and performers to mingle more with the customers. One night a group arrived, among them US politician Robert Kennedy and British actor Peter Lawford, who in turn had arrived in London with Kennedy's sister-in-law Jackie, who according to one of the dancers sisters boyfriends fathers, he was having an affair with. After the show Burnett told Jacqui that Kennedy had asked for her to join his party and then to go back to his hotel. She knew Tony was waiting for her at the rear of the club so she fled through the kitchen and jumped into the cab, upset and frightened.

Burnett had broken the rules: the dancers were off limits. He had hostesses to entertain the punters, but he made the rules then flexed them when it suited. He was also aware how power corrupts, then how the corrupt want more.

The Stork and the Pigalle had politicians, crooks and diplomats and senior police officers sat at the tables most nights, the same table on occasions but not necessarily at the same time. They greased each others palms and probably other parts of the body as well, exchanging favours, covering indiscretions, and generally ensuring nobody was found out. But the times indeed were a changing.

At the rear of Park Lane and just off Piccadilly is an area of London called Shepherd Market, which at the turn of the 20th century was quite badly run-down, then in the 1920s artists and writers started to colonise the area, followed by several high-class prostitutes whose clients were invariably aristocrats, members of the government and certainly most of the males from the Royal Family.

The shops and flats around Shepherd Market had cards in the windows or entrances advertising various unusual services, and educationally, French lessons. The property developers came along buying up the old mansions and large houses from former wealthy families. The buildings were quickly demolished, and new ones began to spring up, the Hyde Park Hilton for one.

The developers became famous in their own right: Charles Clore, Jack Cotton and an associate of theirs called Perec 'Peter' Rachman. Their business ventures and collaborations gained momentum, and what they also had in common was a network of corrupt politicians, in national and local government. They bribed and colluded to gain planning consents and bypass building control regulations.

They also shared two other assets, two girls from Murray's club, Christine Keeler, and Mandy Rice-Davies. Rachman had set them up in one of his flats just off Shepherd Market. The two were also regular visitors at the Park Lane homes of Clore and Cotton.

Tony knew all of this because Sam and his taxi mates told him all about it. When the girls were not being driven around in Bentleys or Rolls-Royces, they would use taxis most of the time, not just Christine and Mandy but a whole group of them. Discretion was not one of their best virtues.

Considering cabbies and their fellow service industry colleagues did not get off to a great start in their working relationships after Immoralitygate all those years ago, they had developed a mutual respect and trust. The drivers generally liked the girls as passengers because they tipped well or made their companions do so, and the girls themselves felt secure and safe. Sam and his fellow drivers were protective and avuncular, but they had rules: no bobbing heads in the back of the cab unless it was for apples which would have been a very rare occurrence indeed.

The lack of discretion meant most of the London taxi drivers knew exactly who was visiting who and where. Christine Keeler had been one of Sam's fares enough times to be on recognition terms; she was by his accounts an attractive and pleasant woman, wearing heavy makeup most of the time but uncomplicated which was Sam's way of saying she was a bit thick.

Sam was convinced that Christine had been set up in a flat back on Pimlico turf at Dolphin Square. She certainly lived there for a time among all the other inhabitants of what became known as a prolific Establishment knocking shop with rooms with two-way mirrors, *ménage à trois*, spies, spying and bugging spies when they were not buggering each other as well.

Sam told Tony that the girls were relaxed with them because the taxi drivers did not subject them to any moral or bigoted judgements. They were judgmental about other subjects of course but not against a group enjoying a lifestyle, however brief and ethereal, that was for them glamorous and fun most of the time. They knew what they were getting into. If Christine and Mandy did not know, they certainly did a while later.

It was all about sex, hypocrisy and lies. The girls lied, the politicians lied, the police and witnesses lied, and after it was all over the politicians, the aristocracy, the judiciary, the Establishment as a whole settled back into its corrupt continuance.

While all that was going on, Jacqui and Tony talked about her future. After the Robert Kennedy incident she had told Al Burnett to stick his job where the sun don't shine. She was looking for work in the theatre, but nothing was around at the time so she was considering working in seaside revues, for 16 weeks on a fairly decent wage. Then Margaret Kelly came to town.

Kelly was the founder of the renowned Bluebell Girls, and arrived in the UK from Paris with her agent Peter Baker. They were recruiting, specifically for experienced professional dancers who were over five feet eight inches tall. Jacqui attended the interview but was worried that she spoke very little French. Kelly and Baker told her not to worry, she would be too busy. The work was explained to her: the dancers would be wearing high heels, tight costumes, and wear ostrich plumes. On the stage they would be a towering, glittering ensemble. Above all else the dancers would need more stamina than they perhaps realised; they were required to do at least 12 two-hour shows a week. The initial contract was for three months, and there were options for renewal or extensions while accommodation would be provided along with chaperones and minders. The couple talked it through; the salary was good and they agreed that Jacqui would sign the contract, so it was *au revoir* to his *petit pois* as she left to work at the Paris Lido on the Champs-Élysées.

Tony thought that Jacqui was more excited than she let on at the prospect of working in France, while he in turn was practical and pragmatic. If he had been offered a three-month tour in a play or musical he would have taken it like a shot. By the time Jacqui had left Victoria Station to catch the boat train to France there was still a lot going on in the UK and London in particular.

Sam had become part of a cabal of very left-wing taxi drivers, so no real surprise there. They were up in arms about a new threat to their livelihoods, the introduction of unlicensed taxi firms into the transport network after a decision by Westminster Council to allow what were termed mini cabs to compete with licensed taxis.

The company given the go ahead to compete was called Car Line, and in the application they argued that the Carriage Act only applied to licensed cabs. If a customer could telephone to a central office for a car to come and pick them up at a fixed point, they were not contravening the act. Car Line bought themselves a fleet of Ford Anglias and began competition against the Hackney Carriage. They stuck advertisements on their cars, so they were pretty much visible.

Car Line immediately got around the law which did not permit people to hail them in the street. If someone did hail the car, the driver would allow the fare in and ask them to use the radio to order a car, when the controller would relay the message back to the driver sitting right next to his passenger.

The black cab drivers' main argument was that the mini cabs, already trying to undercut fares, did not have drivers who had worked through the Knowledge qualification, that they were inexperienced and had no proper vetting. They began a coordinated campaign to disrupt the Care Line operation.

Tony attended the first strategy meeting of the militant drivers with Sam as the main organiser and speaker where they looked at ways to legally obstruct the Car Line fleet. Tony had discussed with his dad that the problem he could see with the Anglia vehicles was because they were only two-doored, the driver had to pull a seat forward to enable passengers to climb unceremoniously into the back. The other cab drivers also had noticed this and they had a plan.

The licensed cabs would follow the Car Line Anglias, wait for them to stop with their fares, then one cab would pull in behind, another to the front then a third at the passenger side so the door could not be opened. The Car Line driver would then have to clamber out, the front passenger would struggle over to the driver's side to get out, while any back-seat passengers would have to do the same. After causing the maximum inconvenience the driver blocking the passenger door would clear off leaving the other two cabs blocking the Anglia.

Another tactic would be to blockade the garage where the mini cabs were based, but eventually a few of the cabbies were nicked for obstruction which did not go down too well with the licensing authorities. The general public seemed to be on the licensed taxis' side at first, preferring the reliability and safety, but eventually the mini cabs came to stay and evolved.

When Tony met up with his dad and the militant tendency in their shelter, they were always in a bellicose mood about one thing or another, but now he also was forming his own political beliefs and they were inevitably left-wing, not necessarily an inherited philosophy but certainly influenced by Sam and his cohorts. He was always the Equity representative in his plays or shows, collecting subscriptions, while he was beginning to attend meetings at the Harley Street headquarters, and as a 'rep' he was also expected to check out working conditions, ensuring wages were paid on time and that the general wellbeing of the company was met.

Around the time Sam and his friends had been terrorising the new mini cab company, Equity became involved in a major dispute with the ITV companies about fees which also affected their counterparts in the Variety Artistes' Federation. Equity had agreed a scale of fees with ITV for actors and a separate but similar agreement was agreed with the VAF. When ITV first started, revenues from advertising were not that huge, but as broadcasts grew more popular that revenue began to soar. Increased fees were demanded.

The variety artists came from a different angle: variety theatres and musical halls had started to close down as a result of falling audiences who were now watching more television, so they in turn wanted increased fees for their TV appearances. Equity and the VAF operated a closed shop policy, like all of the trade unions affiliated to the TUC. In Equity's case a member had to have sufficient paid work to qualify; they would be given a provisional card and had to do 'time' in repertory or provincial theatre runs, then after serving their time they became a full member enabling them to go for West End work, TV or film jobs. The television companies would not agree to a new pay scale so both unions decided to strike.

Tony was one of the main instigators.

At the meetings he spoke out against the ITV companies who had expanded rapidly, as advertising revenues had soared since franchises had been awarded. The actors Ken Haigh and Vanessa Redgrave spoke passionately for the fee increases, but one man really made a major impact. Albert Finney had gone along to the meeting with Tony to offer support and show solidarity with his peers, and when he decided to stand up to speak the whole room fell silent.

'It is interesting that while we are debating strike action for better pay, Lew Grade [a British media executive of the time] is up the road playing snooker at his club for £50 a frame yet, he is saying no increase to our wages. Well let us send Mr Grade a message to his family and shareholders, not only are we withdrawing from television, but we are also going to close theatres, the West End will be dark.'

Grade was furious when he heard Finney's remarks about the snooker, arguing in response,

'Tell him it is not £50 a frame, it's £100.'

Grade and his family had huge investments in ITV and theatre groups so Albert's words did hit home, but Grade didn't believe the strike would last for long.

It lasted nearly for a year and was eventually settled when the television companies agreed to increase fees for both actors and variety artists.

Some of the newspapers had backed the television companies, which was not surprising. They railed against the BBC's ability to pay more to actors because of the licence-payers' revenue, as opposed to independent companies operating free television. Tony was unimpressed by that argument; he believed that the licence fee was always better value than so-called free television and argued that in everything people bought – food, a car, a washing machine or a travel ticket – a significant element of the cost was inclusive of an advertising supplement. If that cost was added together to around five per cent of expenditure it worked out for more than the price of the television licence. With the later introduction of subscription channels, payment was for service and the advertising.

When the dispute was finally over, Jacqui, his *Jacinthe des Boi*, returned from Paris. She had enjoyed the life out there, but the agent had been right, the work had been exhausting. She returned however with a healthy bank balance and little more life experience. There was good news and bad news for Tony – Jacqui would be home for a few weeks, but the bad news was she had signed up to work in Barcelona with the Bluebells; she was about to become 'un-*Jacinto Silvestre*'. They made the most of their time together but he was a little down and jealous when she flew off to Spain. Anne told him to stop moping; Jacqui needed to build her own career, she was still young, they both had a lot to look forward to with him in the future. In other words, get on with things.

Sam, who had just about stopped terrorising mini cab drivers, was now busy shouting and shaking a fist at what he considered as 'toffs' along the new dual carriageway along Park Lane. His perception was that half of the expensive vehicles were being driven by idiots who couldn't drive or shouldn't be allowed to drive because they were morons; the other half were being driven with complete disregard and arrogance towards other road users.

Tony thought that was the same thing.

Sam despised the middle and upper classes, their inherited wealth and estates, private schooling, and the Royal Family. His opinion was intractable which most would consider as that of a typical taxi driver then. However the majority were opinionated right-wingers, so Sam clashed with them also. The fact he socialised with a lot of Tony's middle-class friends, and 'toff' John Villiers, did not seem to Sam a little hypocritical, unfortunately like a lot of his life philosophy.

In the United Kingdom, jobs were plentiful while on the whole wages were good. The young were no longer concerned about conscription while a new generation of 21-year-olds were now able to vote for the first time. They could change things, and more importantly they were more politically aware than their parents' generation.

The Conservative Party seemed remote, unattractive and without dynamism; they were seen as self-serving and anachronistic.

Harold Wilson, the leader of the Labour Party, oozed charisma, the wily Tyke really appealing to the new electorate. Not to Sam, who thought the shadow government was not left-wing enough, Wilson was an opportunist and his shadow ministers too shallow.

Tony asked him,

'What about Anthony Wedgewood Benn'

'Toff turned socialist, never works.'

Barbara Castle?'

'Self Interested'

'George Brown?'

'least said about that idiot the better.'

Tony thought Sam had a point there. His father did vote Labour in the 1964 general election though, there being no revolutionary party candidate standing in Westminster.

12
POLARI, PERIWIGS AND PANACEA

While Jacqui was in Spain, Tony picked up some short-term stage productions and small parts on television. Most of the RADAS were by now up and running. Albert Finney and Peter O'Toole were choosing their own roles, while the others were doing reasonably well in the West End and in films.

Tony would often meet up with his friends at the Buckstone or other watering holes, including the Salisbury pub on St Martin's Lane. The Salisbury was a large Victorian building with its outside features decked out in green and gold paintwork. Inside were huge mirrors advertising beers and stouts, made up of beautifully framed glass etched with elaborate lettering and wall-to-wall glass. The bar area was a vast semi-circle sweeping from the main entrance round to the side, then steep stairs leading down to the lavatories.

Hugh Paddick became a good friend to Tony when they appeared together in a farce called *Don't Just Lie There, Say Something!* which passed on into the void very quickly. Paddick gained great fame in the radio show *Round the Horne* when he and Kenneth Williams played the parts of super-camp duo Julian and Sandy. Hugh called the Salisbury:-

'The ideal venue, Anthony, poofs and actors, a narcissistic delight.'

It was indeed a busy venue frequented by the thespian and the homosexual community. The term gay at that time was an adjective, as in bright, merry, happy, which they were, and queer.

Hugh introduced Tony to several of his friends at the pub. Some worked at the Royal Palace, others as matelots and stewards on the Cunard ships or British Overseas Airways Corporation aircraft. Hugh also introduced him to Polari, the gay community's slang.

Polari has a mixed source of history varying from Romany, circus or from a costermonger background, completely different from Cockney rhyming slang. Hugh explained to Tony that some of the words were backwards, for example 'riah' for hair, and some of the initials were abbreviations,

'naff - not available for fucking.'

Then there was bona meaning good, omni translates as man, palone, woman then palone omni as lesbian so no surprise there.

One night Hugh and Tony were chatting to two of the boys working at Clarence House and who were always the source of scandalous gossip. They told the actors how one of the Royal Family had been found with her lallies (legs) in the air with someone's eek (face) buried in her clevie. Hugh roared with laughter. Tony was lost.

'Clevie?'

'Fanny, dear.'

'Oh right.'

Tony thought of the Queen Mother rather differently for a while until he was told who the clevie really belonged to, but not the eek disappointingly.

Two of Hugh's acquaintances once came over to him with Tony, smiling innocently as they approached. They looked at Hugh then his drinking partner and said,

'Bona omni dear heart, vada the dish and eek on that, wouldn't mind him getting in my farting crackers.'

Hugh didn't translate. He once told Hugh was going up for a play about Napoleon.

'Oh, that's a bona part dear boy.'

Despite the intimacy and relative safety of venues like the Salisbury, it was always a difficult and threatening time for queer folk, who could still be imprisoned if found involved in any sexual activity with the same sex, even in private, but they were to become the vanguard for the future: proud, brave and fearless.

Hugh once said to Tony, 'You can't be jailed for being camp dear, not yet anyways.' He really opened up Tony's eyes to the appalling treatment and persecution from the police who regularly harassed and entrapped the queer community. They also had to endure blackmail or, even more traumatic, the physicality of queer-bashing. Hugh spoke of several married actors who had gone through a few bad experiences, mainly through cottaging – seeking sex in public toilets. Hugh used to go through elaborate inventive ways to avoid detection; if surveillance police officers suspected two people were in the same toilet closet, they would look under the door, and if two pairs of feet were seen the game was up.

As part of a subterfuge, Hugh said one of the closetees would step into a large shopping bag, and when a copper peered under the door only one pair of feet could be visible. Hugh sighed, 'Romance was killed a little bit with the docker next door having a dump, or even worse if he was having a dump while noshing one's knob.' Tony decided he really could not dispute that and chose not to discuss it with his mum over breakfast. The queers and the RADAS and the other flotsam and jetsam mixed happily and freely in their mirrored Salisbury domain.

On the theme of flotsam and jetsam, Tony once met with Ronnie Fraser, Patrick Newell and an actor called Edward Judd who had sprung to fame and brief prominence in a film called *The Day the Earth Caught Fire*, which was a huge box office success. Columbia Pictures quickly signed Judd up on a contract but unfortunately he was a self-opinionated, arrogant individual, and it didn't take long for the studio to realise this. They also realised his acting ability was also limited, so they just as promptly released him with a minuscule pay-off.

It was an early winter's night, as a song might go. The Salisbury had a roaring fire in the fireplace which is where roaring fires should be. The group were all a little in their cups; Judd had been rude and belligerent most of the evening, to the regulars and staff. Fraser was in one of his mischievous moods but also like the rest of them, less than pleased with Judd's behaviour.

'I know I can be a cunt at times, Selby, but this one is out-cunting everyone!' he told Tony.

They had all spotted that Judd's hair seemed a little different, a little more hirsute. Ronnie stared at the top of his head,

'Now Edward dear boy, something different about you, can't seem to work it out. Selby, can you put your finger on it?'

Tony answered,

'You certainly look a little follicly different, Eddie'

Newell decided to join in,

'Is that a syrup of fig we see before us Edward, a splendid Irish jig?'

Judd stared at them, then was more than happy to admit he had indeed purchased a wig from a prominent wig maker on Wimpole Street. The rest of the bar patrons were becoming more interested.

'Sure that wasn't Wigmore Street?' trilled a queen from a nearby table. Edward ignored the remark.

Ronnie circulated,

'A fine periwig if I may say so Edward, it looks so real, authentic. Is it safe? I mean secure, in a strong wind. Or a strong grip even? Would it stand the rigours of a lady in a high state of passion?'

Eddie stroked his hair and responded,

'For £2,000 it's as safe and secure as your wife's minge being out of bounds when you get home!'

Ronnie gripped Judd's head, snatched the wig and tossed it into the fire, which crackled and growled with fiery delight with the addition of new fuel. The rest of the onlookers exhaled an audible gasp of horror, then after the initial surprise and shock came the sound of hysterical laughter.

Ronnie made things worse,

'Edward I am so sorry, I thought the peruke would be fireproof as well, for that kind of money. I do hope it was insured?'

All eyes were on the appalled and distressed face of the man from *The Day the Earth Caught Fire*, rather like the wig one supposes.

'You pricks, you fucking pricks,' he bellowed as he rushed from the pub. Tony thought even by Ronnie's standards, it was a crass thing to have done. Everyone stared at him, but some were still sniggering.

'I'll apologise the next time I see him, in the meantime, I shall have another Fraser water,' Fraser casually said.

Edward Judd wasn't seen around too much after that, and when he did appear his new wig looked as if it had been fitted by a shipbuilder's riveter.

Tony was still living at home in the flat on the Tachbrook with his mother. He argued it was the ideal location to get into town, although it probably helped more that Anne was still doing his washing, ironing, and cooking. He was however picking up the household bills while Anne had a job up in Victoria as a clerk. Sam still popped in from time to time, although it wasn't certain if he was still having a bit of how's yer father with Anne when he was out and about.

Tony was still picking up some roles, jazz gigs or extra work, again nothing of note, when Sam mentioned he had been to the Players' Theatre under the arches at Charing Cross after his shifts a few times. He suggested that Tony might pick up some work there.

The Players' Theatre was something of a legend among the theatre world. It was built into the Hungerford Arches in Villiers Street – possibly named after James Villiers' forefathers. It specialised in Victorian and Edwardian music hall entertainment under the banner 'Late Joys'. It had been founded by Leonard Sachs and his partner, Peter Ridgeway, in the 1930s.

The rather unusual name came from the first owner of the theatre, a Mr Joy. The performances were indeed late, the first at 11pm and the second at 2am, which enabled professional actors to finish work at the theatres then perform in or watch the shows. It also helped that the Players was a private theatre club so alcohol was always available.

The BBC had picked up on the popularity of the shows and from the 1950s it had been televising *The Good Old Days* as a regular series.

It really was a unique theatre with an extraordinary pedigree. In its early days Rex Whistler had designed the sets, while performers of the calibre of Peter Ustinov and Bernard Miles had worked there in their younger days.

Tony attended a few shows and absolutely loved it. His immediate bond was with the songs as he knew most of them from family get-togethers. The shows changed every two weeks and the producers were always on the look-out for new performers. Tony went for an audition and was taken on. The great thing about the 'Late Joys' meant that even if one of the performers suddenly found a job in the conventional theatre, they could still work in the nocturnal hours afterwards.

The format was easy: the chairman of proceedings, resplendent in his Victorian attire, gavel in hand, would announce the commencement of the show with a booming, alliterative introduction to the night's proceedings, then to each act. The only accompaniment for each performer was by a formidable lady called Betty Turner on her stool at the grand piano, or in the chairman's parlance, 'The mademoiselle of melodic cadence, the breathtaking and bewitching belle, the bright and beautiful Miss Betty Turner.' Betty would smile graciously at the audience, then thump away at the first performer's arrangement. When Tony first performed at the theatre, Leonard Sachs, the normal chairman, was away, possibly up in Leeds presenting *The Good Old Days*. Tony followed Hattie Jacques who had just performed 'The Bird on Nellie's Hat'. The acting chairman was Barry Cryer, who was just beginning his career as a comedian and brilliant script writer. He proved to be as formidable as master of ceremonies. Tony's introduction went along the lines of:-

'My lords, ladies and if there are any still left, gentlemen.

We welcome to 'Late Joys', this emporium of entertainment, this salubrious scintilla of sequestered symposium, a young man making his debut in this castle of carousing, a young man who has been described as the Van Gogh of music hall because he is partially deaf, a young man who will thank you for your support, indeed will wear with gratitude.

Ladies and Gentlement, I implore you to applaud, Mr Tony Selby.'

Betty began the introduction 'If these lips could only speak' and he was away.

Tony sang three or four more songs then retired to the wings, and for the finale all of the performers would gather to the stage. Cryer bellowed to a boisterous and more inebriated audience, 'My ladies and gentlemen, unfortunately all the lords are pissed, we conclude tonight's entertainment with a rollicking rendition, a synchronised serenade *sans smorsand* that will end accelerando, achromatic, indeed *agilmente* all at the same time. Please join us down at the old Bull and Bush.' Tony loved working at the Players' Theatre, and spent three or four years guesting there.

Jacqui returned from her stint in Spain tanned, lighter and pleased to see Tony, but there was still not much work for her in London, so she had now the choice of another short-term engagement in Greece. Tony wasn't best pleased about it and made it clear it was possibly time for them to decide about the future. Jacqui had become bored with the routines and living out of a suitcase. They agreed it would be her last European adventure, so it was farewell again to his *kamkpanoa*. Fortunately she quickly became fed up with the olives, vine leaves and moussaka and returned to London, while for Tony it was time to say hello to *Alfie*.

He was offered a part in a play by Bill Naughton which he had adapted as a stage play from his original radio version. *Alfie* had opened at the Mermaid Theatre and then transferred to the larger Duchess Theatre. Tony was to understudy John Neville who played the title role of Alfie Elkins, while also playing his own part as Lacey. Additionally, it gave him the opportunity to work with a young actress playing the part of Siddie, Glenda Jackson.

Despite a relatively short run the play was a sell-out. It was of its day: contemporary, daring, part of the early momentum that began a certain swinging motion attached to London.

Jacqui then had some good news. She had auditioned for the part of Panacea in *A Funny Thing Happened on the Way to the Forum*. She joined the cast at the Strand Theatre, where the star of the show was Tony's old adversary, Frankie Howerd. Howerd's career had plummeted over the previous few years, but he had gained newer audiences after appearing at the Establishment Club and on *That Was the Week That Was*, the BBC's late-night show.

It was a difficult show for Jacqui. Howerd saw Tony picking her up after a show and realised they were in a relationship, so his despicable side went to work. A line delivered by him to her character Panacea went, 'A face that can hold a thousand promises and a body that stands by each promise.' Howerd would then hold on to Jacqui and twirl her around, but his hold on her began to get tighter and the movement rougher until she was marked and bruised. Luckily the director noticed quickly and told Howerd to lay off before Tony came in to punch his lights out.

Everything was going well for Tony and Jacqui, both working in the West End, renewing, and enjoying their relationship so what could go wrong? Probably Jacqui being offered a three-year contract to work in Las Vega in shows featuring Frank Sinatra, Dean Martin and Sammy Davis Jr.

They sat and talked and talked about the offer. In her heart Jacqui wanted to go, it was her dream job, but they both knew if she did go to the States, it would be the end of the relationship. It had survived the disruption over the recent time away, but it couldn't survive a three-year separation.

Jacqui turned down the offer and they got married at Caxton Hall. After a nice, simple ceremony they had a party with family and friends then moved into a small, homely flat in Tachbrook Street.

13
LOACH AND GARNETT

Ken Loach studied law at St Peter's College in Oxford, where he became an active member of the university's drama society. After graduating he decided to try his luck as a professional actor and joined a repertory group touring the United Kingdom.

He crossed paths with and then became close friends with another former student who had read psychology at University College but became far more interested in acting and the theatre, Tony Garnett. The pair were regulars at Joan Littlewood's radical productions at the Theatre Royal, and after being inspired they set up an actors' workshop. Or, more accurately, an out-of-work actors' workshop. Selby heard about it on the grapevine and turned up at a tatty church hall in Wandsworth. Loach and Garnett were really interested to hear about his time working with Littlewood on *The Quare Fellow*, and he became a part of their workshop.

The first collaboration was a first world war play called *Rancour of War*, which was reasonably acted and attended. No one was paid then they all went their separate ways, and although Tony didn't realise it at the time, it was his first introduction to the two men who were to have a profound, historical influence on television productions and would go on to revolutionise television drama.

About a year later, Loach contacted Tony; Ken was to acting what Pinocchio was to veracity. To everyone's relief he had given up the thespian life in a great career move, securing a television director's course with the BBC. Garnett, meanwhile, was still acting, but was also developing as a scriptwriter. He had written a play called *Catherine* which became Loach's pilot or test piece at the conclusion of his course. Loach had asked Tony to take up one of the roles. Tony began to work with them; for him it was apparent from the start that Loach had a unique and innovative style. His direction was calm and controlled which he easily communicated to the cast and crew, and he was succinct without any histrionics or tantrums.

The BBC immediately brought Loach into the Drama Department then Garnett became a story editor with a brief to develop and nurture new drama shows.

It was the most opportune time to start their television careers. The Corporation was evolving from a staid and conservative approach to drama, and Loach and Garnett were also to benefit from the influence and ideas of two other forward thinkers.

The first was James MacTaggart, he of the renowned MacTaggart lectures legacy, who had been a writer, producer and actor in his time. He had produced a series called *Teleplays* but was now looking at developing that concept into a new project to be called *The Wednesday Play*.

The second person was Sydney Newman, a Canadian who had been appointed head of drama and had worked for Canadian and American companies. He had been brought in to bring new ideas and concepts of contemporary social and politically extended drama.

The BBC certainly put great trust in them, particularly because they were more than capable of handling the more eccentric, weird, and wilder of the new creatives. Loach and Garnett had a show called *Z-Cars*, a very realistic police series, an extremely popular and successful drama. They were then asked to become involved with the development of *The Wednesday Play*.

Tony had performed in a few of the *Teleplays*, either carrying a rifle or marching up and down on the spot on the studio floor for whatever reason, lucky to have at least a line or camera shot. Loach decided his first *Wednesday Play* would be from a script by James O'Connor, called *Tap on the Shoulder*. He sent a copy to Tony who immediately decided he wanted in. The storyline was about a crook who had bought a large country house with the proceeds of his many robberies to become a pillar of society. The estate bordered another owned by royalty. He went on to become a local philanthropist and charity supporter to the extent he was being considered for a knighthood.

Tony's character was the leader of a gang involved in a robbery at a warehouse at London Airport (as known before it was renamed as Heathrow), from which his haul was tens of thousands of pounds. His gang hid the cash in a horse box and parked the vehicle on the other crook's land. The police gradually picked up members of Tony's character's gang then traced the horse box back to the unsuspecting landowner who was then immediately implicated, ironically unfairly, by the other crooks, despite pleading his innocence he was imprisoned. Instead of the tap on the shoulder from Her Majesty's sword, it was the tap on the shoulder from the police.

It was an encouraging start for all involved, and when filming had been completed, Tony was in the BBC bar with Loach and Garnett when James O'Connor joined them, immediately putting his arm around Selby and drawing the other two in with a beckoning arc.

'Listen, Tone, I've got a play in my bottom drawer, I think you would be great as the lead.'

O'Connor was born in north London, the son of a wastrel from Ireland and a mother who worked part time as a prostitute, although there is no record of what she did the rest of her time. He became a petty criminal as a kid, left school at the age of 12 and, possibly ignoring the advice of the careers master, decided to become a full-time thief.

In 1941 his life became more complicated when he was wrongly convicted of a murder and sentenced to death. He was taken to Pentonville Prison and had to wait out the three clear Sundays between the death sentence and the execution. The specific timeframe was to allow for any appeal, reprieve or even some divine intervention to prevent the sentence being carried out. Just two days before he was to be hanged there was a reprieve, with the sentence commuted to life imprisonment. O'Connor's hair, as ginger as coconut just two weeks before, had turned to a November night grey. He was eventually released from prison in the mid-1950s.

Shortly after the conversation in the bar, a script turned up for the play, which was called *Three Clear Sundays*. It was raw and rough but utterly compelling, and when they went into rehearsal it became obvious that they would be creating a televisual landmark. Loach and Garnett were looking more and more at realism in their work, so they encouraged improvisation between the actors but for it somehow to look carefully crafted and managed. When they began filming all the criteria fell into place. Tony's role was as Danny Lee, the youngest from a family of petty criminals, and the matriarch played by Rita Webb was the keeper of the purse strings. All the proceeds from the scams and thefts went straight to her, then she doled out 'wages' to the others.

In the production, Danny has chosen not to join the family business, preferring to run a market stall. He has a good steady income and a steady girlfriend who becomes pregnant. Danny promises to marry her.

A pivotal scene takes place in a pub where Danny is having a quiet pint and minding his own business when a detective from the local nick enters, a mean and aggressive bastard who likes to goad and confront the locals and was known to arrest people on a whim. He decides to pick on Danny and makes unpleasant comments about his family. Danny, not the brightest of characters, promptly clobbers the cop and is sent down for six months.

Right from the start Ken Loach decided to push for more location filming, so they did some shots of Tony's character on a stall in Shepherd's Bush and also included the genuine stallholders and customers.

Tony himself said Loach was keen to capture the conflict between working-class people and authority. In the pub scene with the assault on the police officer, he had deliberately created a sympathetic point of view for the simple and naive Danny, while in the scenes where the rest of his family were portrayed as scheming reprobates there was a black humour, with almost reverence to their utter lack of morality.

As the film progresses, Danny is lonely and isolated in Wandsworth Prison when his mother goes to visit him. She displays little emotion or sympathy for his incarceration; her main observation is about his plea in court as he had not followed the family's 11th commandment,

'Thou shalt not plead fuckin' guilty.'

Danny is also visited by his girlfriend who is not getting much support or sympathy from either his family or her own in her pregnancy.

While Danny is left to mull this over he is suddenly befriended by a couple of old lags who listen with interest to his unhappy situation. They see an opportunity to gain an early release from their sentences, and promise the hapless lad that they will give £500 to his girlfriend if he agrees to a little ruse. Danny would attack one of the prison officers and his new friends would drag him off. He would just get a few weeks added to his sentence while the two heroes would be commended by the governor and gain early release. The assault goes horribly wrong, the prison officer is killed during the attack, and at his trial Danny is sentenced to death.

Unlike O'Connor's experience there was no reprieve, and inexorably *Three Clear Sundays* reaches a fateful conclusion.

Tony and the other actors had really enjoyed the location filming and were about to move to the studios at Television Centre, but they had not viewed the sets because they had been utilising rehearsal rooms elsewhere. Once they did arrive at their studio Tony felt a real charge in the atmosphere, a surge in the collective sense of purpose.

On an adjoining set, cells had been constructed on one side, while on the other was the condemned cell concealed by canvass sheets; this was off-limits to everyone. Loach had also skilfully arranged for camera shots lining the cells by simply removing part of the construction.

Tony's character is housed in the main cell block because the three-week rule is progressing. He interacts with the other prisoners who are all commiserative to his impending punishment, and even the screws show little aggression considering he has killed one of their own. Tony told O'Connor and Loach this all brought back memories of *The Quare Fellow*,

'Yeah, but you never saw him Tone, did you?'

Jimmy replied, meaning the condemned man.

'You didn't see you Tone'

On the third clear Sunday there has been no reprieve, no pardon, all hope has gone.

Danny's girlfriend visits when she reveals that the £500 meant for her was passed to his mother for 'safe keeping' and she has not seen a penny of it. Just after this visit he is transferred to the cell for the condemned for the final scene which is both shocking and brutal.

The final night is spent with a priest and two prison officers, and after breakfast one of them offers Danny a hip flask for a sip of whisky. As Danny reaches out, his hands are grabbed and he is handcuffed behind the back while simultaneously a hood is placed over his head. A door opens at the side of the cell then Danny is rushed through straight to the scaffold where the rope is placed over his neck, the hangman pulls the lever, and off camera the sound effect of a body plummeting through the trap door concludes a scene of astounding brutality.

The speed of that final scene was intentionally shocking, the most absolute denouement. Tony was drained afterwards. They had rehearsed it fairly quickly to get the urgency, but without the cuffs or the hood, so he had gone through the last act exactly as a condemned man or woman would: bound, hooded and terrified. The other members of the cast and crew were also drained but all convinced they had completed the most extraordinary of dramas.

What they were unaware of, however, were the clashes going on in the background between James MacTaggart, Sydney Newman, Ken Loach, and Tony Garnett. While the senior heads had been supportive of the production as a whole, they were less enthusiastic about the conclusion and were reluctant to broadcast the film as it stood. MacTaggart was under no illusion about the execution scene: the BBC would be under enormous pressure, not only from the right-wing press owners such as the Rothermere or the Beaverbrook publications, but also from some of the licence payers, pressure groups like Mary Whitehouse's fledgling organisation, and the corporal punishment lobby.

Tony soon realised there were many intriguing strands and sub-plots attached to the production, while James O'Connor was always going to be part and parcel of any tangled web.

The fascinating O'Connor was then still trying to prove his innocence over the murder charges against him from some 25 years earlier. While incarcerated in Dartmoor prison he had enrolled on a writer's correspondence course, and when he was released, he returned to London and talked himself on to the staff of the *Sunday Empire* as a crime reporter which, of course, was entirely apposite, even more so when he met up regularly with his old cronies and contracts from whom he secured some very good stores, even the occasional scoop.

He was a natural raconteur, very funny but had a certain gravitas when required. He met up with a man called Bob Fabian at a press dinner and they bonded. Fabian was a former police chief who had fronted a television series called *Fabian of the Yard*. He had some excellent television contacts, and one of them read a script O'Connor had submitted to the BBC for which was paid 15 guineas. O'Connor immediately handed in his notice as a hack and became a dramatist.

Tony and O'Connor became close for a while, although Tony felt he could never really trust him. O'Connor told Tony he was once in a pub when a voice he recognised called over his shoulder,

'James O'Connor, five feet eight inches, ten stone and four pounds, neck size 15 and a half.'

O'Connor said he had turned to face a grey-skinned face with cold eyes staring at him. It was Albert Pierrepoint, the state executioner, the hangman. This rather unpleasant person still mentally retained O'Connor's drop statistics. O'Connor had looked back into the eyes of death.

'Yeah, got away from you Albert you cunt, now fuck off back to Manchester and play with the bones of the dead.'

Other than that, O'Connor was good fun to be around, and he had met a most remarkable woman of great beauty and intellect, Nemone Lethbridge. In his continued quest to clear his name, he had met and befriended several lawyers and solicitors who gave him advice. Most were eager to help because his case was a *cause célèbre* in the criminal law world, many convinced he had been the victim of a miscarriage of justice. It was also a testament to O'Connor's character that he had cultivated such a disparate group of friends and supporters.

He had been introduced to Nemone by a barrister who had shown an interest in his case. She was one of only six female silks employed in chambers; from the moment they met they became lovers then husband and wife. The thief and the brief.

Sadly, after the marriage became public knowledge, Nemone was promptly asked to leave her chambers, which she did with pride and elan, telling the partners they were a bunch of fuck-faced Neanderthals. Nemone had a much better vocabulary than that but preferred to use O'Connor's. She proved to be a gifted writer, starting to write her own scripts for television, then several books about women and the law, womens' rights, and feminist thinking. In later years some people suspected or suggested she had crafted O'Connor's work. Tony thought she certainly helped to improve him as a writer but he was certainly an original, innovative story teller. Tony also recalled her being around and about when filming *Three Clear Sundays*, and she also wrote the lyrics and music for some of the songs. He also believed she had become aware quickly of the six degrees of separation between some of the main players around the production.

Nemone had represented some of the Kray gang in her early career. They seemed to be everywhere around London then, slithering between the showbiz and theatre world, the sporting arenas and the periphery of the political establishment. Tony had also come across them over the years, at opening nights or entertaining celebrities somewhere, but he managed to survive with face and sphincter intact.

What Nemone did not know at the time was the remarkable number of not guilty verdicts returned for her clients was not necessarily down to her brilliant advocacy: they were more down to Ronnie and Reggie and their mates scaring witnesses and jurors, not to mention paying off bent coppers.

During his prewar criminal career, O'Connor had been an associate of a duplicitous character called George Sewell. Sewell had been a prominent figure in the prosecution case against O'Connor, providing the police with a witness statement incriminating him in the murder and theft from the jeweller that he was subsequently arrested for. Many years later Sewell provided another statement retracting his original comments, then implicating the detective superintendent who had been in charge of the original murder investigation as the individual who had fitted O'Connor up. Shortly after that, Sewell went to the office of the solicitor looking after O'Connor's appeal, saying he wanted to check on a few things on his statement. The secretary gave him the original, so he put it in his pocket and shot out of the building. There was no copy of the statement. Fast forward a couple of years and Sewell's son, the actor George Sewell junior, was playing the role of the man who had set up Danny in *Three Clear Sundays*.

Tony asked Sewell about the irony or if he was aware of the coincidence, and he replied that it didn't really matter,

'Just another job to me, Tone.'

Tony remained convinced Jimmy had persuaded Loach and Garnett to cast Sewell deliberately, and Nemone certainly concurred.

The reaction to *Three Clear Sundays* was astonishing; it was no coincidence it was broadcast before the third reading of the Abolition of Capital Punishment Bill.

O'Connor used his press contacts to gather a posse of journalists and photographers then smuggled them into the set at the studios. The whole set was still awaiting to be dismantled for another production, so he arranged the meeting so they could meet deadlines for their editors the following day.

Meanwhile, in the House of Commons, the Honourable Member of Parliament for Nelson and Colne, Sydney Silverman, was preparing for the debate in the House. A parliamentarian since the 1930s, he was considered something of a political maverick.

He had been part of the Attlee government, yet despite his great socialist commitments, Silverman was not necessarily an Attlee devotee. He was, however, a magnificent campaigner for the abolition of capital punishment and was one of the founders of the movement against it. Silverman had made people aware of the appalling miscarriages of justice that led to the executions in the cases of Derek Bentley and Timothy Evans, or the prejudicial case of Ruth Ellis.

In 1956 Silverman piloted a private members bill through Parliament, although it was passed, the bill for abolition was defeated in the House of Lords.

When the Labour Party came to power in 1964, Silverman had several supporters within the elected government, and also some significant support with the opposition groups. His new bill progressed quickly through the system. The day after *Three Clear Sundays* was broadcast, the bill was passed, and it received Royal Assent a few months later.

At the BBC, the reaction to the film was either ecstatic, ambivalent or one of deep concern.

O'Connor's coup and clandestine visit to the studio with his media mates had provided immense coverage in the popular newspapers where all the editors had seized on the shock aspect of the production. The more serious broadsheets praised the *Wednesday Play* as a triumph of social realism, with one of the most thought provoking story lines.

Tony didn't have the opportunity to work with James O'Connor or Nemone Lethbridge again, but he met up with them socially from time to time. O'Connor died without ever proving his innocence.

On the day after the bill was passed, Sydney Silverman hailed a taxi at Westminster and gave his destination as the BBC studios where he was to debate the passing of the bill on a current affairs programme. The driver recognised him and asked how he was feeling after his great success.

'You know cabbie, the BBC film made all the difference, the performance and ability of that young actor who play the prisoner…' He trailed off and sat back. The cabbie nodded in agreement. His name was Sam Selby.

14
UP THE JUNCTION

Maurice Aza, first met Tony in the late 1950s and agreed to become his agent. The Fraser and Dunlop agency had not really delivered anything for him and while they had Sean Connery, Terence Stamp, and later Michael Caine on their books, Tony was down their list of priorities so it was time to move on. Tony had met up with an old pal, Johnny Briggs, who had been at Italia Conti, and who listened patiently as Tony complained about the lack of work. Briggs suggested he called his own agent and sign with him.

Aza invited Tony over to his office in Golders Green, which in reality was part of his large house. Tony met a delightful and sartorially elegant – small, but as they say, perfectly formed – gentlemen. The agency had been started by Aza's mother Lillian who represented a whole stable of variety acts, the biggest of whom was Gracie Fields. Maurice had come into the business straight from school, confident and outgoing. Lillian immediately encouraged him to develop the theatre, film and TV side of the agency, which he did quickly and without too much fanfare, into a thriving operation.

After a longish, agreeable lunch, Aza decided to take Tony on as a client, and a few years later he was taking the actor out to lunch again. The success of *Three Clear Sundays* changed Tony's professional and personal life immediately and profoundly. Over the previous few years he had enjoyed minor celebrity status, but after the transmission of the Ken Loach/Tony Garnett film the reaction to him proved to be rather life-changing. People wanted to shake Tony's hand in the street; he was recognised amid nods and smiles and autograph requests including one on a piece of Izal toilet paper which proved tricky. When Tony entered the restaurant with Maurice heads turned to stare as they made their way to their table. He realised with a thrill of joy that vicarious celebrity feeling when Albert Finney made his way through the White Elephant; it was now his first frisson of fame and he wanted more.

Aza was doing what all good agents did, keeping Tony's profile in the right places, ensuring the media attention was progressing positively, then waiting for an anticipated deluge of work offers. While they awaited, they planned Tony's development as an actor. Aza felt the direction would be for more television than theatre, then major film work.

Tony felt his progress as a television actor had soared with working with Loach and Garnett, but he now wanted cinema work for a more attractive and lucrative future. Unfortunately nothing much happened.

At the age of 27 his CV was certainly considerable and varied, but his contemporaries such as Richard Harris, Albert Finney, and Terence Stamp, not to mention Peter O'Toole, were all box office stars. Tony was a good actor, but he was considered as a London actor, in danger of becoming limited to that sort of role, which was not necessarily a bad thing.

A few weeks after that triumphant lunch, he was sitting in Aza's office with his secretary Sheila fussing around, shuffling her files. She told them that nothing of note had come in but Loach had contacted the office, asking for Aza to call him back, which he did.

Loach had met up with the writer Nell Dunn, who came from a very well-to-do family who lived in and owned some real estate in Chelsea. Nell started her writing career in the early 1963 after moving from SW3 to Battersea with her husband Jeremy Sandford, an old Etonian and also a writer and experimental composer. Most people would refer to him as 'eccentric'; others, including Tony, felt he was a complete nutter.

Nell worked in a local sweet factory to gain what she once told Tony a 'feel for the south London vernacular'. He kept his thoughts to himself on that one, then as he heard more of her progress, he became more impressed.

Nell and Sandford became regulars in the pubs around Battersea and Clapham then began a series of stories about the areas and people, which were featured in the *New Statesman* magazine and then published in book form. It was called *Up the Junction*. Tony had read it, so had Loach and Garnett, and the story was to be adapted as the next *Wednesday Play*.

Loach and Garnett wanted to include what was now being regarded as their ensemble, a group of actors they could rely on. The book itself was a thin tome, no more than 100 pages, but Nell had indeed captured the South London nuance and dialect while being accurate in her descriptions of her observed lifestyles. Tony told Aza to let Loach know that he had read the book and liked it, so Loach offered him the role of Dave, another ne'er do well.

When the script eventually arrived, Tony smiled to himself. It was really an outline of a very lean storyline, and although Nell was credited as the writer, Loach's influence was evident. Garnett was the story developer and would also edit.

On the first day of rehearsal in yet another dusty church hall, they sat around a refectory table drinking lots of tea and eating Arrowroot biscuits which they all thought were dreadful for dunking because they melted away anywhere near a hot drink. There were no Badoit or Evian bottles, water was from a tap sipped from chipped glasses from a draining board.

The essence of the film centred around three girls who worked in the local sweet factory, Nell's research coming to the fore here. Rube, Sylvie, and Eileen were played by Geraldine Shorman, Carol White and Vicky Turner.

They became involved with three local men, Ron (Ray Barron), Terry, (Michael Standing) and Dave, played by Tony, a married man who cops off with Eileen. Rube falls pregnant, so with the connivance of her mother and her friends she decides to terminate the pregnancy which at the time was illegal. It could only be carried out legally if there was a serious medical problem that was confirmed by a doctor.

Backstreet abortions were being carried out in every town and city by the knitting needle and gin specialists while in Harley Street gynaecologists were doing very well carrying out abortions on a private basis.

The significance of the storyline for Garnett was profound and personal because his mother had gone through a backstreet abortion and had died as the result of an infection. Garnett's dad, who had agreed to the termination because they could not afford to have another child, was interviewed by the police who were going to charge him with aiding and abetting. Two weeks after the death, Garnett's father put a few shilling in the gas meter, and drank a bottle of whisky as the unlit gas hissed its poison fumes into his lungs. Tony had very strong, forthright views on the issues of abortion.

Rehearsals for *Up the Junction* began and for the first day or so they read out parts from the book, slowly improvising the dialogue. As the process developed, two shorthand specialists transcribed the words verbatim, then Garnett would edit, then he and Loach would further develop the original outline they had sent to the actors. The result was a considerable deviation from the book.

The actors developed a measured, insouciant approach to a work in progress, but they bonded well, and although as a whole they attended rehearsals together they would be working in separate units once filming began.

Tony, from his experience of working with Loach and Garnett, suspected when filming began that there was a cloak-and-dagger atmosphere around the duo, a little cloak of deceit perhaps. He also knew that James MacTaggart had seen the outline script, and other than a couple of comments and suggestions, he seemed relaxed about the project. MacTaggart also assumed it was to be mainly studio-based, but unfortunately Loach and Garnett had been economical with the truth. The success of the film would entirely be reliant on 16mm film with lights, far more flexible cameras than the traditional Mitchell 35mm cameras in the electronic studio. While they were much more capable technically, they would be unable to capture the filmic documentary or realism of 16mm; more importantly, the 35mm cameras were heavy and clumsy to manipulate.

The Drama Department at the BBC had always been prominent in appropriating funds and resources, but money was becoming tighter and under more scrutiny because of the imminent arrival of BBC 2, while there was also a growing trend for series-based dramas or serials. These were more cost-effective and achieved economies of scale as continuous performance. Granada Television was leading the field, an example being the great success of *Coronation Street*.

Loach and Garnett would also have the problem of explaining why half of the technical crews and camera operators were out on location. Garnett manoeuvred around one issue by booking studio time even though it would be unused, but before filming began the head of drama still needed to peruse the shooting schedules, locations, and budget.

While Loach was thinking about this, he discovered that MacTaggart was about to go on holiday, so he got around things by postponing meetings and becoming unavailable. Selby thought MacTaggart must have suspected something dodgy was going on, but as the Caribbean beckoned, off he went and as MacTaggart's aircraft lifted its nose wheel upwards, filming began.

On the first day's schedule Tony met up with Rita Webb again, his screen mum from *Three Clear Sundays*. She had been a late addition to the cast so had not attended any of the rehearsals. Rita was probably in her 60s then and was about five feet tall with a fabulous *gross poitrine*. She had been in show business for most of her life, from music hall to early television, and despite her bag lady persona, she was a well-dressed woman and one of the most fragrant. Rita was also very funny and at the BBC she would breeze through the doors and say 'Hello love, how's it hangin?'

In the lift, 'Hello sir, how's it hangin'?'

'Er, very well Rita, thank you,' replied the Director General.

While waiting for a scene to start, she walked up to Selby and asked, 'Hello Tone, how's it hangin?' before offering him one of her Rothmans.

Rita also had a laugh like a cuckoo's cackle when it lays an egg, and it rasped out when Tony Imi, the head cameraman, came over to say hello. Imi, who was about six foot four inches tall, gave her a big hug.

'I won't ask how it's hanging dear, I can see for myself,' Rita said.

'Ere, there's a lot of fucking Tones on this gig.'

Rita also loved gossip, the more salacious the better, and she also liked a bet. Within minutes of her arrival she had made a couple of wagers on 'who would be 'avin it orf' with each other among the cast and crew.

Rita had just finished working with Frankie Howerd, so Tony confided to her his unhappy experience with him.

'Oh, he'd fuck a vomiting dog, dear,'

Rita replied, then paused.

'No disrespect Tone.'

The cuckoo cackled.

There was an extra on the shoot named John Binden, a tough, cold man with something of a reputation in the criminal world. He provided the muscle and intimidation for the gangs, a sort of agency thug. Ken Loach, for some reason, hired Binden after meeting him in a pub, where Binden told him he had ambitions to become an actor. Loach used him as a background extra in a few pub scenes.

Rita knew Binden from around the pubs and clubs where her husband Al 'Mr Banjo' Jeffrey worked. Binden, by many accounts and certainly confirmed by Mrs Jeffrey, had the most enormous todger. She had seen him unroll it at a party and balance half pint glasses on to it, she didn't mention if they were full.

'He could probably balance 14 budgies on it, Tone, well if the one on the end stood on one leg,'

She also revealed:-

'He's been porkin' Princess Margaret as well Tone.'

A rumour spreading far and wide for years.

'Ere, you could say he's got a big part in *Charlie's Aunt*, cackle, cackle.'

Binden went on to work on the fringes of the entertainment world, and was then involved in a trial when he was acquitted of murder. He was the subject of much speculation about his involvement with Princess Margaret; he was also a proven misogynist and violent partner. Perhaps the only group that mourned his death were 14 yellow and green Australian avians deprived of any more gainful employment.

Tony's first scene was in the pub, along with the actors and extras. The pub was also crammed with the regulars, mainly because the production was picking up the drinks bill. Loach would set up the scene, wait for everyone to be more or less ready, then without the use of a clapper board or the shout of action, he would wait for a hush to descend then gently say, 'In your own time, when ready.'

Tony recalled that the pub scenes reflected accurately the social changes happening. The divide between the older and younger generations was palpable; most of the older pub patrons were sitting gap-toothed or toothless, singing away self-consciously to the old songs played on the old 'Joanna', and occasionally an old fart would get up, grab the crackly pub mic and croak out a song, a precursor to karaoke. Later a guitar group would be recycling pop songs with the younger farts dancing and swaying. His character Dave is first seen chatting up Eileen even though she is aware he is a married man she really fancies him, then Ruby and her friends are suddenly on screen at work in the sweet factory. They endure the dead-end job in the dreary workplace sharing their whimsical dreams of a life they would like to live and the man of their dreams to fall in love with. Then romance takes a back seat as they talk about men and sex, shagging men and men they have fucked, sounding like a raucous aviary of exotic birds.

Loach and Garnett suddenly inserted random scenes with peripheral characters seemingly having no direct link with the story.

Rita acted out a scene where she led a posse of local battleaxes rummaging through a pile of second-hand clothing being sold by a passing rag and bone man. They gossiped and complained to the vendor about where his wares were from then asked for a price reduction on pairs of piss-stained drawers. Tony watched the scene and loved it. Rita was working with some of the locals, one of whom said,

'Oh, you smell nice dear.'

Rita replied,

'Thanks love, I was thinking of buying a couple of pairs, I've got holes in the knees of mine.'

After the scene she went over to Selby who laughed loudly, gave her a hug and stuck a Rothmans in her mouth.

In another extraordinary segment, a tallyman played by George Sewell was followed closely, filmed by a handheld camera as he drove his car. The camera was behind him on the rear seat showing the driver's point of view. Sewell turned his head to another camera to the left and sported a litany of vile racism about 'yids' and 'darkies'.

Probably the worst and most racist moments came when Sewell's character was delivering a new suit to a West Indian man. The suit was clearly ill-fitting, but the tallyman convinced him it was fashionably cut, then in a hideous line Boris Johnson would be proud of, he looked at the purchaser's son and said,

'What a lovely piccaninny.'

Back in the car, Sewell turned to the back seat camera and said,

'That lot have only half the brain cells of us lot, proven fact.'

Tony asked Sewell how he felt having to say those lines, and got the response,

'Just another job, Tone.'

The filming moved on with the characters Eileen and Dave consummating their relationship. The coupling was filmed after midnight at the Brockwell Park Open Air Lido, so to do this they had to climb into the lido over a wall where the cameramen were waiting, and as they were frolicking in the pool a nightwatchman appeared and told them all to,

'Fuckin, fuck orf.'

A fiver soothed his anger.

From the Lido the lovers were driven to a building site up the road where they were lying on rubble and freezing cold. Vicky Turner and Tony had to simulate a very uncomfortable leg-over; intimacy coordinators where were you? They could have helped pick out the bits of concrete and brick residue from their various hairy bits afterwards.

The abortion scene is suddenly there, a sudden switch to the whole point of the film. Ruby is seen preparing herself for the procedure in the front room of a kindly Vera Drake-like lady, the conversation matter of fact.

'How's yer mum, Rube?'

'Well, fanks.'

The shot slowly fades into a new, harrowing scene Ruby is screaming in agony, her cries searing into the very soul. She does recover, life progresses, and she goes back to work with her friends. Sylvie and Ron get married and row a lot, then Ruby has another tragedy in her life when Terry is killed in a motorbike accident. As for Tony's character, Dave, he is nicked for stealing £800 and gets a five-year sentence, but at least Eileen visits him.

At the conclusion of the film, there is an extraordinary narrative given by a doctor listing in chilling detail the number of abortions that were carried out in the UK each day, all of them illegal. He then extended the numbers to each month, then to each year. He then slammed home the statistics of the number of deaths and critical injuries women suffered. The doctor was Tony Garnett's GP.

Tony Selby was not allowed into the screening room when the edited film was first shown but by all accounts, there was mayhem. Tony and the rest of the cast were well on their way to other possible projects by then, but he was still close enough to Loach and Garnett to hear the eventual fallout.

It seemed that when James MacTaggart returned from his holiday, he had a queue of technicians and studio managers complaining about subterfuge and the misuse of the BBC resources, then after the screening there were arguments the edited work was not fit for transmission. It was argued that the production used music instead of dialogue and the film itself was of poor quality, lacking any continuity, that it was in fact more of a documentary rather than a drama. A drama-doc then?

MacTaggart was really furious and agreed that the work was not fit for transmission. He was also even more angry at the perceived breach of trust from Loach and Garnett, which was reasonably really. The furore spread forever upwards and the Director General demanded answers from his senior managers, a faction, of which, wanted Loach and Garnett to be sacked immediately.

It was a very near thing, but they were not.

MacTaggart, when he slowly calmed down, gave things a little more thought. He knew despite the clandestine operations; they were both brilliant pioneers and innovators. He then began to argue in their corner.

Up the Junction had already been placed in the BBC schedule, so it would have been necessary to find a replacement drama or face a blank screen for the *Wednesday Play*.

MacTaggart decided to proceed, and after transmission it was received with acclaim but also predictable outcry. Mary Whitehouse and church leaders were outraged, and although she agreed that backstreet abortionists should still be prosecuted, she gave no insight on how this could be achieved. More importantly, she did not indicate if abortion should be legalised. She was just outraged. It was also significant there was no comment about the racist or misogynist parts of the film. The Catholic and Anglican church leaders condemned any form of approved abortion legislation. In the secular world there was a much more positive reaction, followed by a swell of support for an Act of Parliament to legalise the termination of unwanted pregnancies.

Others were not necessarily critical of the content but rather its style, mainly from within the BBC but also from the television industry generally. Was it a documentary or drama?

Tony argued that it was a drama, but shot in a documentary style, the precursor to the common television docudrama. Whatever the debate, *Up the Junction* received outstanding reviews, reaching an audience of 12 million. A year so later the Abortion Bill was passed, and Tony Garnett's smile became a little warmer and wider.

15
THE ROYAL COURT

The Lord Chamberlain's office is part of the Royal Household. It has the responsibility of organising the main activities of the Royal Family. In the early 17th century it became responsible for the licensing and censorship of all plays performed in theatres, specifically to prevent or limit political satire or any hint of ridicule aimed at the Royals.

In the 1950s John Osborne and his contemporaries were in frequent conflict over what they considered the moral conservatism and artistic restrictions being imposed on theatre productions. These censors were also the same people who had been regulars at the Windmill.

The Selbys, with lots of immature tittering, were delighted to discover the Lord Chamberlain at the time was named Sir George Titman, while one of the inspectors was called Moorcock. Tony was soon to be more involved with the censors than he bargained for.

The Royal Court Theatre was the home of the English Stage Company, formed by the Royal Court's artistic director George Devine. The company, which relied entirely upon donations and subsidies for its funding, was set up to produce plays by young writers and performed by young actors.

One of the first productions had been Osborne's *Look Back in Anger*; his two other plays had also received the full reprobation of the censor's office. Some of their decisions were farcical, including objection to the use of 'up periscope' in one play because the term had been perceived as a euphemism for the act of buggery. Perhaps someone in the Lord Chamberlain's office had been a submariner and knew about that sort of thing. Mr Moorcock, maybe.

Tony had worked at the Royal Court in two plays both directed by Lindsay Anderson, the first a version of *Antigone*. The initial production had been adapted by Christopher Logue, and his second show was a satirical piece also by Logue, *The Trials of Cobb and Leach*, in which Mary Ure played a prostitute who had entertained a client in a field, during which time the act of orgasm had been witnessed by a horse.

Mary's character was then arrested by a policeman and, for some inexplicable reason, the horse was summoned to the court as a witness. Bryan Pringle, one of the RADAS, played the front of the horse and the unfortunate Tony performed in the hind quarters. During the court scene the horse broke into song, the final line being, 'Everything comes out of the horse's arse!' Before the first performance Lindsay had called the cast together and read out a letter from the Lord Chamberlain's office. They had licensed the performance but with the caveat, 'You are allowed to whack the horse's arse, you can touch the horse's arse, but you shall not allow anything to come out of the horse's arse!'

During that first show, Pringle and Tony, hot and sweaty in their equine costume, rather unprofessionally made their colleagues lose track because of the loud farting noises emitted from the horse's rear end. Tony had been invited to audition with the English Stage Company by Bill Gaskill, who had succeeded Devine as the artistic director. He had seen Tony's work with Ken Loach and Tony Garnett, when they met up the audition became a general chat about how Gaskill wanted the project to develop and his ideas for future productions.

Gaskill was also recruiting some very good young actors, which appealed to Tony as like him, they mostly came from working-class backgrounds. More importantly they all recognised the structure and progressive framework Gaskill would be leading.

Tony was offered a part in a play called *Saved* by Edward Bond. Gaskill told him, 'I was poking about in a cupboard and found the manuscript just sitting there, all alone and neglected.'

It was quite a find.

The setting for the play was in a bleak part of south London, with the plot centering around a young couple. The girl had conceived a child by another man while living with her partner and her somewhat unstable parents. A nice dysfunctional household then.

Tony was to play one of three young men; the other two actors were Ronald Pickup, about to appear in only his second professional stage production, and Dennis Waterman who was around 18 years old at the time.

Their main dialogue was about girls, football, finding work; they were aimless young men devoid of ambition or a sense of purpose, very dated for modern times, corny perhaps then, but they all liked the script. Tony recalled that it was well crafted, and written with a wry, dark humour.

The scene is set in a park. The young couple are observed exiting the stage leaving the baby behind in its pram. The three young men skulking in the background notice the unattended pram and child, at first they have a peripheral interest, then less so. Slowly the pram becomes the centre of their attention and their mood changes becoming brutal, then savage.

The pram is prodded and probed, then it is rocked, then rocked with menace, and the action becomes cruder. A baby is removed and waved around, comments are made about the child's genitals, then shockingly a stone is lobbed into the pram, another follows then a whole fusillade of them increasing in violent velocity. The baby is stoned to death. The actors all knew the play was going to be controversial. Bond had watched them in rehearsal and thought they instinctively understood the play. To an extent he was right.

Waterman and Selby were both from south London, they knew and recognised the vernacular, they had both been actors from a young age, they had been around for a while. Pickup, unsurprisingly, was more apprehensive.

Pickup came from a middle-class background in Cheshire, and because of his limited stage experience he would be reliant on the others to guide him a little. They in turn felt he was astute enough to realise the play touched upon very difficult aspects of human nature: futures with no prospects, violent families, and environment. Rather sadly that culture still exists in Britain in the 21st century.

Decades later, when Tony was interviewed about the play, he thought he understood it intuitively from his own background although that was certainly not as violent. *Saved* was about ignoring young life; the baby is sacrificed in a way, it is saved from an awful future life.

Waterman was more circumspect, but he had a similar intuition. They both remembered seeing bored, scruffy kids around the local parks chucking stones at squirrels and ducks, really trying to hurt or kill them. It only took a small leap of imagination. Pickup had also started to understand the nature of the work, and although he had difficulty with the south London accent at first, he proved a good mimic. The play was ready to open but alas the Lord Chamberlain's office stopped them by refusing to approve the performance licence.

They demanded a huge amount of cuts and script changes, no use of the word 'arse' was allowed (although it had been in *Cobb and Leach*), while 'crap', 'shag' and 'bugger' were to be taken out.

Saved also contained a very sexually suggestive scene in which a character played by John Castle had to darn the stocking of a much older woman played by Gwen Nelson, who by her own admission was well past the flush of late blooming.

Castle had to raise her skirt, put his fingers into the stocking top at the inner thigh then slowly darn the hole. Bill Gaskill decided not to rehearse the scene until the very last minute, primarily because he thought Bond had not really finished the play. Bond said he had finished, and this scene had to be performed in complete silence. When the rest of the cast watched the scene, Waterman summed up the general mood by breaking the silence, 'Fuck me, that's a bit near the mark.' The censors had agreed with Dennis's summation. They also wanted to cut the stone scene completely.

Gaskill, Bond and the Royal Court trustees went into a collective huddle, emerging from it with a good plan. They decided that the Royal Court would become a private members' club theatre, with membership to be given on the purchase of a ticket.

On the opening night when the curtain rose there was a full auditorium, the critics were out in force too with their pens poised like a heron's beak about to spear a fish.

Selby thought everything was going well, they'd had a confident start with just a few murmurs about arse, bugger and shag, then it came to the stone scene. The first cry heard was 'revolting', the second 'how dreadful', then came the smack of angrily vacated seats as they lost a fifth of the audience. By the time the darning of the stocking had finished half the audience remained plus the critics, although those who remained gave rousing applause, even one or two 'Bravos' at the end of the performance.

The majority of the Royal Court's regular audiences were loyal and knowledgeable theatregoers; they expected daring innovation and certainly found it. The reviews inevitably were mixed.

One found the play's depiction of the working class leading awful, desperate lives as sensitive, even compassionate, while another praised its remarkable delicacy, but many others were damning. They were vituperative towards the characters; one referred to Bond's 'slavishly literal bawdiness', accusing the playwright of a lack of artistry in his writing. The *Daily Telegraph* condemned the play as the ugliest, nastiest, most sickening and revolting exercises in brutality ever seen on the modern stage.

When the company read that one, they thought they were doing something right and were looking forward to a sell-out season.

Shortly after the opening, leading critics and figures from theatre and the arts held a debate at the Royal Court Theatre. It was chaired by Kenneth Tynan, a man not known for mincing his words, nor his modesty.

Tynan orchestrated the debate brilliantly. Selby and Waterman both attended, and at the end all agreed that censorship of the theatre was stifling writers, actors, directors, and producers while most importantly, restricting the public's right to decide for themselves. The argument that the Theatres Act was anachronistic and antediluvian was put forward with such fervour that it carried the movement to end censorship forward and rapidly gained momentum.

The English Stage Company worked as a repertory company. *Saved* was performed half a dozen times then rotated with two other productions; one was Edward Bond's adaptation of *Chaste Maid in Cheapside*, the other a version of *The Voysey Inheritance*.

Selby was elated to be involved with such a group of talented people. Other than Waterman and Pickup, Jack Shepherd and Tim Carlton were working there, along with a great character and actor called Victor Henry. Victor and Dennis became really close friends.

The group were all regulars at the King's Head pub, conveniently next door to the theatre. Tony would have two or three beers then, as a happily married man he would dutifully travel home to Jacqui, leaving the younger men to continue into the night. The following day at work, he would have no choice but to listen to their exploits and be amazed at their astonishing energy and libidos.

Selby was suddenly offered a part in another BBC *Wednesday Play*, *Silent Song* by the great Irish writer Frank O'Connor (no relation to James). It was to be a rather unique work in that it was devoid of any dialogue.

Fortuitously there was a gap of eight days between Tony's next stage appearance. Bill Gaskill was happy for him to take the role, but his only misgivings were about the tight shooting schedule and the effect on Tony's stamina. Jacqui probably felt the same.

Silent Song was set in a monastery, with Tony's role would be as a former gravedigger who had joined a silent order of monks, outside Dublin. He flew over to Ireland for two days of filming then, in a frenetic schedule, back to London to complete the work at the BBC studios.

The two other principal actors were Leo McCabe and Jack McGowan, and with those two it meant the scenes would be completed quickly because the hotel they were staying at was next door to a very Irish and very boisterous pub. Tony, in all honesty, felt the scenes were completed with speed because the castle location was freezing cold.

After the day's work the actors were grateful to be sat in a pub with a roaring fire toasting their toes, enjoying a pint with a whisky on the table, then craic.

McGowan had been in the most famous film ever made in Ireland at that time, *The Quiet Man*, starring John Wayne. Tony sat back to hear his story.

Jack and John had bonded immediately, the booze contributing most to the bonding. Once the filming was over, Wayne insisted that McGowan was to visit him in California the next time he was there, which in reality Jack was unlikely to be. Then, unexpectedly Wayne got in touch as he wanted his Irish pal in his next film. McGowan turned up on Wayne's doorstep and was welcomed with open arms.

When in Ireland, Wayne was enthralled by McGowan's stories and tales of Michael Collins, Éamon de Valera, and the struggle for Irish independence. When McGowan arrived at Wayne's place with his suitcase and a smile, he was led to a guest house on the estate, later meeting up for dinner. McGowan had arrived in the United States just as another Jack had been nominated to become the Democrats' presidential candidate. They were all having a pleasant dinner, recounting the wonderful time filming together in

Ireland when Jack mentioned how exciting it was that a man of Irish ancestry could well be the next president of the United States. The whole table froze; Jack said he looked on as icicles froze the candles, the suntanned Californian faces turned puce, and cold winds from the north blew around the room.

Wayne of course was an out-and-out Republican, a fascist, red-neck bigot. He just stared at McGowan.

'I tort he was going to draw his feckin' gun on me,' McGowan later said.

The gunslinger bellowed at him,

'Get the fuck out of my house, we don't associate with fucking communists.'

McGowan eventually arrived back in Dublin completely broke, but his agent threatened to sue Wayne and he paid up Jack's contract. Roaring with laughter, McGowan said,

'That's how I paid for me feckin' house.'

The night in the pub progressed, the ubiquitous Irish fiddles arrived, and McCabe had an idea. Tony played the spoons and as McCabe knew he could sing, he finished up the night singing folk blues while cracking bits of metal on his elbows and kneecaps. McCabe joined in at first before deciding to fall asleep on a comfortable chair.

They flew back to London the next morning and the makeup was applied heavier than normal, then they were straight into the studios for a day's work then home to the flat, where Jacqui was less than impressed as Tony fell into bed without showering or brushing his teeth. There was a scale model of the Berlin Wall between them when he woke to go back to the studios the following morning.

When *Silent Song* wrapped Tony said a fond farewell to McGowan and McCabe, but it was with relief that he returned to the relative tranquillity of the Royal Court. The tranquillity did not last for long as Victor Henry had suffered an awful, dreadful accident. He had been walking along happily and soberly, minding his own business when a car mounted the pavement and hit a lamp-post which fell on to Henry, smashing his cranium into pieces. Henry survived for a few days before he died. The actors were all devastated, particularly Dennis Waterman. Tony really took care of him after the loss of his close friend, but it took Waterman a long time to come to terms with Henry's death.

A few weeks after *Saved* had opened, an official from the Lord Chamberlain's office had made his way to the theatre for a performance. He then pointed out he had not been given a membership when purchasing his ticket and argued that the performance he saw was not under the auspices of a private members' club. The Lord Chamberlain's office issued a summons against the theatre.

Bill Gaskill and Alfred Esdaile, who was the leaseholder of the theatre, were the names on the summons to appear at the magistrates' court. The actors were all waiting for them when they returned to the theatre from court. Bill and Alfred said the magistrate seemed very sympathetic towards them but as the law stood, he would have to find against the Royal Court, so there was a fine of £50, while the two theatre representatives were given conditional discharges. *Saved* had come to the end of its run but had now become in its own right the clarion call for all activists to bring an end to theatre censorship. This was eventually achieved by the Theatres Act 1968.

Shortly afterwards, Ken Tynan filled the London stages with as many bare breasts, buttocks, penises, and vaginas as he could. The actors also said arses, shags and fucks, a lot.

The Royal Court was not the most luxurious of venues, and sometimes parts of the inner-stage area flooded, while the dressing room shared by Tony, Waterman and Ronald Pickup was always damp and cramped. After one performance of *Saved*, Tony was standing in his underwear trying to shave from the tiny sink, the room was hot and steamy. There was a knock at the dressing room door and the other two decided he was the nearest, so he had to open it. A well-dressed, distinguished-looking man smiled and shook Tony's wet hand, while the other two out of curiosity stood behind their part-shaven colleague.

'A splendid, brilliant performance from all of you, thank you,' said the man, who turned quickly and headed down the stairs.

Waterman laughed, 'You know who that was, don't you?' Tony blinked the sweat and steam from his eye and replied,

'No, I didn't really see him, who?'

'Only Laurence fucking Olivier, you prat Tone.'

So another Pimlico boy knew that Tony was not left-handed.

16
FILMS

Tony and Jacqui had settled happily in their fine but smallish flat at number four Tachbrook Street. Their careers were going well, if not spectacularly, while socially they had many good friends, including the Ken Loach/Tony Garnett team of actors and crews.

After work on the *Wednesday Plays*, Jacqui could always be relied on to cook up a huge amount of lasagne – or Italian cottage pie as Rita Webb called it. Everyone would pile in after work to eat the food and drink some decent red wines. One night Jacqui's agent dropped by for a social visit, he told her that a new musical was in the pipeline, and asked if she would be interested.

It was written and composed by Lionel Bart, produced by Bernard Delfont, and directed by Joan Littlewood, so with that grouping involved Jacqui didn't hesitate to express her interest. It was at this time the couple had decided it was time to start a family. Since the marriage, life had become busy and hectic, since her stint in *Forum* she had been busy organising the household, actively in contact with her old dancing colleagues around the West End or socially active at the Buckstone Club or Gerry's.

In the meantime, Tony had been working non-stop so their choice of contraception had been the circadian rhythm method, with work and sleeping patterns restricting opportunities. When Jacqui was offered a part in the new musical she discovered she was pregnant, which was great news for them of course, but bad news in terms of the new job. Her initial contract was for three months which was not too restrictive, and she could probably get through the early pregnancy stage reasonably well, then again it would depend on how physically exacting her part would be. Unfortunately, Bart, Delfont and Littlewood were not aware of how exacting and demanding everything would prove to be, even with their great pedigree.

With Bart, the composer of many fine songs and the brilliant musical *Oliver*, Littlewood the doyenne of Stratford Royal and Delfont, from the legendary theatre family, the new show had to be a surefire hit. The musical was called *Twang*; that alone should have set off alarm bells.

It was to be a spoof and a satirical look at the legends surrounding Robin Hood and his Merry Men cavorting around Sherwood Forest. Tony recalled Jacqui coming home from the first rehearsal a little less enthusiastically than when she had set out in the morning. By her account it had been completely disorganised with absolutely no cohesion, not helped by the fact the script was weak and that Bart had turned up for work spaced out on Valium and half-pissed on vodka. The schedule for *Twang* was for it to preview at the

Palace Theatre in Manchester for a week then open in London at the Shaftesbury Theatre. By the time the company arrived in Manchester nobody knew what the hell was going on.

This was a production with a cast of very good and well-known actors including Bernard Bresslaw, Barbara Windsor and Ronnie Corbett. By the time they returned to London, Joan Littlewood had quit, her successor John Bryan also quit after a couple of days, the music director Ken Moule had collapsed from exhaustion while Bernard Delfont was changing his underwear ten times a day. To make matters worse, an increasingly substance-reliant Lionel Bart had overall control assisted by the lead actor Tony Booth.

On the opening night at the Shaftesbury the script had been changed yet again, with some of the songs cut so that the continuity of the songs no longer fitted into the scenes, then to make things even worse, at the curtain up all the stage lights faded then flickered on and off all through the opening act.

Twang closed after three weeks.

Windsor and Bresslaw went off to 'Carry on', Booth went on to *Till Death Us do Part* and Corbett to *The Frost Report* where he teamed up with Ronnie Barker.

Jacqui had frequently helped out behind the bar of the Buckstone Club. They relied on volunteers to man the bar but the accounting and transactions were not particularly stringent; patrons were supposed to have tabs or accounts, their drinks purchases added up and paid for each week, but everything was very lax. Occasionally, when it looked as if the club might have to close because bills could not be paid, somehow there was always a rush of late payments or even a generous cheque to clear the debts.

Jacqui remembered Corbett working behind the bar; they knew each other from the Windmill. It was at the Buckstone that the two Ronnies first met. Jacqui said she could more or less recall their first conversation.

'Hello, my name is Ronnie.'

'Good heavens, so is mine.'

'Gin and tonic please Ronnie.'

'Two shillings please.'

'Can I pay you next week Ronnie?'

'Certainly Ronnie.'

'Good, then have one for yourself and one for the delightful young lady with you.'

It wasn't all bad news then for most of the cast of *Twang* after it closed. The main sad loser from the debacle was Lionel Bart, who was made bankrupt by the whole sorry debacle.

Just after *Twang*'s bow string snapped, Tony Selby was offered a part in the film adaptation of *Alfie* which would star Michael Caine. Filming was to start in Brixton at a club owned by the Howard brothers, a hard-as-nails family of 'businesspeople'. After the first day's filming Sam came to pick Tony up and offered Caine a ride back into town which he accepted, then for the first few days of the shoot Sam then became their driver. Caine remembered staying over at the flat and enjoying the free supper in the cab shelter. He gave Sam a generous tip at the end of the week.

Tony would not have called Caine a friend, or even a colleague. Caine was always professional and courteous but somewhat distant, probably because he knew of Tony's close association with the RADAS.

Tony learned some time later from Peter O'Toole and Albert Finney that a sort of feud had developed between them and Caine and certainly with with Richard Harris over an alleged remark Caine had made about them that they were unpleasant, unreliable drunks.

To make matters worse, Caine had included Richard Burton in his tirade. Tony could only assume this had all started after Caine's film career began to soar, particularly after *Zulu* and then *The Italian Job*, but it wasn't as if they were going for the same parts. It was, in Tony's opinion, more to do with their acting range and abilities.

Caine was essentially a film actor and had appeared in only a few theatre roles including understudy positions for all of the RADAS who were proving to be hugely adaptable in stage, film, and television work. It was possible that the feud was also related to the number of film awards the other four had achieved in relation to their body of work as a whole.

O'Toole once told Selby,

'We might like to get pissed, but unreliable, unprofessional, never, well other than once or twice!'

Richard Harris made the most explosive outburst.

'The point about Michael Caine is that he can say what he likes, I don't mind him shouting his mouth off but he can't categorise Richard Burton or Peter O' Toole and me as drunks, as if that is all we have achieved in our lives. He could live or have twenty fucking lives without ever achieving as much as we have. He is a flatulent windbag, a master of inconsequence now masquerading as a guru passing off his vast limitations as pious virtue.'

Michael Caine probably decided this was all very unpleasant and declined to make any further comment.

When *Alfie* was released, the Selbys went to the premiere. Jacqui's bump was now showing proudly and she was in full sail, but enjoying the showbiz glamour. After an uneventful confinement, Samantha was born in Westminster Hospital on 27 July 1966. The Selby and the Milburn families invaded the maternity ward with gifts and flowers and beaming smiles.

Tony and Sam were now in a dilemma, Tony more so because three days after the birth of his daughter, England were to play West Germany in the World Cup Final at Wembley. Sam had two tickets.

It was normal for first-time mothers then to be kept in hospital for a few days, so it was probable that Jacqui and Samantha would still be confined to the ward on the day of the match. Tony and Sam approached the subject gingerly. Jacqui of course knew they had the tickets as her mother and Anne had told her.

On 30 July Tony and Sam stood on the terraces at Wembley, watching England win the World Cup. They were both a little hungover when they picked up the girls from the hospital the next day and took them home to Pimlico.

The film industry in the UK, like all other areas of music, fashion, and sports, was attracting a lot of interest, and more importantly finance. Tony was offered more film roles, so he talked things over with Peter O'Toole and Albert Finney. Albert was perhaps more forthright, telling Tony he had a niche, but it would be as a quintessential British actor, a character actor; Finney felt Tony would always be in work but rather like Bryan Pringle, James Villiers, or Ronnie Fraser, never the star, just blessed with the talent he had. Tony took a role in a film called *The City Under the Sea*. As far as cinema history goes, he is still down at the bottom of the ocean tied to a stake.

Tony also heard that his more famous thespian mates had suggested him for roles in their films but for reasons best known to themselves, casting directors or producers had not pursued interest.

A film career still seemed the way forward for him though, and Maurice Aza called him to ask if he would like to appear in a film with Vincent Price, called *Witchfinder*

General. Tony talked over the offer with Jacqui; because of her own career she knew how opportunities could be missed, and in a somewhat brutal admission, as she sat at home and with a baby, her decision to turn down the job in Las Vegas had become one of regret. With that in mind, he signed up for the film.

Witchfinder General was based on a novel by Ronald Bassett about the life of Matthew Hopkins, a 17th-century lawyer who claimed, falsely, to have been appointed the Witchfinder General by Oliver Cromwell during the English Civil War. With social order breaking down, Hopkins had charged around England with his assistant torturing completely innocent women who were suspected of being witches.

Hopkins would then charge the local magistrates for his services before moving on to the next hunting ground, an example of Puritanism at its very worst.

Tony was cast as Salter, Hopkins' main assistant. When he met up with the 25-year-old director Michael Reeves, they initially got on well, with Tony being impressed by his ideas. The other actors included Rupert Davis, Peter Haigh and Ian Ogilvy who happened to be a close friend of Reeves. Patrick Wymark had agreed to play Cromwell although he would only have short periods of filming.

The part of Hopkins had originally been written for Donald Pleasance, but the American producers insisted on a more international star so they brought in Vincent Price. Reeves went ballistic; it meant the script would have to undergo a complete re-write to reflect Price's more flamboyant style and mannerisms.

The producers also wanted the script to be toned down, as within the first drafts there were scenes of bodies tied down to stakes, beheadings, stabbings, people being impaled on spikes or being thrown over walls. When Reeves asked if there was anything else they wanted to cut they told him, 'Yes, the rape scenes.' A lot of time had been lost when the script was finally re-drafted; it was September before filming began so it was going to be a race to complete all the exterior shots before autumn and early winter set in.

Tony was there when the shit really hit the fan when Reeves and Price met up for the first time; it was volatile. Tony watched on as Price, then in his mid-50s heard from his director – less than half his age – that Reeves really didn't want him in his film, he wanted an actor who could act, not one typecast and limited.

Tony and a couple of others stood back. Price hit back: he had more films than anyone could remember, at least 80, and asked how many had Reeves made. Reeves waited, then spat out,

'Three, all of them good films.'

Touché.

When filming began at last, Reeves did not just bitch and bicker with his lead actor, he bitched and bickered with everyone – cast, crew, caterers, drivers – with two exceptions, his mate Ian Ogilvy and, for some reason, Tony. Despite the histrionics, the two of them thought Reeves was a good director as he let his actors get on with it, he encouraged improvisation, and he did listen for preferred ideas. He let actors act, but unfortunately Reeves still had this pernicious, vicious streak mostly directed at Vincent Price.

Tony loved Price from the start as did the rest of the cast and crew. They found him endearing, funny and very generous. The star of countless horror films, he played it campy and hammy, camp because he was and hammy because he completely sent up the genre.

He told Tony,

'I call it the Hammy House of Horror, dear boy.'

Price was indeed camp despite his marriages and propagation and as Rita Webb might have explained,

'He goes for the pink and the brown, Tone.'

While Price did, of course, he seemed very discreet to Tony by not trying a Frankie Howerd on him or to any others.

Price was a knowledgeable collector of art, antiques, and of antiquarian books. Suffolk and Norfolk were a collector's paradise for him. On the increasing extra days off as the production problems continued, Price had hired a car and driver to tour around the two counties looking for curios and paintings, so he asked Tony to accompany him on his expeditions. This was mainly, he said,

'For you to translate, and to ensure I am not overcharged too much.'

On the first journey into the wilds of East Anglia, they stopped off at Farkham Hall, and the Hollywood legend looked at Tony in astonishment when he heard the local station master herald the arrival of a train.

'Fark-en Hall, fark 'em all.'

They hurried off to find the local antique shops a little more welcoming and Price quickly chose a few items. Tony helped him to get some favourable deals. Price caught Selby looking at an old copper teapot which he thought would make a nice present for Jacqui but it was a few more shillings than he could afford. They returned to their hotel to meet some of the other actors for dinner before they all chose an early night for an early call. When Tony picked up his room key he was also handed a bag, containing the copper tea pot.

When production finally began to gain some momentum, it became more and more apparent that it was going to be a Reeves versus Price battle, then Vincent fell off a horse.

It was during an important scene and messed up a whole day's filming. Price was a very accomplished rider but his mount had reared, probably as a result, as Vincent proclaimed,

'Of its fucking enormous fart, too much hay.'

The day was lost however, and Reeves accused Price of being inept. They squabbled as the technicians, not to be outdone, decided they were going to go on strike.

Most of the film interiors were set in an old aircraft hanger the producers had leased at a site in Bury St Edmunds. The sound quality was appalling and the technical crew were badly understaffed, so they decided to walk out. The dispute was eventually reconciled when everyone realised the sound quality was awful anyway; the acoustics within the hanger were crap, so the soundtrack was to be re-engineered back in the London studio.

Other than that, everything went swimmingly and they eventually wrapped towards the tail end of the year. When the film was released in the spring of 1968, the British Board of Film Censors insisted on the heavy cuts because in their opinion there was too much exploitation of sadism and violence.

Michael Reeves was proud of the film, even giving grudging praise to Vincent Price, and told Tony that he had been offered a few projects in Hollywood and he would certainly like to cast him for one of them. Then the director flew off to Los Angeles where he decided to kill himself. C'est la vie, or not in Reeves' case.

Tony met up with Vincent Price a few times in later life, once when he was on his third marriage, to the actor Coral Browne, a formidable woman who was also bisexual which must have made a very interesting union. Tony's uncle once stopped for her when she hailed his cab, and as she was getting in a City type clambered in through the other passenger door, the uncle told the man,

'The lady was first mate.'
The man stared across and asked,
'What lady?'
Coral looked back at him and fluttered her eyes,
'This fucking lady, now fuck off.'
Price told Tony one of the great stories about her; a producer in Hollywood had once said to Browne,
'Coral, I would love to get into your panties.'
She looked back at him seductively and replied,
'Sorry darling, there's a cunt in there already.'

After *Witchfinder General*, Maurice Aza called Tony with the news he had been offered a role in a film starring David Niven. It was to be made in Austria with a two-month schedule.

Tony was a little concerned about being away for any length of time because Jacqui was pregnant, which also meant they would have to look for a larger place to live. Jacqui said that he must take the part as the money was good and it would get them enough for a deposit on a house. This became less of a problem when Sam heard they were looking for a house as he lent them the money for the deposit. Things moved quickly and they found a terraced house just off Tooting Bec Common. Just after they moved in Tony went off to work, arriving in Salzburg on a cold February morning.

The film was called *Before Winter Comes*. Based on the book *The Interpreter*, it was set in an Austrian transit camp housing refugees from the war. It had been set up to assign displaced persons to the Allied or Russian Zones in Europe.

David Niven played a British officer in charge of the camp, while Chaim Topol played a refugee who was a gifted linguist who had proved immensely helpful to the processing of the refugees. The plot in a nutshell reveals he is in fact a deserter from the Russian army, and he is sent back to face the consequences.

The film's director was J. Lee Thompson whose credits included *Ice Cold in Alex*, and a film he and Niven had previously worked together on, *The Guns of Navarone*. The unit had taken over the Anif Hotel in the foothills overlooking the lake where Tony met up with the rest of the cast, including Anthony Quayle and John Hurt whom Selby knew peripherally from around London. After work each day they all dined together; Thompson encouraged them all to socialise. Niven and Quayle had no pretensions about their star status, happy to mix and share their tales and anecdotes, particularly Niven who was a natural raconteur. He had been great friends with Errol Flynn, indeed he had shared a house with him. They had also appeared together in many films. The younger actors and certainly Quayle encouraged Niven to spill the beans, which he did. Tony and Hurt were particularly impressed when Niven told them he was making a pirate film with Flynn, another lot of swash and buckle. They were about to continue a scene after a lunch break when the director bellowed,

'Where the fuck is Flynn?
 Go find find him Niven'

Niven wandered off set and heard familiar sounds emanating from behind a props cupboard door. It was obvious that Flynn was engaged in an enthusiastic bout of sexual intercourse and from the noise it was seemingly nearing a mutual conclusion.

Niven wandered back on to the set where the director barked again,
'Well?'

Niven replied,

'I believe he is just coming.'

Niven and Quayle were both generous in the time and advice they gave to the others, Niven even more generous in a financial way. Tony found him a man who was always intrigued by other people, in what their plans were, their backgrounds, futures. Tony mentioned that he and Jacqui had just moved into their new home; it was just before Easter when the film production was to have a few days off. Niven asked Tony if he was going back to London for the break, but Tony explained he couldn't really afford it as all his fee would be going towards the house. Niven paid for Jacqui to fly out and join them for the Easter holiday.

Although the production had been free of any personality clashes or animosities, there had been one little fly in the ointment: one of the electricians, was a very opinionated mouthy sparks. One of the gaffers had called him out a few times for being rude or disrespectful. He had not done this in front of the director or the main stars, just around Tony and Hurt and other cast members. Towards the end of location filming, several of them decided to take advantage of a day off by taking a boat out on to the lake, and among them was the fly. He started to mouth off, saying that all actors were 'mollycoddled puffs who would be too fucking scared to even jump into the water'.

Tony stripped off and challenged him to a swimming race, from the boat to a metal buoy bobbing about some 50 metres away. There was not only the challenge, but he also bet him £20 he would win, triggering a lively round of side bets among the crew. The challenged one seemed a little hesitant. Tony taunted him,

'Let's see if you can beat one of us puffs then.'

They were both stripped to their underpants, and on the count of three they dived over the side as the others on board noticed the two of them were right-handed. The water in the lake was freezing, Tony's testicles shrank to the size of peas, and after the initial shock he was away, speeding towards the buoy. Strangely he could not hear anyone splashing about with him, but he kept his head down and reached the base of the buoy, then when he glanced back, the fly was nowhere to be seen.

Back on the boat, the others were animated, waving, and beckoning him back, so thinking his opponent had gone under he swam back to the boat and was dragged back aboard.

The fly was lying on the deck, deathly white and wrapped in a blanket. It transpired he had hit the water and the freezing temperature had caused him an asthma attack, which was probably a little worse than having pea-sized bollocks. They quickly headed back to shore where the asthmatic was offloaded and rushed to hospital, and after treatment he was sent home. Tony never received his £20. When he returned home in the early spring, Jacqui had organised the house into a stunning home, Sam was toddling around happily, and they were enjoying being a family again. The fee from the film enabled them to pay back his father. The future was looking bright and all was well in the world, or so they thought.

17
GOODBYE SAM, HELLO MATT

On his return from Austria it was time for Tony to catch up, firstly with his marriage and responsibilities. Jacqui had been lucky in that both her mother and mother-in-law had been more than helpful and supportive, enabling her to have time to herself when they took on babysitting duties, giving her freedom to catch up with her friends but it wasn't really helping her state of mind. She was now really starting to miss the old days, the glamour and remembered fun. Tony sensed this and it would have to be talked through, but he wasn't quite sure how to deal with it so he let it drift. He was seeing his father more, they would get together for a beer regularly, but his dad had become more enthusiastic in his politics again.

There had been some incredible demonstrations, the most startling and violent of which was in Grosvenor Square in London where thousands of people tried to storm the American Embassy in protest about the war in Vietnam.

The postwar generation had started to grow up, the 'Summer of Love' quickly faded, and people had become more pragmatic and astute. They were more informed and politically active than previous generations, not having to fight wars or suffer from conflict made a great difference, and thousands now felt encouraged to march in protest.

Tony himself had been aware of the growing revolutionary zeal for a while, especially within the acting world, with Vanessa Redgrave specifically in the UK and Jane Fonda in the United States, both speaking out openly and regularly attending rallies against US policy on Indochina. Tony liked their commitment and so did Sam.

They were also getting excited about the political situation in France where a communist and socialist alliance was forming with a growing number of disaffected students ready to take on the Charles de Gaulle government. Sam was exuberant at the way the mood seemed to be changing so rapidly, so he told Tony he could taste revolution in the air, even while driving his taxi.

Sam was still living over in Fulham, working long days, but he seemed more cheerful and relaxed, still enjoying his football, and although not playing any more he still was a regular at Stamford Bridge. Just at the end of that 1968 season he became more excited when the French kicked off, not in the football sense though. The alliance started their rebellion, they ripped up the cobbled streets of Paris using the cobblestones as a weapon of choice against the police, then when the army came in they used Molotov cocktails to get themselves noticed. The French people then decided to have a General Strike. Anarchy ruled; Sam rather liked the French.

'That French hero de Gaulle, he's fucked off out of the country, Henry,' he told his son.

Tony acknowledged that observation. De Gaulle had run away like a frightened *lapin*. Vive la France, *vive les evenements*. While France was in revolt and Tony was still thinking about his pregnant wife's dis-satisfaction, he started work on a six-part series called *The Inquisitors* at Wembley Studios.

Tony was the other half of a partnership investigating corruption in the judiciary, alongside Alan Lake. The first episode was called 'The Peeling of Sweet Pea Lawrence' with a storyline around a corrupt judge and a bent copper.

Sweet P. Lawrence, the titular glamour blonde, was an inspired casting, Diana Dors.

Dors had once been touted as Britain's answer to Marilyn Monroe. She had been to Hollywood to make some films but none of them were of any significance. There had been a scandal or two, several affairs, then she produced two children before returning to the UK to try to revive her career. She had been financially robbed blind by ex-husbands, lovers, and managers, and on her return she had to spend time working in cabaret on the northern club circuit to pay off her debts.

Dors was still a very attractive woman, seductive and to use that fine tabloid term, slinky; she had maintained her figure while her appearance was immaculate. She radiated stardom and all the men, well most of them, fancied her immediately, especially Lake. On the first day of filming they both seemed to be getting along very well indeed.

On the second day Tony was having a cup of tea and cigarette with some of the camera crew outside the studios when Diana arrived in her Rolls-Royce. Lake was driving, and he was wearing clothing that belonged to one of Dors' previous husbands. By the third day of filming Lake had moved in with her. On set Tony found that Dors was flawless, totally professional, and he had not realised what a really good actor she was.

Lake also proved to be a very competent actor and endeared himself to everyone with some very funny, rude and self-deprecating stories. Sadly in later life he experienced awful addictions to alcohol and drugs.

Selby also bonded well with the series writer Trevor Preston; they went on to become firm friends. Preston had studied at the Royal College of Art before starting his writing career on the Arts programme *Tempo*. He then started writing for children's television before progressing to become an ingenious writer for grown-up telly.

The Inquisitors had a good feel to it. Selby thought the scripts were strong and contemporary, a feeling that was mutual with the rest of the cast and particularly Patrick Magee, who was playing the dodgy judge. Work progressed well, always finishing on schedule, which meant they would all relax with a drink at the end of the day. Patrick, Alan, and Diana were always affable and amusing.

Diana Dors' real name was Diana Fluck, and when she told her audience that, fellow actors and crew laughed with disbelief.

'Exactly,' she replied,

'Just think what I went through at school.'

She said her first agent suggested she change it to another perhaps simpler name. Her parents were with her in the agent's office, they could not see what was wrong with her given name, rather surprisingly saying they had had no problems with the name Fluck. Thinking quickly, her agent suggested it could be a problem if, for example, her name was up in lights at a theatre or cinema where a circuit malfunction could black out the L, or there could be an unfortunate misprint on a contract or agreement.

Diana sat back, drew on her cigarette deeply and blew out a long plume of smoke, elegant yet mischievous at the same time, admitting,

'It could have been worse of course; I could have been named Diana Clunt.'

Miss Fluck was the subject of many lurid stories in the press, some she had leaked herself, others from ex-lovers, husbands, or 'friends'. Diana made no secret of the fact that she liked to party, she was on her own admission a highly sexual person and enjoyed an energetic adventurous sex life. The parties at her home became the stuff of legend, stuff being the operative word: orgies allegedly filmed on eight-millimetre cameras capturing film stars, politicians, and royalty (of course), all maintaining with great stamina and enthusiasm some very unorthodox positions.

Tony was told later by a well-known comedian who had attended one of the parties,

'The problem with the sexual scrum at Diana's house, with all the lights down, you didn't know who to thank afterwards.'

The production was way into the second episode when one morning they had cut for a short break. There was a telephone just off the set linked to the production office and when it rang, Patrick Magee was the nearest and answered the call. He nodded, then beckoned Tony over to him, telling him,

'Terribly sorry Tony, I'm afraid your father has died. Sorry dear boy.'

Tony thought it must be a mistake, that whoever had phoned must have meant his grandad, who was always choking on a fish bone or had some obstruction.

Magee patted him on the back,

'It seems he had a heart attack, so sorry'.

Tony immediately called Jacqui who confirmed Sam had indeed gone to the long cab rank in the sky. In the studio car taking him home, Tony thought to himself wryly that it must have been all the excitement of the French riots, his dad's newfound socialist optimism, but then he told himself it was probably an aggregate of a crap diet most of the time, long and stressful working days with a complicated secretive personal life thrown in. Sam died at the flat he shared with Maude and her son. It seemed he had been suffering from chest pains for some time although he had not mentioned it to Tony, and his blood pressure had suggested because of the irregular lifestyle the pains were more than likely due to a prolonged bout of indigestion. Sam was taking the dustbins out for collection then just dropped down dead, which cured the indigestion immediately.

Sam had expired as a result of a coronary occlusion, a partial obstruction of the flow of blood to the heart. It produces just mild pain, like indigestion but the condition causes a hell of a mess to the heart tissue. Coronary occlusion is a common condition, and had it had been diagnosed correctly a heart bypass could have been performed. That was certainly not as simple an option then, but it should have been done. Tony would know a lot more about this procedure in later years.

When he arrived back at the house, he immediately called his mum. Kathy was with Anne, who had received the call from Maude who gave her telephone number to Kathy. Tony then called her at her home. It was a rather odd feeling for him, bizarre even, that he and Maude had never met. Sam had never discussed his relationship with her, the family knew nothing of their life together, now for the first time the Selby family had to come to terms with Sam's duplicitous life. They had to have the two women in his life attending the funeral. The good Catholic side to Anne's character agreed that Maude should be at the service.

The funeral was held at Anne's local church which was crammed with mourners; as well as the Selbys and the Weavers, the Milburns were there, a crowd from the Tachbrook Estate, and people from his football life. Sat together in a small huddle were Maude Brown, her son Mike and a few of her friends.

When the cortege left for Streatham Cemetery, the roads leading up to the gates were lined with dozens of taxis, each cabbie wearing their official drivers' hats with the green badges attached. Tony's tears ran like an early spring rain.

He didn't keep in touch with Maude and Mike, although he did hear that Mike had become involved in the film industry as a technician but their paths didn't cross. Tony always felt it fitting that the two parts of Sam's life should remain separate.

They tried to gather the threads of their own lives as quickly as they could but they weren't allowed to because Grandad Selby passed away a few weeks later. To help relieve the sadness, Mathew Selby was born at Westminster Hospital. Tony also had to find some more work.

18
ALL THAT JAZZ AND HULL

The Inquisitors had ended ingloriously. After three episodes were in the can, London Weekend Television pulled the plug, leaving the cast and writer bewildered and frustrated. LWT felt the plots were far too political and the dialogue too racy, in fact just like many other shows and series being shown on other channels. The cast and crew were paid off and were all now looking for new horizons. In Tooting Bec, Jacqui was coping well enough with the two children, but Tony could see she was becoming frustrated by domestic restrictions. This was time to talk things through.

Jacqui had always been a spontaneous, carefree individual from her early childhood. In Austria, Tony had seen how much she enjoyed her time with the actors and the film crew, and she also missed the closeness of the RADAS and her Bluebell line-up. She wanted more time for herself, to catch up with friends, to have more freedom.

Tony and Jacqui decided to employ an au pair.

Her name was Rita and she was from Basel in Switzerland, and when they interviewed her, she said she wanted to be more fluent in English, although it was already fluent when she started work. Rita also spoke German, French and Italian. She proved to be intelligent, capable, funny, and fantastic with the two children. Her colloquial English also improved considerably during her time with them, particularly the swear words and expressions.

With Rita proving to be a godsend, Tony and Jacqui were able to attend a few of the jazz venues around town. Whenever they left the house Rita always wished then well,

'Have a fucking good time.'

Tony's own music career had taken off a little more, certainly since entertaining Mrs Goody. He was introduced to a producer called Bernie Stringell, who had contacted Maurice Aza to ask if Tony would be interested in appearing in a beer commercial. It was to be big-budget and made for television and the cinema. They went over to see Stringell at his home for a casual drink and a chat with a few of the creatives from the advertising agency. Stringell was a big jazz fan, and while they were mingling and chatting Tony heard the most haunting piano music from along a corridor. He asked Stringell if he was playing an Erroll Garner record. Bernie smiled and nodded to the room from where the music was delightfully dancing from, Tony followed the melody.

The pianist sitting at the piano was playing just like Garner to perfection. Tony wandered over to stand by the piano, when the playing finished with an ivory flourish. Tony nodded and applauded in appreciation to the talented tinkler, Tony Lee. The two of them discussed Erroll Garner, and jazz generally, then Lee returned to the piano to play a George Gershwin number and Tony sang the vocals. The room began to fill with the other guests as the two of them entertained for the rest of the evening. Tony also blagged the beer commercial.

Tony Lee had regular gigs at the Bull's Head and also at the Leather Bottle in Merton. They found it weird that their paths had not crossed before. Lee gigged on a regular basis with the double bass player Tony Archer, so they asked him to join them as their vocalist and christened themselves the Three Tones; when drummer Tony Mann also joined them, they became the Four Tones. Unfortunately Mann left fairly quickly to work full time with Ronnie Scott and was replaced by Martin Drew. The Three Tones and Non-Tone played on and off for several years.

Jacqui was approaching that time in her life where she realised her future in the theatre was unlikely to develop further. Although still extremely fit and active, her years of pounding the stage as a prominent dancer had reduced her stamina, and her motivation; it had been a strenuous lifestyle for her. Their lifestyle was busy; work for Tony had been regular for the last year or so of the decade, nothing outstanding but good fun, especially when he teamed up again with Dora Bryan for her television series *According to Dora*, which was to go out live on Saturday nights. Jacqui could come over for the transmission then they could go off to the West End to catch up with the gossip and the scandal at the Buckstone or Gerry's but Tony could sense some discontent from his wife. This wasn't helped when he was offered a part in a new play by the prolific author and playwright Robin Maugham, who was best known for his play and subsequently film *The Servant*. The producer was the much-feared Doris Cole Abrahams who asked Richard Eyre to direct, or possibly insisted he did so.

Tony had met Eyre at the BBC a few times. Eyre had the reputation of a very talented writer and director, and was also a contemporary of Ken Loach and Tony Garnett.

Enemy was devised as a two-act play about two soldiers, one German, one English. Both were lost in the desert after being separated from their units, and after wandering around aimlessly they eventually met up at the hulk of a disabled abandoned tank. Luckily, it had been left with some food and fresh water. The soldiers' first instinct was to try and capture each other but they recognised the ridiculousness of their situation. It made sense if they were to survive, and it made much more sense to become friends rather than remain enemies.

As the two got to know each other, the German in a lengthy and poignant speech confessed to the English soldier that he was a homosexual.

In the second act another actor appeared, a British officer out on a lone reconnaissance who eventually shot the German.

The producer and writer had originally wanted Dennis Waterman to take the role of Ken, the English soldier, and when he had visited Doris Abraham at her flat to discuss the role, he surprised her by saying he wanted to play Paul, the German. Maugham and Eyre, who were also there, were less surprised and after Waterman had done the read-through as Paul, he was immediately offered the part. Tony became Ken, and Neil Stacey was offered the role of Decker, the British officer.

After a four-week rehearsal they opened at the Yvonne Arnaud Theatre in Guildford, after which they were then to go on a six-week tour before opening at the Saville Theatre.

Waterman and Tony were of course old mates from their Royal Court days and quickly took on their characters. Tony was surprised by how convincing Waterman was as a gay German.

Waterman at the time was married to his first wife, Penny, but was involved in a passionate affair with the Oscar-winning actress Romy Schneider whom he had met on a film set. He was about 22 at the time; Romy was ten years older.

When they opened at Guilford it was Romy who arrived for the first night, not Penny. Tony made no comment, preferring to accept the situation even though he felt sorry for Penny whom he had met and liked. He would always wonder how Waterman managed over the years to keep his extraordinary and complicated love life together but concluded that his pal couldn't and wouldn't, but he certainly had stamina.

After the week in Guildford, they went on to Swansea, Cambridge, Bath and then Hull, and by the time they arrived on Humberside they had formed a strong working relationship and friendship. Tony and Waterman were the social secretaries: they would find the best pubs, clubs, and eateries while Stacey, on the other hand, was the teacher and tour guide.

Neil was a Norfolk boy who had taken a first-class honours degree in Modern History from Oxford University. His great hobby was researching early medieval estates around Glastonbury Abbey so would have found evidence of the Rolling Stones' first gig down there. Neil proved to be a thoroughly nice person and he gave the other two slight philistines a guided history tour as they travelled the country.

Then they arrived in Hull.

Dennis was a good friend of the comedian Les Dawson who once told him,

'If God ever wanted to give the world an enema, he would do it in Hull.'

When they arrived in the city it a was cold, grey November day in East Yorkshire. Neil had told them the city had been the most bombed in the whole of the United Kingdom during the second world war, but on the plus side it had its very own telephone system with white telephone boxes. Despite these fascinating facts the whole place seemed to be closed down.

Hull was indeed pretty well run-down, the fishing industry was failing, and no real investment was coming in, while Phillip Larkin was complaining about being 'fucked up' by his mum and dad and the poor timing of sexual intercourse in his life. Fellow Hullians Tom Courtenay and Maureen Lipman had already escaped to London down the M1.

When the three actors shuffled into the New Theatre that Monday morning, they agreed it was perhaps not suited for an intimate three-hander cast. They had been playing to audiences of around 600 but this in comparison was huge; the auditorium held an audience of 1,500.

The theatre manager told them that ticket sales had been healthy, but that matinees were proving to be somewhat low. Most actors dislike matinees at the best of times, more so when there was a poor house. There was an unwritten rule that if the cast outnumbered the audience then the punters got their money back. The actors would then have the afternoon off, but with only three of them in this cast, it would be unlikely.

Their opening night was encouraging: the theatre was full, with an enthusiastic receptive audience, but by Wednesday for the first matinee they had an audience of 20.

Tony had a glance from the side of the stage just before they went on, and saw an old bloke shuffling to his seat. He turned to Waterman who was peeking over his shoulder, 'At least he's brought the average age down to about 80, Den.' Waterman was in one of his mischievous moods. Actors are selfish at times, well a lot of the time actually, but with the poor attendance and the knowledge of another performance that evening, they tended to speed up the dialogue and the action a little or a lot and running time could be reduced by up to 20 minutes. They could also be very immature by trying to make each other corpse.

Tony had great pride in his self-control and discipline while performing. He very rarely needed a prompt or properly corpsed although he had been near it a few times.

The *Enemy* set was basically the shell of a tank tucked into a mound of sand, in the western desert near Gazala. Tony was lying down in the sand as Waterman launched into his coming out of the closet speech; Paul telling Ken about his lover Rolf left behind in far off Berlin, about how much he loved him and missed him.

After three months of hearing this speech, Tony instinctively knew there was something going on. The delivery, tone and accent was changing, so he started to worry, and suddenly Paul became a German Larry Grayson impersonation that turned into a teutonic Lily Savage, then even more scarily a prototype Julian Clary. Ken could not look at the super-camp Paul.

Tony felt himself going; a slight splutter followed, then he pretended to cough, which turned into a stifled scream and when he heard Marlene Dietrich emanating from Paul, he lost it, or more embarrassingly his bladder did. He actually pissed himself laughing.

They finished the show with the colour of his shorts slightly darker at the front although the sand helped to disguise the sizeable stain. The audience, or those of them still alive or awake, gave a ripple of applause. The shorts had dried out for the evening performance after a good wash.

The last matinee was on the Saturday, with a similar audience. Tony decided to get his own back. Ken started as a London boy, then turned into a Belfast lad with an accent so thick no one could understand a word, then Glaswegian before turning into Dai of the Valley.

When they left Hull, which quite deservedly became the City of Culture in 2017, they headed for the south and a week in Brighton, thinking they were to open at the Saville Theatre after they had finished on the coast, it suddenly became unclear if they were going to do so.

The Saville had been the subject of a takeover by Brian Epstein who had been using the venue to put on live Beatles gigs, and also other bands he managed. After Epstein died other promoters were using the theatre for pop and rock bands, and it was becoming unclear which way the theatre would be heading as an entertainment venue.

When *Enemy* finished the run in Brighton, the cast had a couple of weeks off until the transfer to the West End was sorted out, or so they thought.

Waterman decided to continue with his complicated love life, Tony went to catch up with Jacqui, Samantha and Matt, while Neil could go back to Glastonbury and perhaps advise Michael Eavis about how he could earn some extra revenue to supplement his earning for the dairy farm.

Doris Abrahams had other ideas. Although they were not sure if she had got wind of the pissy pants incident, or the round-Britain accent tour, she told them the play needed more of an edge for a London audience. Their time off was considerably reduced when they were asked, indeed commanded, to spend a week, in her words, taking part in a 'more disciplined rehearsal' with a slightly revised script.

When they eventually opened at the Saville, they did so with a feeling of uncertainty., Waterman felt they had been on tour for too long a period and Neil agreed, while Tony felt that the excitement and nervousness normally felt for a London opening was lacking.

The first night proved to be tremendous. A new play by Robin Maugham was in itself an occasion of great anticipation and because it was Maugham, Noël Coward and his whole entourage were there to support him. Jacqui, her parents, and the Milburns were there, Neil's family also. Penny Waterman had been invited for the opening night. It was a little awkward, but she seemed cheerful and chatty to everyone.

The performance was politely received, and afterwards Maugham brought a mince of friends into the dressing room. In trooped Coward, Trevor Howard, Helen Cherry and a few other confirmed bachelors.

Enemy was not a great success. It probably broke even but unlike Hull's improved performances, it didn't capture the London theatregoers' imagination. Rather sadly, it was also the last play to be performed at the Saville Theatre, which closed shortly afterwards and became a cinema.

Selby and Weaver families 1948.

Skippy Smith goes to the circus.

Sam dropping "Sir Henry" at Lime Grove.

Sam Selby MaCaTra goalie.

A 21st birthday at the Garrick Theatre.

Jacqui (top) at the Windmill.

Jacqui (far right) in Spain.

Jacqui Windmill debutante.

Jacqui and Tony's wedding at Caxton Hall.

The condemned cell. Three Clear Sundays.

Final scene. Three Clear Sundays.

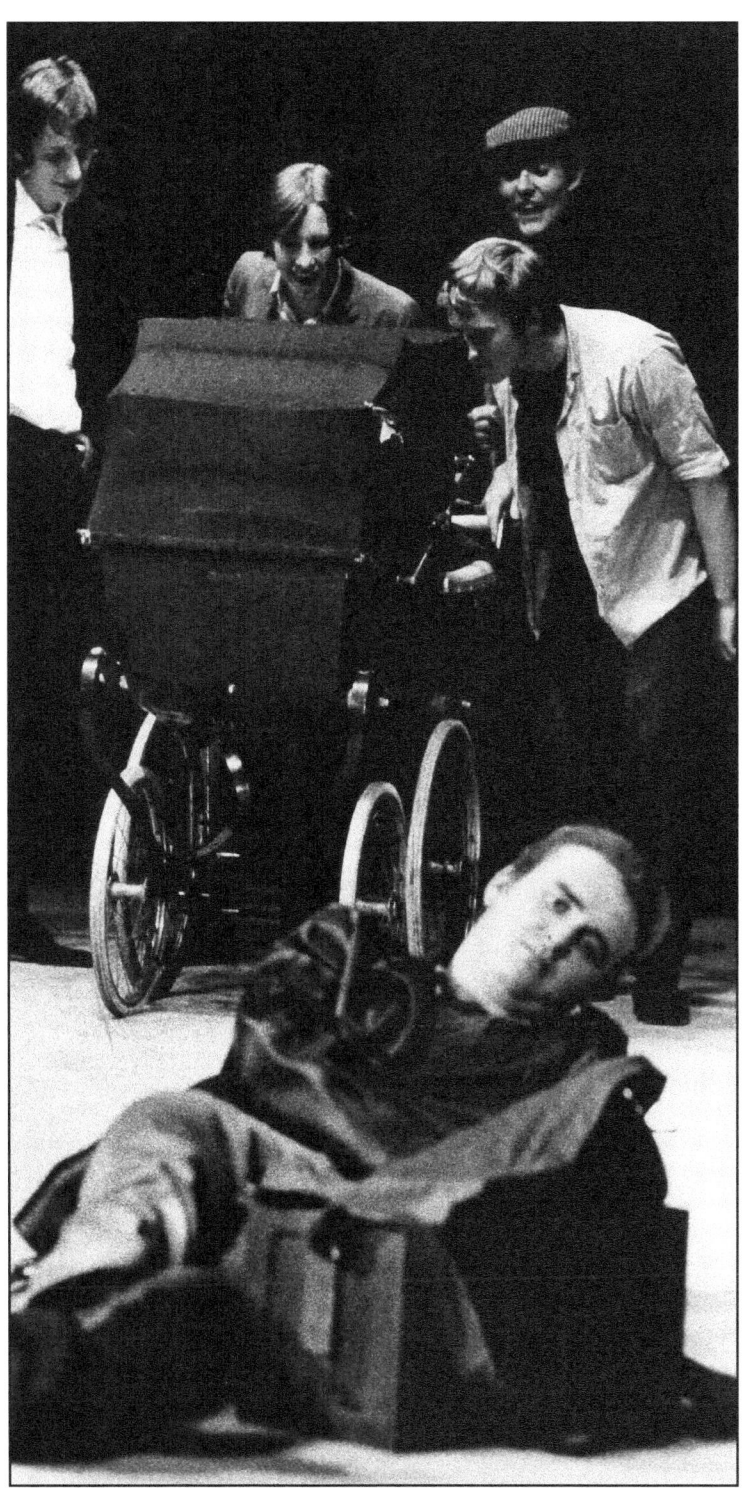
Saved at the Royal Court with Dennis Waterman.

Alfie. Tony, Sam and Michael Caine.

Not many people knew this. Sam dropping Tony and Michael at the Alfie set.

With Jim Dale in Adolf Hitler - My Part in his Downfall.

Corporal Marsh - Get Some In.

Another view of Marsh.

Midfield dynamo for the Entertainers XI.

Selby the Striker.

Showbiz football squad.

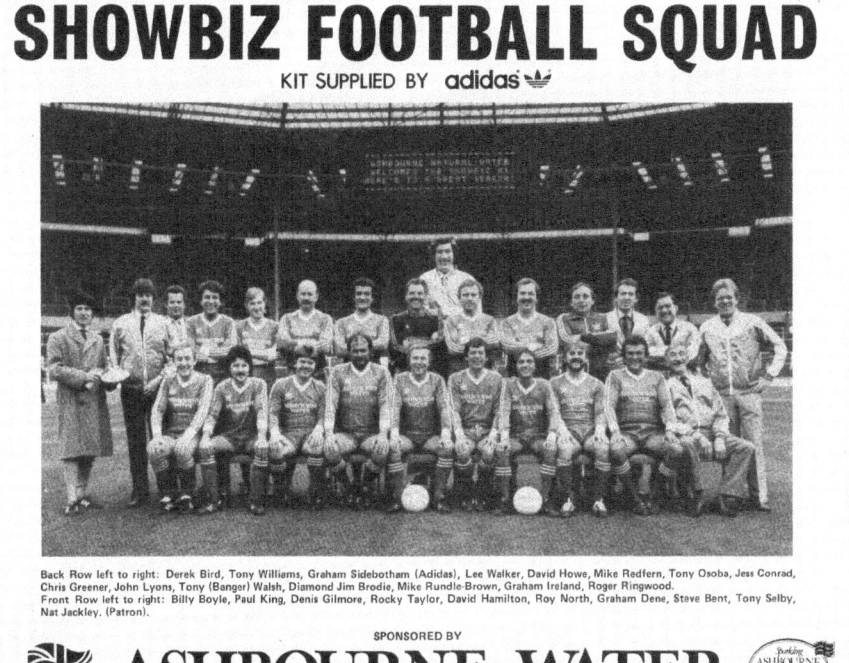

Entertainers X1.

In Minder

Gina and Tony with Dick Emery.

Run For Your Wife (Australia).

Sabalom Glitz.

Glitz again.

With co-stars Bonnie Langford and Sophie Aldred.

Glitz with Dr Who - Sylvester McCoy.

As Tevre in Fiddler On The Roof.

*Gina and Tony
on their wedding day.*

Love Hurts.

Regents Park- Paint You Wagon

Sir Henry Irving.

19
MR AND MRS BURTON AND SPIKE

When Tony and Jacqui woke up on 1 January 1970, they would have been able to go hang gliding on the new size of shirt collar while an old tea clipper would have sailed to the Far East in about three days with the width of material of their flared trousers.

The voting age had been reduced to 18, Karl Marx's grave was vandalised, and later in the year the Beatles disbanded, the Conservatives won the election with Ted Heath becoming prime minister although the events were incidental rather than connected. While tripping over his bell bottoms and sulking about the Beatles' breakup and Heath, Tony was suddenly overwhelmed with opportunities.

The first was for a Yorkshire Television series called *Shine a Light*, which was centred around two lighthouse men, set in a lighthouse, and he was to play one of them, Ken Robinson. Six episodes were shot very speedily, but the lights went out very quickly and the series crashed into the sea below. When he had dried out Tony had a call from Trevor Preston who had been writing a new series called *Ace of Wands*; the main character was a super detective battling fiendish villains with the use of magic and tarot cards. The Ace of Wands is the name given to the tarot card Minor Arcana, *Arcana* being the Latin for mystery. The main character, Tarot, played by Michael MacKenzie, had a pet owl called Ozymandias. Tarot also had two assistants, Lulli (played by Judy Lowe) and Sam Maxstead (played by Tony).

Lulli had a telepathic link with Tarot which could be transmitted over great distances. If for example he was in Croydon she could let him know what time tea would be ready. Sam was a reformed convict who wanted to put his criminal knowhow to better use and rehabilitate himself into society, although he had to guess what time hot beverages and crumpets were to be served without help. Tony also thought Ozymandias was possibly contacting a very young J.K. Rowling. Lulli and Sam were there to help Tarot solve heinous crimes through his cabalistic powers and also to have a jolly good time.

The show proved to be a great children's television hit for Thames despite the unstable poorly constructed sets, and although it was not perhaps Preston's best dialogue the television company commissioned a third series which was a pity for Lowe and Tony because they both suddenly had other, and in Tony's case, more exciting commitments.

Maurice Aza asked him to come over to see him as the director Michael Tuchner was casting for a film written by Dick Clement and Ian La Frenais loosely based on the life of Ronnie Kray. Tuchner wanted Tony to play one of the henchmen.

Tony wasn't sure and thought the Kray story had been done to death, rather like some of their victims, however out of curiosity he asked Maurice who was starring.

'Richard Burton in the main role,' came the reply.

Before he had completed the sentence, Tony was in.

When he received the script, he was less enthusiastic, not necessarily by the script itself but by the concept. The storyline was that a tough, psychotic, homosexual East End criminal called Vic Dakin had his gang carry out a massive payroll robbery, after which they all headed to the south coast, soon followed by the police. Dakin has an alibi provided by his boyfriend, played by Ian McShane, and when the police catch up he tells them they were both elsewhere when the crime had been carried out. He is backed up by a Lord Boothby figure who also confirmed he had been with them, mainly because he was being blackmailed. This was the concept Selby was concerned about. The Sexual Offences Act permitting two consenting adults of the same sex to have a sexual relationship had only just recently become law, and his opinion was that the scenes of Burton and McShane, two very heterosexual virile actors would not be believable or accepted by filmgoers, nor would the public have a more liberal attitude towards gay couples. His opinion didn't pay the rent, so he prepared for filming. Tony travelled down on the train to Brighton on the same train as Burton and other cast members; they checked into the hotel then agreed to meet up at a pub in The Lanes for lunch. Burton was already sitting at a table with an actor who had come into prominence in the *Z-Cars* series and would go on to win an Oscar as a writer. He stood and shook hands with Tony.

He introduced himself,

'Colin Welland, I'm known as the sixteen stone rabbit who can eat an apple through a tennis racket!'

Tony could not really contradict him; Burton roared with laughter. The waitress came over, looked at them, stared at Burton, then screamed and fled. Shortly afterwards, another girl came over to take their order. Selby whispered to her,

'Is your friend all right?'

'Yes.'

'What happened?'

'Well, as soon as she realised it was Mr Burton, she weed her knickers."

'Ah.'

Burton raised an eyebrow of interest.

'I'll tell you later,'

Tony told him.

Burton was sympathetic when he did.

While the young lady was changing her clothing, one of the world's great actors, together with two workmates, were demolishing a huge plate of steak pie and chips.

They started work the following day, waiting to begin filming just by the West Pier entrance. Ian McShane and Donald Sinden, who was the Lord Boothby character, were with them when a horde of shrieking kids charged towards the actors. Sinden looked toward them, 'God, how awful'

Some of the crew moved in around the thespians to keep the kids at bay, but it proved to be unnecessary. The mob formed a large, rowdy circle around Tony brandishing bits of paper for his autograph. They were all *Ace of Wands* fans.

After the adolescent adoration, it was time for a lot of graphic violence and homoerotic action which the director really wanted to ramp up.

When the gay love scenes were being filmed, Burton and McShane really went for it. They had a fag and a Scotch before the scene, a couple of mints then a long lingering snog, all pointless as in the end as it was cut in the film's final edit.

Villains was not a great and fulfilling experience for Tony. From an acting perspective the London accents from some, including Burton, were not altogether convincing; a few of the actors were struggling or inconsistent with their dialect.

Tony also felt the shoot in Brighton was all a bit seedy, as if Tuchner wanted to recreate *Brighton Rock*, but with his own role in the film coming to an end he was preparing to head home.

It seemed some scenes had been re-written then a couple of extra ones added so they asked Tony to stay on. He agreed and asked what fee he would receive, only to be told they would let him know.

On the first morning of his extra days he was told there would be no extra fees, just hotel and *per diem* rates. He told them to eff off and stormed off to the trailer he had been sharing with McShane and Welland, then locked the door and sulked. They sent over one of the production runners who knocked on the trailer door and bellowed that the director was angry and waiting to start the day's work, but the runner was told to fuck off. Then an assistant director arrived and repeated that the director was waiting but he was told to fuck off as well. Shortly afterwards there was another knock on the door.

'Hello Tony, it's Richard.'

Tony decided not to tell Burton to fuck off and instead let him in. They sat down at the table and opened a very nice bottle of whisky Burton had brought with him, poured two generous measures, clinked glasses and had a good talk. Burton knew the RADAS well of course. The two of them swapped stories, they talked about each other's backgrounds and the acting profession's ups and downs. Tony's singular industrial action was not mentioned.

Two hours and an empty bottle later Burton headed out leaving Tony groggy and sleepy with his immediate future still to be resolved. He was awoken by another bang on the door: it was the assistant director again who told him Burton had spoken with Tuchner and they had an offer for him, a three-week retainer on £75 a day, to which Tony quickly agreed. He discovered later that Burton's fee for the film was $500,000.

Shortly after the stand-off, Welland and Tony had completed their schedule by late morning, Burton had also so he invited them to have lunch with him. He told them he had some 'fat bird' coming down from London and had booked her into the Grand Hotel on the Brighton seafront.

The three of them gathered at the bar and drank a few beers but there was no sign of the plump female. The head waiter then met them and led the trio to a small private room overlooking the sea, where on a side table there was a bottle of champagne, and a white Bordeaux in the ice buckets with a bottle of burgundy standing guard behind. A few minutes later Burton stood up, the other two looked behind the door, and entering the room with the most radiant of smiles, her vivid violent eyes reflecting the sea, was Burton's 'fat bird'.

'Gentlemen, this is Elizabeth,'

Tony stood up quickly, his knee catching the corner of the side table causing the bottles and the ice bucket to clink like an exaggerated wind chime. Welland rose more slowly and quivered.

Elizabeth sat down slowly and gracefully as the head waiter confidently poured her a glass of Veuve Clicquot. She asked how the film was going, Burton told her of Tony's one-man stance. She also made the comment that Richard had suggested that the movie was all thuggery and buggery which they both agreed was a succinct summary. They began to relax with her, probably the most famous woman in the world after another Elizabeth, one of whom said 'fuck' more than the other possibly. Tony couldn't recall all of the conversation; he remembered he and Welland were completely captivated, then suddenly the actor and his bird had flown, possibly for some afternoon delight, leaving them to finish off the burgundy before the head waiter kicked them out. They drifted back to their less salubrious hotel around the corner.

Villain concluded filming in Kentish Town and then there was a wrap party at the Assembly House. Over the years there were stories of Liz Taylor serving behind the bar. Tony said she didn't, she was too busy in front of the bar ordering rounds of drinks and passing them back to the crew.

The film received mixed reviews. It had reasonable success at the box office while making the producer a decent net percentage. From his own experience, Tony had benefited in two ways, one having worked and dined with the two most famous actors of the time and secondly, thanks to Richard Burton, he had almost doubled his wages. The film, though, had hardly enhanced the reputations of the cast, but despite that the next couple of years were busy for Tony. In the early 1970s he had appearances in several television shows, then he was offered a role in another film based on Spike Milligan's book, *Adolf Hitler – My Part in his Downfall*. It was to prove, not unexpectedly, to be a bizarre experience.

Spike was a co-writer of the screenplay, along with Johnny Byrne and Norman Cohen. Milligan was also cast to play his own father, while Spike himself was to be played by Jim Dale, a man with an astonishing varied career. Dale had worked with the National Theatre and the Royal Shakespeare Company but had sealed his acting credentials by making his name in the *Carry On* films, most memorably as Dr Mucky. He was also a singer and songwriter having composed two top-ten hits, 'Georgy Girl' by the Seekers and the rather less creditable 'Dick-A-Dum-Dum' for Des O'Connor. Unfortunately a majority opinion agreed he was the wrong actor to play Spike.

The rest of the cast was a who's who of prominent television sitcoms or *Carry On* films. Arthur Lower played the Major without stepping out of his Captain Mainwaring role from *Dad's Army*, except for his higher rank perhaps. Windsor Davies played a Sergeant Major so no change there then. Tony Booth, who had recovered from being Twanged, played a Scouser, which was not too exacting for him. Pat Coombs played Spike's mother, a role she was born to play, while Bob Todd, who played the pop-eyed madman with Benny Hill, was just that, a complete nutter.

Tony had met Milligan a few times over the years, mainly through their interest in jazz. They had come across each other at Ronnie Scott's in the early days then at most of the major jazz venues and concerts. Tony thought he was always an enthralled and appreciative listener. Milligan was also an enthusiastic and fairly good trumpet player, and when he first turned up for filming that was exactly what he was doing. Most of the scenes had already been completed in the studio, then the whole production moved down for location filming around Bexhill-on-Sea. The whole crew assembled in a field, then in the adjoining field they could see and hear a large herd of cows loudly munching grass, mooing, and expelling volumes of methane and shit.

Then, unanticipatedly, 'When the Saints Go Marching In' suddenly assailed the air. They all looked over to see the whole herd of cows ambling over happily to the figure playing the instrument. It was Milligan.

The cows completely surrounded him, and he was last seen lying down serenading the bovine jazz enthusiasts. When Tony looked over a short time later, the herd had gone back to its day job but Spike had just disappeared.

Tony found Milligan a very funny man but often depending on his mood; when his depression set in he could be dark as the inside of Fingal's Cave on a winter's night. The few instances of his cruel illness manifested itself during filming he just left for home, which was fortunately just around the corner in Rye.

He continued to make unexpected chaotic appearances though, and once found Selby and Bob Todd innocently walking along the street. He dragged them into an adjacent undertakers, rang the bell, then lay down on the desktop, crossed his arms across his chest and yelled 'shop'.

Later Tony was in a tea shop with Pat Coombs and others when Spike stumbled through the door. Suddenly Pat had a tea cosy on her head, he was playing a teapot through its spout, Tony played spoons while Milligan was using the cake stand as a percussion instrument.

When the film was eventually released it was a sort of *Carry on Spike*. It wasn't as funny as it could have been while the reviews would not have helped Milligan's depression.

The only good thing heard afterwards was that 'Dick-A-Dum-Dum' had been voted one of the worst songs of all time; that would have cheered Mr Milligan up immensely.

20
GET SOME IN!

Tony had always liked Christmas. When he was a child the Selby and Weaver families always made it special, singing carols and the songs of old. It was always warm and fun. Now as a father he found it even better with his own family. Samantha, at eight years of age, had strong suspicions about Santa's existence and was possibly trying to influence Matt's opinion about the man in a red suit and splendid white beard. As a result they spent most of the days leading up to 25 December looking into cupboards or wardrobes for a possible stash of gifts.

On the morning of Christmas Eve, Tony was trying to have a lie-in while his children were crashing about downstairs. Jacqui brought him up some tea and the mail, and among the late cards was a large manila envelope which he opened first. He withdrew a script with a note attached, began to read it and started to laugh. It was read out loud to Jacqui who also started to laugh, but then she whacked him with the envelope with a reminder that they had to complete the Christmas shopping.

Despite the busy preparation, Tony found himself constantly thinking about the script and that evening, with the two less hyperactive children in their beds, he had another look at it. After another loud snigger Jacqui confiscated it, then put it in a drawer with an embargo until after Boxing Day. On Christmas morning the kids rushed about with their presents amid the detritus of wrapping paper, ribbons, and boxes, then they were on the road visiting relatives and friends before arriving in Pimlico for lunch; on Boxing Day everyone descended on Tooting Bec. The following day the embargo was over; Tony could read the script in full without interruption.

It had been sent to him by Bob Larbey who was becoming an in demand sitcom writer together with his co-writer John Esmonde. They were both South Londoners from Battersea and former classmates at grammar school. The duo had been writing together for a few years without much progress, but they persevered and eventually were commissioned to provide some radio scripts. They eventually gained recognition with a television series called *Please Sir!* which starred John Alderton playing a beleaguered teacher at a run-down school trying to teach a group of disinterested, loutish pupils. The series also became a feature film, and when it finished its run, the writers were asked to work on a sequel, following the lives and fortunes of the former pupils after leaving the school.

Tony had first met the two writers in the bar at London Weekend Television and they all hit it off immediately. Larbey mentioned they needed an actor for a part they were recording the following day, giving him a brief outline. Tony agreed to do it, but as he was already working there on another programme, he would have to get permission from his director. As luck would have it in many ways, he was not needed on set that day so arrived at *The Fenn Street Gang*'s studio. The episode was based on one of the *Please Sir!* characters called Frankie Abbot who had joined the army after leaving school. Tony was to play the drilling instructor, Corporal Elliot. They quickly completed the scenes, and he then finished his other job.

Shortly afterwards the writers sought Tony out in the bar again at LWT. They had a good chat about things generally then specifically about a series they were planning which was based on their time completing national service. It was to be focused on the character he had just played, Corporal Elliot, but they had a bit of a dilemma. There had already been shows based on army conscripts, most notably *The Army Game*. Larbey had been in the army for his call-up while Esmonde had served in the Royal Air Force. They decided to base the series on a group of conscripts called up for their service in the RAF. Thames Television loved the concept, and Corporal Elliot from *The Fenn Street Gang* metamorphosed into Corporal Percy Marsh. He and Tony were to become very close over the next few years.

The series was called *Get Some In!*, the title based on the phrase the compulsory enlisted used to yell at civilians of their own age who they thought should be in uniform, like themselves – rather like Tony – those few years before. The storylines revolved around four young recruits, all from different backgrounds, called up to have two years of their lives dominated by Marsh. Marsh was a bully, liar, and an unscrupulous cheat; these were his good points.

The writers said the Corporal was an amalgam of the men they had experienced some two decades or so before. Now they had to develop Marsh's character, agreeing that men like him would not change; they loved the power over vulnerable or inexperienced people, they were misogynists and bigots, intimidating and threatening the tougher recruits who were insubordinate or offered dumb insolence with the punishment of extra chores or duties. After all, they had no one to complain to.

Tony had a good retrospective think about past regimental ogres in television and films, William Hartnell or Bill Fraser for example, but because Marsh was more flawed than most, and cowardly, it was decided the character would evolve with the storylines. The series producer and director Michael Mills agreed.

Mills was the former head of comedy at the BBC where he had commissioned and produced *The Liver Birds* and *Some Mothers Do 'Ave Em* while being peripherally involved in developing *Monty Python's Flying Circus*. He had a good track record and experience in television comedy, and as a result he became invaluable in the casting of the supporting actors who became the four hapless recruits.

David Janson was the former grammar school boy Ken Richardson, immediately dubbed by Marsh as a 'posh poofter'; Gerard Ryder played Matthew Lilley, the harpsichord-playing vicar's son; Brian Pettifer was hired as the maudlin, taciturn Scot, Bruce Leckie. The fourth member of the quartet, Robert Lindsay, was to play Jakey Smith; he was an actor who originally wanted to be a drama teacher before he obtained a grant to attend RADA. Other regular characters were Marsh's long-suffering wife Alice, played by Lori Wells, and David Quilter the CO, Flight Lieutenant Grant, all together based at the fictional RAF Skelton.

Michael Mills brought in a drill instructor to teach them to march in formation and to react to commands. The instructor barked at them like a Doberman, quickly organising them into a disciplined squad. Tony watched the instructor with interest, picking up his body language and mannerisms. Location filming was at the Hobbs Barracks in Surrey which had variously accommodated Women's Royal Army Corps, Royal Electrical and Mechanical Engineers and at one point became a temporary accommodation for refugees fleeing from Idi Amin's Uganda. The barracks still had a 1950s look and feel which probably did nothing for the confidence or optimism of the displaced African community when they arrived.

The internal scenes were completed at the Thames Television studios in Broom Road, Teddington, a fine location on the banks of the River Thames, which must have been a difficult decision for the executives when they had to choose the franchise name.

At the studio, the scenes were rehearsed in the afternoon, then filmed in front of a live audience in the evening. The cast and crew gelled really quickly, working well without any disputes or rancour, they were also wrapping on time.

The first series of *Get Some In!* became an immediate success with an audience of 14 million. The cast went into an urgent rehearsal for a Christmas special then they were all signed up for a second series, more importantly with vastly improved fees.

The impact the show was having in popularity came home to Tony just after the first series broadcast. He took the children to school as often as he could, the other parents and kids all knew him as a face off the telly but there was no unctuous or sycophantic behaviour towards him, but Corporal Marsh immediately changed all that. Tony had gone through a public recognition period in the 1960s after his Loach and Garnett collaborations, and to a certain extent from his *Ace of Wands* juvenile audience, but this form of acknowledgement proved more startling. Now when he took his children to school, the other parents and kids started to call out the show's catchphrases:

'Stand by your beds'; 'Fag for the corporal'; 'Light for the corporal'.

It proved to be a little scary for Matt, who knew his dad was a reasonably well-known actor and accepted it as a matter of course, but now things had changed perceptively. He did not want to share his dad with anyone else and he was bemused; Samantha understood things more and realised she now had a famous dad.

When Tony turned up for work on the second series the others recounted their own experiences. Robert Lindsay had been called out as 'Jakey' when he had been out and about, and a few times in a pub or restaurant people were trying to pick a fight because of his hardcore persona. The first time he said jokingly:-

'Was by my bloody mother.'

Brian Pettifer was hailed as 'Jock' wherever he went; he was used to that anyways but not 'Jockstrap'. The scripts for the second series were still strong and funny for the time, while Michael Mills was as encouraging as ever. They also became Teddington residents; some script meetings were held in the Tide End pub, as were after-work pints, then each Thursday they had a regular dinner table at Spaghetti Junction on the High Street.

One of the first reviews had referred to Tony as the star attraction. Mills and the others called him that at every opportunity:

'What is our star attraction up to at the weekend?'

'What does our star attraction want from the wine list?'

The average age of the younger actors was about 25, so Tony was a good 12 years older, but he felt, as did they, that there was no discernible age gap. They shared the same sense of humour and interests, including football, so they always took advantage of an impromptu kick-about at the adjoining Lensbury Club or the St Mary's University pitch just over the road from the Thames Studios.

Although *Get Some In!* retained its popularity after series three and four were made but the momentum was no longer being maintained. Larbey, Esmonde and Mills and most of the actors realised the format had gone as far as it could. While the writers and producer decided which way they could take things forward, Tony had some time on his hands, so he caught up with a few jazz gigs with as many of the Tones and Non-Tones who were around, but after the intensity of being the star attraction for a while it was time to face a major problem: things on the domestic side were not as warm or as natural as they used to be.

For a while now the couple had started to snap at each other, and it was a serious concern. Jacqui was fiercely independent, and he knew it had been a coin toss between him and Las Vegas. Jacqui had worked whenever she could to boost his own feast or famine earnings, firstly starting a keep fit dancing school and a few other dance-related fitness schemes. They started to live separate lives, and when Tony was at home his wife started to frequent her old haunts in the West End, until the early morning or all night. She was still ensuring the children were loved and cared for, but she now wanted her independence back; she was no longer content to be on the arm of a celebrity.

Towards the end of the screeching hot summer of 1976, Tony went back to work at *Get Some In!*. It had been decided to move all the characters to a different level, from the bullied recruits on to more balanced roles with the other actors having far more individual storylines. For a series about the RAF, as in reality, most of the service personnel had never been near or even up in an aircraft, which gave the writers a bit more scope. They sent all of them into the air on a training exercise.

The plot was that Corporal Marsh, in the skies, completely bottled it. He shouted, then panicked before hiding in the lavatory. When they greased calmly on to the runway, he tried to regain his control and composure. Of course it was all an act to demonstrate to his young charges what could happen if someone did lose control, so they could all recognise the symptoms. To the relief of the actors it was not filmed in the air, it was filmed in a very grounded aircraft in a hangar at Northolt. It was becoming a more challenging time: how many more awkward, embarrassing situations could they create for Marsh?

The cast as a whole were a creative group; they all had a good input and a voice. Larbey and Esmonde had the ears and perception, and because the series was not about planes and dashing pilots, they could take it anyway they wanted, though not vertically. In an inspired turn of direction they were all part of yet another fictional RAF station called Midham, a medical unit set in Lancashire, although the location looked suspiciously like the old one in Surrey. They all worked hard on the new ideas, but Marsh was finding himself increasing in the shit, again down to his own incompetence, until he was eventually denoted for cheating in his examinations and having to share the same accommodation as his former changes with the predictable consequences. There was really nowhere to go from there. Well there was; Marsh and his wife were eventually posted to Labrador and the four conscripts to a very pleasant posting of Malta. The cast would wait to see what would happen next.

What came next was the proposal of a very lucrative offer to perform a summer season at the Princess Theatre in Torquay, which they all agreed to do, but it was going to be hard work. The promoters wanted two performances a day with just Sunday off.

Get Some In! had been a funny, happy series. It had been getting top ratings, but by the time they went into theatre production, Thames had not indicated if they would be picking up their option for another season.

Before the show opened Tony had rented a house in Torquay, and Sam and Matt were going to go down for some of their summer holiday, but Jacqui decided not to. She wanted a break from him for a while. It was time for some honest, straightforward talking.

Tony, despite his love for his wife, had been away on tours or locations long enough to find brief interludes with other women; even in his early days it was not difficult for him to resist the advances of attractive girls.

His first encounter had been on his *Peter Pan* tour when one of the local cast in Glasgow had him walk her back to her parents' house. He discovered how pleasurable the knee tremble dance first witnessed on the Tachbrook all those years before really was. Unfortunately for him on this occasion, he realised his partner was being pushed against the large doorbell, and just on the vinegar stroke he heard her father clopping on the tiled floor towards the door. He escaped, he blew a kiss and she smiled at him the following day.

In Austria, despite David Niven's kindness in flying Jacqui out there, Tony had been having a dalliance with one of the hotel staff, a very attentive catering manager who soon liked him to enjoy her Wienerschnitzel and she his Krainer sausage.

On the road with Dennis Waterman he had enjoyed vicariously the benefits of his friend's magnetism and appeal to females. It also became apparent that Jacqui had been herself involved with a few extramarital adventures herself.

The show had been performing for two weeks before his children arrived, and while it became a concern that while the evening figures were very good, the earlier shows were less well attended. As the senior actor, indeed the special talent, Tony was nudged by the others to write to Bernard Delfont's office arguing for a less-demanding working week.

He pointed out that from the production company's interest, it would be to their benefit to consolidate the audiences, and it would lead to better performances by reducing exhaustion in the cast. Delfont's office agreed.

When Sam and Matt eventually arrived in July he was overjoyed to see them, tthen he had two heavy hits to contend with.

Robert Lindsay announced he was leaving to move to the BBC to work with a new writer called John Sullivan on a show based on the life and antics of a delusional revolutionary based in Tooting, whose name was Woolfie Smith. It worked out rather well for them both.

The second hit coincided with the first; Thames Television announced they were dropping *Get Some In!*, possibly in part because Lindsay was leaving. The Thames announcement caused an unprecedented backlash: the *News of the World* began a campaign for *Get Some In!* to be continued, petitions were signed although it is doubtful questions were asked in Parliament, and in a quick *volte-face*, Thames decided to have a fifth series.

The Selbys were up early most mornings, and after breakfast they were straight down to the beach, lots of swimming then with the rest of the company, or around at each other's temporary homes for barbecues on rare time off.

On matinee days, Sam and Matt would go over to the theatre, at first to watch the show until they were bored, then they were allowed to destroy the dressing room. For the evening performances there was a network of babysitters and chaperones taking care of things until after the finish.

One Sunday Tony hired a boat for the day and set off for a cruise up and down the coast. It proved a lovely sunny day with the proverbial clear-blue sky, and the bow of their vessel pushed effortlessly through the waves. The boat had a cold box for the beers and pop for the youngsters who were quickly raiding the picnic baskets. They wanted to dive off the boat and swim, but the skipper advised against it; he told them the waters were dangerous with strong currents which changed rapidly and were unpredictable. Similarly the weather was likely to change very quickly to sudden squalls and storms, which it immediately did.

That particular part of the south Devon coast played host to the Fastnet yacht race. Starting in Cowes on the Isle of Wight, it headed off to Fastnet Rock off Southern Island, then from there the yachts travelled back, spinnakers billowing, to Plymouth where the race ended, and everyone cheered heartily, had lots to drink and fell over. It is now called the Rolex Fastnet, so the timings are more reliable. On their boat, they were told dramatically that there was a worrying storm creeping towards them, of high intensity, so rather than stay out on the sea it would be wiser to shelter in one of the nearby inlets. They just about made it before the storm hit.

Non-seafarers often hear the shipping forecasts of force six or seven threatening the progress of mariners. What the occupants of their boat did not know was that a force eight with winds of up to 88 kilometres an hour was blowing across Torbay to Plymouth. When they arrived at the inlet, they looked back at the thunderstorms – a black maelstrom of fury. They were stranded for several hours. Meanwhile Jacqui had been due to call them that evening for a catch-up with Sam and Matt who had told her they would be on a boat trip that afternoon but would be back by teatime.

Jacqui had called the house several times, then she learned from the evening news about the storms around Torbay, so she found the number of the coastguard and phoned them. The diligent skipper of the boat had already reported their position and that everything was fine aboard, and the coastguard passed on the good news.

A few days after the great adventure, Sam and Matt returned to London. Tony saw out the last couple of weeks of the season and left for home. It was not going to be an easy time.

On his return there was an awkward, uneasy atmosphere between husband and wife; they found things difficult to communicate but they made a mutual decision, they both agreed the marriage could not continue. However, whatever happened, the children would be cushioned and protected from the fallout. It was also decided that Tony would stay in the marital home until he had finished the last series of *Get Some In!*.

When they began series five, Lindsay's character Jakey Smith was replaced by another up-and-coming actor, Karl Howman, who quickly fitted in with the regulars. For this final series, with the storylines having to regroup from Labrador to Malta and the transformation of one of the actors, it was agreed the plots would have to be as stretched as a bungee elastic. Esmonde and Larbey kept things open for a reasonable and plausible reconnect. Percy Marsh had been shipped out to Labrador for being a cheat; they decided to return him to the UK as a hero, but nevertheless still a cheat. He returned as a hero because he had reportedly risked his life in the frozen wastes of Canada when rescuing his commanding officer from death. He hadn't of course, the senior officer had saved him, but his exertions from carrying Percy had caused him to pass out, just as Marsh came around briefly before rescuers arrived and assumed he had saved his boss.

Corporal Marsh continued to be a devious arsehole, continually stealing credit where he could, being economical with the truth and an obnoxious bully, but there was really nowhere else to go and despite Howman injecting some life into proceedings, *Get Some In!* had run its time and ended without any outcry from the newspapers or the general public. In truth, comedy series were now coming under more scrutiny; younger writers and performers were starting to come through, comedy and indeed social changes were influencing the old guard and younger audiences wanted more realism in television, more dynamic, contemporary stories, rather like that time in the 1960s when Tony Selby represented that dynamism.

Tony now found himself typecast, out of work and going through a marriage break-up as a fortieth birthday present. After a bleak winter with little work and a difficult home life, an offer came in for another season of Get Some In!, this time in Blackpool. The pay was much better and just nine shows a week.

Tony stayed in digs for the first week until he could find a house to rent. Sam and Matt would be visiting for part of the school holidays again, so when the estate agent told him a well-known client of his had a place for rent, he snapped up the offer. The house belonged to Sir Stanley Matthews, the legendary footballer who would have been in his early 60s then but seemingly enjoying playing away because he had left his wife 'Lady Betty' for a 'foreign woman' as the estate agent explained.

Stan and Betty still owned the house, but it was rather tatty and in need of some TLC. There weren't even any wardrobes, just lots of clothing racks that looked as if they had been nicked from Marks and Spencer. On the plus side the rent was not too extortionate, and the house also had a massive garden, a mini putting green and an old tennis court. The garden had lots of trees, hidey-holes for hide and seek and enough danger areas to guarantee a visit to A&E sooner or later.

Despite *Get Some In!* no longer being on television, the stage version was still a big draw, with full houses and responsive audiences. By the time Sam and Matt turned up they immediately loved the slightly tatty house and garden and Blackpool; the furthest north the two of them had been was probably Enfield. They had certainly not experienced anything like the piers and the Pleasure Beach. Torquay was a minnow in comparison, except for the storm.

As they had done in Torquay, those of the cast with wives and children organised minders and guardians for critical parts of the working day, while some of the more mature youngsters were allowed some independence, and some of them became a little bit feral. Tony was keen for his children to go off on their own, to discover new experiences, in perhaps a more relaxed and trusting era. Fortunately Jimmy Saville wasn't in the area at the time.

Sam and Matt were not too mischievous and were only mildly rebuked for small misdemeanours, on the other hand Tony's own misdemeanours were catching up with him.

Some weeks before opening in Blackpool he agreed to appear in a play for a short run in Cambridge, then at the Key Theatre in Peterborough where he met up with an old friend, John Barnwell, the former Arsenal footballer who was managing Peterborough United. Barnwell invited Tony to train with the team, have a kick-about to keep him fit and out of trouble, which went well, until on a night out with his friend, he was introduced to Carol. They chatted and flirted then woke up the following morning in her bed, the start of an energetic affair which enhanced his fitness programme. It was still going on by the time the show had opened at the Winter Gardens; Carol had been up to Blackpool and returned to Cambridge by the time Sam and Matt arrived.

There was an agreement that the cast's offspring would be allowed to go to the theatre for matinees, so before the performance they were used to children clambering over stuff in the dressing rooms or farting about with props, not necessarily running riot but more undisciplined playtime. Sam always had a curious nature; some would say intrepid, others nosey. In the dressing room stuck to the mirrors or walls were messages and cards from fans or friends; she had seen and read them all dozens of times before that afternoon, her natural curiosity looked up to the top of a cupboard near the makeup area, just about in vision she saw the corner of a postcard so she stretched up to retrieve it. Tony watched then he froze. He had placed it up there to avoid prying eyes, particularly those of his daughter, her prying eyes glared at him.

The message on the card read:-

'To my darling Tony,

best wishes for a fantastic show.

All my love Carol.'

Sam handed the postcard to Matt and the searing look of shock from his children burned into Tony's skull. David Janson was in the dressing room with them. The tannoy beckoned Tony to the stage, then Janson put his arms around the two angry youngsters. Tony looked at them and muttered,

'Sorry, I'm on.'

After his crass departure from the dressing room he returned from a rather distracted performance to face his distressed children. He had not returned at the interval, nor had he considered putting on his understudy. Tony tried to explain about his relationship with Carol, but it felt shallow. He tried to explain to them how things happened, but he couldn't. He then began to feel sorry for himself which he would later confess was one of the most selfish things he had ever done.

To a certain extent, the marriage difficulties had been reasonably well disguised, but while Sam and Matt were not really aware of their parents' disintegrating relationship, they both sensed something, an intangible feeling of insecurity, a fear almost

The two of them returned home to Tooting Bec to restart their school life, while Tony hung on for the final few weeks of the Blackpool season then prepared to return to London to face the sadness and heartbreak. After the last of the *Get Some In!* performances, the cast had a final kick-about on Blackpool beach and said their goodbyes. Tony would always have football as some comfort.

21
SEE YOU AT THE BUSH, 11 O'CLOCK

The *Get Some In!* cast and crew had some rather good footballers. Robert Lindsay, David Janson and Tony had turned out a few times for the Thames Television All Stars while over the years Tony had also been involved in celebrity games.

The original celebrity teams had been about in many forms over the years, probably beginning during the first world war when the variety and musical hall performers played in matches to boost morale or raise funds for various charities. With the appeal of football increasing within the working-class communities, these games attracted huge crowds.

The women's team Dick, Kerr Ladies were always a huge attraction, then there were the top dance bands playing against each other. By the late 1950s actors and comedians from theatre, film, and radio were taking part, and by the turn of the decade the momentum slowed until things got a little bit silly. A mish-mash of teams evolved, mainly boxers, wrestlers and jockeys continuing the tradition, so there would have been some very interesting line-ups and formations.

Tony had still been playing with the taxi teams or the pub teams from his jazz venues, then in the early 1960s things began to change. With so many actors from working-class backgrounds making progress in the industry, it was inevitable they would get a team together. Well, not them exactly, piss-up and brewery comes to mind, but a man called Pat Sherlock did. He worked for Chappell Music; a few of the early pop performers like Joe Brown and Tommy Steele had turned out for his teams, the Show Business Football XI was formed and then came another offshoot, the TV All Stars, formed by Mike and Bernie Winters, two of the worst comedy partnerships ever.

In the words of a Glasgow Empire heckler,

'Oh fuck, there's two of the wee bastards.'

Despite that rather succinct analysis, the brothers brought together a rather talented team, then various combinations of the teams mixed and matched depending on work commitments. They also played to a high standard; a good number had been courted by professional or semi-professional clubs until finding fame in other areas. When Tony started turning out for the show business teams the football started to suffer, not because of his involvement but because in his words, 'They started fucking about and it became silly.'

The matches were turning into comedy routines and rather like Mike and Bernie they were not that amusing. During the matches, clowns would suddenly appear and throw buckets of water at the players, which was fine in summer but not on a cold November in

Leeds. Then, even worse, they would start throwing buckets of feathers creating the effect of a mass poultry slaughter.

Unfortunately the boxers were still about, and in one of the games Tony played in Dick Richardson and Terry Downes – both champion fighters – started a pretend bout then began baiting the spectators, provoking them to take them on. Anyone showing any bravado, as in the old fairground boxing booths, was promptly decked.

Eventually the players became a little fed up with the shenanigans; they wanted to play a game of football at a higher, better standard while the spectators could watch a decent match without a bunch of fuckwits falling over or punching people.

The more serious and committed teams started to merge through friendship and contacts, and gradually an organised team was formed and became good fun. Tony also was to make two lifelong friends.

The first was an actor he met in the back of Sam's cab on the way to an England v Scotland game at Wembley Stadium. Johnny Wade was then one of television's most popular actors, indeed one of the most well-paid. He played a character called Stan Millett in Britain's very first soap opera, *Compact*, set in the offices of a high-quality women's magazine. Wade was from Bethnal Green and had been variously a market trader, a skilled carpenter, a semi-professional with Wimbledon FC in the Southern League and then a singer in the West End clubs; this was the job that brought him to the attention of the producers of *Compact* who needed a good East Ender who could sing. Sam was driving along Wembley Way because taxi drivers were allowed to drive right up to the stadium where they had their own car park giving them the opportunity to pick up punters after a match had finished. All other drivers had to park vehicles further away then have a longish walk to the ground.

As Sam's cab drove slowly through the crowds, Tony saw Wade walking on his own just beside the cab. He nodded at Johnny who recognised him immediately, and the next thing the soap star knew he was in the back of a crowded London cab with some English and Scottish men pissing into bottles or plastic bags. When he sniffed the air it was an interesting mix of booze and urine, oranges and peppermint.

The second lifelong friend he made through football was Tony Osoba, a tall handsome man, the son of a Scottish mother and Nigerian father. Osoba had been born and brought up in Glasgow, then lived for a while in Nigeria before he and his mum returned to Scotland. Osoba could not remember if they had first met at the Buckstone Club or at a football game, but football was certainly a common denominator rather than acting. Osoba was a member of the Royal Shakespeare Company for several years and became an in demand television and film actor. His TV career had bloomed when playing Jim 'Jock' McLaren in *Porridge*, not the most politically correct of parts but at least he was acknowledged as the first Scottish actor to star in a television series as a psychotic hard man who was not ginger or had freckles. It was also ironic that Osoba, who possessed a marvellous baritone voice with a unique received pronunciation cadence found fame playing a Glaswegian sociopath, but at least he knew the accent.

They became part of a celebrity team known as the Entertainers XI and managed to recruit some ex-professionals, including Tony's old friend John Barnwell, Frank Worthington, he of the well-known STD, and Stan Bowles, the main financier of Ladbrokes. The balance of the team was impressive but they just needed someone to organise them, then an extraordinary individual by the name of Hugh Elton suddenly filled that role.

Many years later none of the team or their families could work out when or where Elton first appeared. His biography had to be taken with a large pinch of Saxo; he had variously claimed to be a singer who had toured with Frankie Vaughan, and that he had been part of *The Black and White Minstrel Show*, but who could tell?. Then he claimed to have been Peter Sellers' stand-in but more importantly as 'man in court'/barman/visitor, the result of his many roles as an extra.

One thing for sure was that Elton had the most comprehensive and unusual contact lists, together with an uncanny ability to track people down. Each Sunday during the football season the Entertainers XI would assemble outside the BBC Television Theatre at Shepherd's Bush, then clamber on to the maroon Rickards coach; coincidentally and conveniently the meeting place was just around the corner from Elton's house.

Then the coach would be off to various parts of the south-east, and every so often up to the Midlands and the north-west where they would stay overnight. The opposition was always a good standard, either lower non-league team or an amalgam of experienced amateurs and former professionals, and the games were also expected to be hard, robust, and played at pace with no holding back on challenges. The only problem with that was insurance: even Hugh Elton could not arrange any, those of the team under contract for a production were always going to have an issue.

One of the team, who will have to remain nameless, did break his leg in a game but refused to go to hospital because he was working in a very lucrative theatre production. After a night on very strong painkillers provided by a contact of Elton's, he was smuggled into the theatre the following day. His mates laid him at the bottom of the stairs where he was found by the theatre staff moaning and groaning after 'falling down the stairs'. It was deemed an accident at work, therefore he was insured, so he drew his pay and smiled as people signed his plaster cast.

The main nucleus of the Entertainers XI, other than Selby, Wade and Osoba were actors Richard O'Sullivan, Roy Holder, Jack Shepherd, and Dennis Waterman before Waterman left to set up his own team, entertainer Dave King, and a true narcissus, the vague, early 1960s pop non-icon by the name of Jess Conrad.

Elton would phone around during the week to find out who was available; if they were in a play or filming around London, most would be about on a Sunday. Hugh's message to them all was, 'See you at the Bush, 11 o'clock.'

Elton was a good organiser. Freshly laundered kit was laid out in the dressing room, the team would be introduced to local dignitaries and press before kick-off, and after the match they would all sign autographs, have a few drinks in the clubhouse or hotel then be on the way back to the Bush.

That was normally the plan, but sometimes they had problems before the Rickards coach had even left. Roy Holder was a charming, funny character actor, and despite him being the captain of his golf club, sitting on various charitable committees and being an outstanding drama teacher, he had what might be called a major flaw. His concept of time-keeping was the same as Keith Richards' concept of abstinence. On arrival at the Bush, cars were normally parked by the BBC Theatre or in one of the side roads, and those without cars would organise to be picked up. Roy once agreed to pick up Selby who saw him approaching in the distance and waved in recognition, then Holder suddenly shot by him, did a U-turn, and set back in the direction he had just come from. It seemed Roy had promised his long-suffering wife Pauline that he would prepare the family lunch and pop it into the oven for when she returned from whatever she had been doing. He had forgotten to do that but remembered when he was about to pick up his mate, and instead of stopping to explain he just sped back to his house. Luckily Tony managed to thumb a lift and joined the coach party.

The coach began its journey up the A1 when a car started to flash its lights and have a good beep of the horn, so they eventually pulled into the layby and the car tucked in behind them. Roy Holder clamboured out of the car and on to the coach where he immediately told the driver to wait while he went back to his car to retrieve his boots and bag. Roy climbed back on to the coach with everyone shouting to the driver,

'Just fucking go.'

They played the game, then journeyed home and all disembarked at the Bush, but they had forgotten Roy's car was still in the layby – and sadly so had he.

It was said of Jess Conrad that if he wasn't near a mirror, he would pray for rain in order to catch his reflection in a puddle. He was one of the mainstays of the Entertainers XI and agreed with himself that he was the vainest person in entertainment. He had started his career as a singer and was voted the most popular singer of 1961 after such well-known songs as 'Cherry Pie' and, believe it or not, 'This Pullover'. Conrad was the goalkeeper, and like most custodians he kept a towel and spare gloves in a place at the side of the net. Unlike most other goalkeepers though, he also kept a makeup bag which he applied at every opportunity so, as he told his team-mates, his fans would always have a good photograph. One of his fans actually turned up with an LP of his called *Jess for You* which even then was about 15 years old. Conrad signed with a flourish, holding it up for all to see.

One of the most famous team members was Dave King. An all-round entertainer, a comedian, and singer, he had a hugely popular television series in the UK, then at that time, went on to became one of the few British stars to have been successful in the USA, which baffled everyone. Dave loved football, the only problem being that he wasn't very good. Selby summed things up by saying he had a very deceptive speed: he was much slower than people thought. Selby did think he was a trier, but that attribute was aligned to his sense of self-importance: he was very pompous. During a half-time break King began complaining he was not receiving enough of the ball and when he was about to kick off for the second half, he was distracted while one of the team picked up the ball and stuffed it into the back of his shirt. A bewildered King looked around asking,

'Where's the fucking ball gone?'

'You had it last Kingy, you said you wanted more of it.'

At another match, the team were awarded a penalty and normally it would be a cultured left foot of Osoba or a mighty belt from Selby to convert, but King grabbed the ball and waved his team-mates away. After placing it on the penalty spot, he picked it up and rubbed it on his shirt before replacing it, then raised his hands and cracked his fingers before carefully measuring his paces for a run-up. He then rubbed his boot instep on to the back of his socks, did a couple of touch your toes then spotted a microscopic bit of disturbed earth between the ball and the goalie who by this time had taken the opportunity to have a brief nap. King walked up to the offending divot, pressed it into the earth and returned to the very patient football. He looked around the stadium, rolled his neck a few times, then hands on hips stared at the now-awake goalkeeper. By this time there had been two military coups in Asia and the Americans and Russians completed two Moon landings.

King then stepped to one side, knelt down, and put his thumbs in the air as if measuring the angles of the goalposts.

While King was working at the geometry or trigonometry, a mad figure rushed up behind him moving faster than anyone had seen him move before, it was Roy Holder. Roy, along with the rest of the team had had enough of King's farting around, he hit the ball hard but sadly not that true, it was already six feet over the crossbar as the seagulls screeched out warning signals. The ball continued over the terracing then out of the stadium where it landed with a plop on a previously undiscovered cow pat in the adjoining field. The goalkeeper, the opposition, King's team-mates and 5,000 spectators roared with laughter. King did not see the funny side and jumped up and down on an imaginary hat.

Although not related to his penalty ignominy, possibly though, Dave King had decided to sell up his house and move to the countryside. He told Selby that he quite fancied being a country squire. Selby was with Johnny Wade at the time, and they exchanged glances. Wade, as well as being an accomplished actor, vocalist and carpenter, also had another interesting sideline. Together with his co-star from *Compact*, Bill Kerr, and another mate, they had over the years built a business interest in architectural reclaiming. Well they didn't reclaim the items as such, they nicked them. They would discover old houses that had been empty or abandoned for some time, then wander into the garden and reclaim ornate pots together with any other interesting garden ornaments and furniture. One time, they had piled some lovely cherubs and bird baths on to the pavement when a police car pulled up, the officers climbed out of the car and immediately recognised the two of them from the telly.

'Everything all right, gentlemen?'

'Fine thank you officers, we are just moving some stuff for my, er, uncle,' said Bill.

The coppers helped them load the loot into the back of their station wagon and then bid them good night. Shortly after King had moved home, he turned up for a game, and seemed a little preoccupied so Selby asked him if he was feeling OK..

'Yeah Tone, but here's a thing, you know I've just moved.'

'Yes Dave.'

'Well you know those two Greek statues we had by the pond, they were to stay as part of the sale.'

The rest of them became interested and crowded round. They all nodded, most of them had been over to his place for the odd party.

'Well in between me and the missus moving out and the new lot moving in, someone nicked the fucking statues and the bloke who bought the place thinks it was me.'

King was looking forlornly at his boots as Selby and the rest looked at Wade who said sympathetically,

'Sorry to hear that Kingy, some bastards will nick anything.'

It was not Wade though; it was some other bastards.

Hugh Elton, in the meantime, would be busy behind the scenes, liaising with the local dignitaries, pressing the flesh as it were, wheeling and dealing. The rest of them were blissfully unaware of any of the financial arrangements; they assumed it was making a few bob on the side after all the expenses had been dealt with and for all the effort Hugh put in. He organised sponsors, provided all the playing kit, tracksuits, footballs and even got them deals on their football boots. On the times they had a night stop, all the accommodation, meals and drinks were taken care of, while he also dealt with the local press or TV publicity. Elton really was the ubiquitous Zelig character, he was able to track anyone down when required.

Over a pint Dennis Waterman told Selby he was convinced Elton was stalking him, he seemed to be everywhere he went, Elton was there, it had got to the point he tried to hide if he saw Elton nearby.

Once on location he was having a contemplative moment on the toilet, his newspaper open at the sports pages and a newly lit cigarette between his fingers when a note appeared under the door. It read,

'Sorry to disturb you Den, but see you at 11 at the Bush?'

Tony Osoba was once working on a film at Pinetree Studios. David Niven was there working on a different project, but they met up during the lunch break and were having a genial chat when Elton appeared,

'Hello Tony just thought I'd give you a little reminder about the game on Sunday.'

Osoba confirmed he would be there. Hugh then nodded at David Niven,

'If your mate fancies a game, bring him along as well'

When Tony Selby heard this, he roared with laughter, then it happened to him. He was in an episode of *The Sweeney* playing a gang boss who lived in a large house. He was playing a scene when he was in the bath being massaged by two attractive girls when the telephone was due to ring. His character, angry to be disturbed, then had to answer the call in his dressing gown. As he climbed from the bath the director called 'cut' leaving Tony standing near the phone awaiting the director to resume the scene. The telephone rang, Tony looked thinking it was a prop, but it was actually the house phone. He answered, 'Hello, yea OK Hugh, see you at the Bush.'

Waterman was hanging about the set and he laughed like a drain when Tony told him who it was. Dennis said,'Told you, he is fucking stalking us.'

Hugh also organised the entertainment after each game when it was possible. It became a fairly simple formula: generally it would be held at the football social club or local pub or hotel, and after a meal and a mingle the entertainers would entertain.

Inevitably, Jess Conrad would take to the stage first, 'Hello ladies and gentlemen, I know you can't really believe it's me, bet you all thought it was my much younger brother.'

He then chatted away to the audience, about himself, then would go into a limited medley of his hits, including 'This Pullover'. Selby would normally sing a couple of classics, duetting with Wade on 'Chicago' or 'I Left My Heart in San Francisco'. One night they were interrupted by the MC who announced with pride the engagement of his daughter to one of the local team footballers. Without any prior thought or contemplation, their next song was 'The Lady is a Tramp'.

Afterwards Selby thought about it then hoped the happy couple were not related to Mrs Goody.

In the middle of their entertainment, Hugh would come on. Experience had taught them it would be a wise move on their part for him not to end the show. When he did appear they all trembled with a macabre anticipation. He had in effect a drag act which was painful in its delivery and tasteless in its content. An apparition wearing an unwashed frock, an exploded straw bale of a wig, lips smothered in vivid red lipstick and would give a 'thanks for having us speech' then go into a routine.

'Hello mate, why is your wife not wearing any knickers, has she got holes in the knee?'

Then to the audience generally,

'Cor the toilets here really stink, but must remind you of home.'

Then, if possible, he became even ruder and viler,

'Look at you love, what a big arse, must be the size of Rutland. Thought there had been an eclipse when you came in.'

Selby's personal favourite he heard by Hugh, was to a couple who were sitting innocently and unobtrusively near the stage

'Hello mate, your missus reminds me of Sophia Loren.'

This was followed by a pause and another comment,

'Because she looks like Carlo Ponti.'

Fortunately, Elton's routine only lasted for five minutes before he was off the stage. The rest of the group had inevitably gone outside for a fag while when was on, even if they didn't smoke. It always amazed Selby that Hugh had not been smashed extremely powerfully in the face. It might have been even more relevant if they had tried to stop his routine, but it was that time, misogyny and sexism was fine and all the women loved it really, sipping their gin and orange or warm white wine!

At the end of the football season, if they could not get hold of any tickets, most of the team would meet up in someone's home to watch the FA Cup Final. It was always a great occasion, a barbecue or picnic then around the television for the big game. It was an all day telly event and from lunchtime there was an analysis of each team, then the teams leaving their respective hotels, on to the coaches to make their way to the stadium with everyone glued to the screen. There was a moment when the FA Cup itself was being carried up towards the Royal Box ready for the engraving and presentation. They all looked at the individual carrying the trophy. Wives, husbands, children, boyfriends, girlfriends, lovers, and mistresses, even passing strangers cried as one, 'It's Hugh Elton.'

The Entertainers XI began to attract more actors, fortuitously slightly younger and fitter. Tony Osoba persuaded Richard Beckinsale, the co-star of *Porridge*, to join them, immediately adding a couple of thousand to the gate, the majority of them young women. The veteran goalkeeper Jess Conrad was delighted because he could chat up their grandmothers and talk about knitwear. Tony found Beckinsale delightful with a fine dry sense of humour, but alas he was with them for only a short time. They were all devastated when he died from a heart attack at the age of just 31 in March 1979.

They also recruited Peter Duncan, the *Blue Peter* presenter, actor, chief scout and all-round good egg. Peter was a really tenacious footballer who would just not give up. If he lost the ball he would chase and chase until he won it back; if he was hit with a hard tackle he would be up quickly and ready to go again. Duncan formed a good partnership with a tough Yorkshire lad called Dai Bradley, who had worked with Ken Loach and played the main character in the film *Kes*; indeed he had won a BAFTA award for what was his very first film.

There were a few show business peripherals who were either mates of the team or were known to Hugh Elton. These included a professional wrestler, Tony 'Banger' Walsh, and Rocky Taylor who was a film stuntman; they were both decent players. Hugh also tried to introduce some of the old comedy or novelty acts but the team insisted these were confined for half-time entertainment or after the game when it was normal to see the world's tallest man walking around collecting money in a bucket from the crowd. He would have made Peter Crouch look like Ronnie Corbett, then Ronnie Corbett would walk around collecting money in a bucket making Dai Bradley look like the world's tallest man.

Hugh Elton eventually retired and died shortly afterwards. At his funeral his wife Daphne was deeply moved to see a group of actors forming a guard of honour, holding aloft jock straps and football boots. Jess Conrad took over the management and would go on to receive an OBE in recognition of his work with the Entertainers XI, or as Tony called it the 'Order of the Botox Eyebrows'.

Between them, Hugh and Jess raised over £25m for various charities, they also gave Tony Selby a great time in helping to achieve that.

22
THE REDHEAD

Tony moved out of the family home shortly after his return from Blackpool, and lived with Tony Osoba and his girlfriend Sally for a while in their flat in Maida Vale. On one of the football trips he was sitting with Dai Bradley, who told Tony he had heard about his relationship problems and commiserated. As they continued their chat Dai listened as Tony explained he was now staying temporarily in Maida Vale, but he felt uncomfortable imposing on Osoba and Sally, intruding on their privacy. Dai immediately told Tony he could move in with him in his flat in Ladbroke Grove, so he did, into the attic bedroom. He also continued his relationship with Carol for a while, he travelling up to Peterborough or she going down to London for a few days, but the affair gradually petered out.

Selby became a little depressed and melancholic then claustrophobic at Dai's place, it was also the first time he had lived on his own as he had rather a comfortable time of it living with his mother taking care of things and then Jacqui looking after him; even on the road he had friends and colleagues who took care of him.

Work was now proving a little slow in materialising while his bank balance had started to dwindle rather too quickly. On the plus side, Tony was meeting up with Sam and Matt regularly. He still had the keys to the house and had access at any time, and he slowly started to build up trust again with the two of them, in terms of his marriage however, there was no chance of a reconciliation.

While he was moping, he had a call from Maurice Aza. An advertising production company called Adventure wanted to cast Selby in a television and cinema advertisement for a computer games company called CGL who, at that time, were one of the major players in computer games technology. They were launching a new product called 'Why did the chicken cross the road?' And while Selby didn't know the answer to this age-old philosophical question, he knew the manager of his bank would be more than happy with the fee so agreed to do it. Selby sauntered along to St Martin's Lane and into the Duke of York Theatre for a daytime shoot. He ambled in early through the theatre entrance and into the stalls where the production company, crew and director were finalising the day's schedule. After shaking hands with everyone he was pointed towards the stage where the makeup area had been set. As he made his way down the steps he noticed a very attractive woman wearing a fur coat who smiled at him; he assumed it was the director's wife.

The makeup technician was Stella, who gave Tony a big hug. They had worked on a lot of shows together so he felt more relaxed to have a familiar face around, particularly as Stella was about to change him profoundly. The character he was to play was an old-fashioned end-of-pier comedian. He and Stella agreed that an Archie Rice character from *The Entertainer* was the look they wanted. His wardrobe was a striped blazer, white slacks then a Panama hat. Stella slapped on the white face makeup, rosy rouge cheeks and heavy red lipstick for his transformation.

Tony was sitting facing the stage. He and Stella had been talking about their love lives, or lack of it in his case, and their children when she nudged him and nodded back to the auditorium, saying,

'There's someone for you.'

He turned and looked at the woman who had smiled when he arrived, he agreed she looked really nice. Stella asked him if he liked redheads and he fell back on the old joke,

'No hair, just a red head, anyway, I thought she was the director's missus.'

Stella laughed

'No, his redhead has got a willy.'

Suddenly the redhead without a penis was walking towards him with the director who introduced him to Gina. They exchanged pleasantries then began the shoot.

At lunch time everyone was going over the road to the pub but Tony couldn't go because he was still in full makeup and costume, so they aranged for some sandwiches and drinks which Gina brought back for the both of them. They talked for an hour or so, she told Tony that she had only recently joined Adventure to run the office for them but she had also suggested to her colleagues, who were looking through agency photos to cast for the CGL job, that he might suit the part. She then admitted that she was also a fan of his.

Tony remembered feeling a bit maladroit. He asked her how the job was going, and her interests apart from the obvious attraction. He was delighted to hear she was a big football fan, and as they continued their tête-à-tête they were more or less oblivious to the chatter and general mayhem of the crew returning to work. Stella returned, brushed a few crumbs from Tony's clothing, touched up his makeup then they completed the filming. By the time the makeup was removed and he was reunited with his civvies, most of the others had disappeared, and as Stella said goodbye, she nodded towards Gina who was completing her notes and timesheets.

The Adventure boss invited everyone back to the office for drinks. Tony and Gina joined them but he couldn't stay for long because he had to pick up Sam and Matt from swimming, so he took her number and she said to call her at the office, which he did, first thing in the morning. Tony then took Gina out for a drink in the evening and then for two weeks they were inseparable, which proved a little difficult because it was just before Christmas.

Gina had two sons from a previous marriage, so they both would have family commitments over the holiday period. She spent hers with her sons and family in north London while Tony was at his sister's place in Croydon after seeing Sam and Matt in the morning. It was a long day, and at some point in the afternoon, the traditional time for when sleepy heads dropped chins on to chests, so Tony snuck into the hallway to use Kathy's phone to call Gina. A brusque voice at the other end shouted out, 'Gina, some man, Tommy I think.'

They met up again on Boxing Day and in the New Year, then there were further complications when Tony discovered that Gina was disconnecting from another relationship. Dai's flat became their refuge while they tried to sort out the complications. Dai, after his brush with fame in *Kes*, had become a very spiritual person. He was a follower of Jidda Krishma Muri and his home reflected a tranquil environment amid the whirling dervish of their frantic liaison. Dai had bought himself an old church in Kent, and for most of the time he was down there renovating the building then only returned to London for an acting job or a short break, so they had space and unhindered time together, but Tony realised they could not really impose themselves on Dai for too long. Gina was also still to move out of the flat she had shared with her previous partner and her younger son Gary.

By chance, Tony and Maurice Aza met up for lunch and Selby mentioned his rather busy and suddenly complicated life. Rather fortuitously, Maurice's mother owned a flat in Fulham, which had two bedrooms and rather conveniently, was available for rent. They moved in, so did Gary who had been away for most of that eventful Christmas but he and Tony got on well. Selby then met the older son, Richard and his wife Tracy and they got on well together too. The move to Fulham worked out well for all of them as it was not too far from Tooting Bec, Gary's college was just around the corner in North End Road, and it was easy enough to get to Gina's office. After this intense flurry of activity, they now had to introduce each other to their families and friends. They chose Gina's first.

They arrived at a pleasant town house in Northwood, and Gina pushed Tony forward. Once inside, the Bright family had their first view of Tony Selby, off screen anyway. Gina's mother was called Irene, but was known as Podge, and her father was Cecil. Her two twin sisters – fraternal but not identical – were Myra and Linda while Podge's mother Granny Goodman also lived with the family. Over lunch the women were chatty and inquisitive but loudly, all at the same time. Cecil calmly and quietly munched his way through the meal.

Tony was impressed when he learned of the Brights' and the Goodmans' sporting pedigree. Both parents had been captains at Mill Hill Golf Club, which was more apparent when he noticed golf trophies dotted around the room.

Irene's father, Albert Goodman, had played professionally for Tottenham Hotspur and Charlton Athletic, while Cecil's dad had been a professional heavyweight boxer. Tony was immensely impressed, and while the ladies cleared the table and disappeared into the kitchen no doubt to discuss Gina's new man, the new man sat with Cecil when he now had a chance to get a word in. Cecil ruefully explained that living with four women – or five sometimes – he was the titular head of the family, and his opinion only mattered when it came to signing cheques and paying for weddings. His girls had six between them, mostly Myra's.

Tony passed his audition with the Brights and the Goodmans, so now it was Gina's turn to pass hers with his lot. He had some unwelcome free time from work around then, mainly because little had been forthcoming. He started performing a few gigs with the Three Tones, Four Tones or Three Tones or Non-Tone, mainly at the Bull's Head. Jacqui still liked to attend the gigs, so Tony thought that might introduce Gina to his fairly recently estranged wife then, rather than to his children first over a McDonald's and large fries. Jacqui recalled when he did contact her about his new paramour, she was delighted for Tony and told him, 'See you at the Bull, I'll bring Sam along.' So that was sorted then, and when Tony told Gina she was going to meet his wife and daughter at the Bull she was completely unfazed. On his own admission his mental process was not necessarily full of clarity then; he had gone from separating from his wife and children, nearly broke and full of self-pity, living in a mate's flat, then another mate's flat to suddenly being head over heels daft for a glamorous divorcee with two boys who was coming out of her own broken relationship, and then living together in his agent's mother's flat, and about to introduce her to his wife and daughter.

They arrived at the Bull fairly early as Selby had to go through a sound check with the rest of Tones. After the checks were completed, he moved a table near the stage area and sat Gina there. Just as Jacqui and Sam arrived, Tony rather gawkily introduced them to each other, then the band started up and he rushed off to the stage. The Tones had changed the playlist, and they smirked as they led him into 'Is You Is or Is You Ain't My Baby'. He looked down from the stage to see his three guests chattering and laughing away, completely unaware of the juvenile joke from the blokes with an average age of 50. When Matt was eventually introduced, his precocity eventually accepted the new parental changes, and while that was going well Tony now had to catch up with his close friends.

Gina had been involved in casting another telly ad for CGL. They chose David Janson then found out he was a good friend of Tony's during the filming, so she told Janson she wanted to arrange a surprise party for Tony's birthday when it would also be a good opportunity to meet his friends. He agreed and made a few calls for them to meet in a pub on Kings Road. Gina then booked an Italian restaurant nearby. As they sat in the pub for a quiet birthday drink, Tony was delighted when Janson and his wife unexpectedly appeared, then Johnny Wade and his partner turned up. By a delightful coincidence, his incredulity soared when Tony and Sally Osoba then appeared. He had not been in touch with them since the first Gina meeting, and he had been feeling some guilt. The Osobas had a suspicion something was afoot; Sally's intuition knew for certain something was going on. Whenever more friends started to appear, Selby suddenly twigged something was going on as well and became splendidly pissed on the boisterous night out.

Their first summer together approached so Tony and Gina decided to have a family holiday together with Sam, Matt, and Gary. They booked a trip to Greece, flew out to Athens then sailed on the ferry to Erminea on the Peloponnese. Matt and Gary shared a room, with Sam next door in her own room as any 16-year-old should be, then the two lovebirds not too close, up the corridor. They loved the local Taverns and shops and above all the beach and the sea. After one carefree afternoon, they arrived back at the hotel to shower and change for dinner when Gina noticed her bracelet was missing. It was gold though not hugely valuable; it had been given to her by Albert Goodman, and she was distraught. The last time she remembered wearing it was when they were out swimming. She was consoled over dinner, but there was not a lot they could do about it other than thank Dionysus and his mate Bacchus and make a toast to dear old Albert.

In the morning Gina woke a little more excited than normal, 'I know where the bracelet is, exactly where it is.'

Tony, who was wanting to come around a little more slowly, asked where she thought it might be, 'In the sea.'

Not wanting to appear too sceptical, or thinking it was fairly obvious, he remained patient. She repeated in the sea, adding 'It landed on a rock or boulder, or are they the same thing?'

'How do you know Gina?'

'Cause I had a dream.'

When they met over breakfast, they all agreed that they must follow her dream and find the missing trinket. They returned to the beach and clambered on to one of the larger pedalos, and within seconds they were thrusting through the sea with Gina providing enough power on her own to get them to Athens and back in ten minutes. She suddenly screamed and they stopped, which Tony remembered being grateful for because his knees were creaking like a sycamore in a high wind. Then they all watched as Gina dived over the side, arse following shoulders in a perfect dive. She swam a few metres then dived like a guillemot, and within seconds she broke the surface holding aloft the bracelet. The others looked at each other incredulously, then hauled her back on the pedalo. She breathlessly explained she dived in after seeing a ray of light passing down through the water to a flat ledge, and the light was illuminating the bracelet. She said it was the spirit of old Albert. They could not really disagree; his spirit had played a blinder.

23
'IT IS A FEARFUL THING TO LOVE WHAT DEATH CAN TOUCH'
– JOSEPHINE JACOBSON

Just after his return from holiday, Maurice Aza called Tony and asked how he had got on with the comedian Dick Emery when they had worked together on *The Dick Emery Show* a few years back. Tony couldn't really recall anything negative; it had been very professional and disciplined during the few weeks of recording. Emery had been a huge television star but at the beginning of the 1980s his popularity was waning.

Comedy and television comedy in particular was moving on, younger audiences were now being entertained by *The Comic Strip* and *The Young Ones*. The alternative comedy circuit was thriving.

Dick had come from a family of vaudeville performers; his parents, who had a double act, used to take him on tours with them before he too started to perform, firstly in variety theatre then on to the Windmill before eventually radio shows where he variously worked with the Goons, Peter Sellers and Tony Hancock. He also, for a time, worked with Charlie Drake in a comedy pairing, a short-lived venture which provided him with less than fond memories, as it did to the unfortunate audiences who paid to see them.

The Dick Emery Show was character-led; Emery played a toothsome vicar, an old tramp, Hetty a frustrated spinster and Maudy, she of the 'pneumatic chest' and line after line of double entendre. The show had become dated and repetitive, and more seriously, the ratings were falling, so it was in danger of being dropped. Sensing this, Dick and his two main writers, John and Steve Singer, pitched an idea to the BBC for a new show, *Dick Emery Presents*. The main character was a Jewish private detective called Bernie Weinstock who ran Crimebusters International from a battered old caravan, but business was slow, mainly because Bernie was so inept. The first series had gone well but Emery wanted a change of sidekick and new actor to play his new business partner. Selby read the scripts, loved the part and signed up to play the exotically named Norman Lugg on *Jack of Diamonds*.

Selby's only concern was that the entire filming would be on location, with lots of travel and hotels. He and Gina had been inseparable from the moment they had met, and now they had to face reality: he had to go where the work was. He also had another major issue to deal with, his divorce from Jacqui.

They had talked things through then attended the court together, and the divorce was granted quickly with the decree nisi following a few months later. They also had company at the hearing: *The Sun* had a reporter and photographer there, probably because they were tipped off about celebrity names. Quoted in the newspaper, Jacqui said,

'There is no animosity between us, although we are still the best of friends, our marriage is now over.'

Tony said,

'We have two wonderful children which will always be the great bond between us.'

The two of them went for a quiet drink afterwards and made a toast to their new lives. Selby travelled down to Cardiff for the first episode of *Jack of Diamonds* and met up with Emery for a read-through. Emery had a reputation for being difficult to work with, at times appearing to be stand-offish but Tony found him courteous and delightful company, deciding he was a private man but like many good comedians he lived through his work and characters without having the inner turmoil of, say, Tony Hancock.

Emery also had a charm about him which had led him into five marriages, and countless sexual affairs and encounters. Johnny Wade, who had also worked on *The Dick Emery Show*, told Selby that in a break in filming, Emery had spotted an attractive woman at the bus stop, then went over to chat her up and within minutes she dragged him into a nearby house presumably to discuss her shopping list.

Jack of Diamonds was a story of a cache of diamonds which had been buried somewhere in Holland by a British soldier during the Second World War, he had stolen the gems from a retreating German fleeing back to his homeland. On his deathbed he told his daughter where they might be, then she in turn hired Bernie Weinstock to find the gems. Dick was playing several characters including a dodgy geezer called Cyril Blockman who was shadowing Weinstock and Norman Lugg, and also Inspector Dearlove who seemed to be shadowing everyone. The reason they were all in Cardiff was because of the castle, then more practically Castell Coch up the road in Tongwynlais because it looked like a German schloss, which was to prove convenient as the episode was set in Germany.

Tony was delighted when his old friend James Villiers turned up. Villiers was to play a character by the name of George Billyard, a sort of upper-class toff, so he was playing himself really. Dick Emery had not met James before, but within minutes they became instant pals. Emery was even more impressed when Villiers was always ready to go, and was word perfect, although he once admitted, 'I might be a bit pissed sometimes luvvie, but I always know my lines.'

This was true and rather fortunate because Villiers did indeed get pissed on occasion, sometimes twice a night.

The first few days of filming went well. Gina went down from London on the Friday then checked into the hotel and was invited to have dinner with them all that evening.

Emery had an overly complicated schedule as he had to film several scenes as his different characters which then had to be edited together, and it meant he was a little late arriving for the meal. Villiers was in his cups by then, and the others were not far behind. When Emery did arrive, he was in the company of an attractive companion at last 30 years younger. He waved to all and plonked himself down. Dick was still married to his fifth wife at the time but was about to leave her for his new partner, Fay Hillier. Dick was five foot four inches tall, and Fay towered above him. Emery confided to Selby,

'They may be taller Selby but not in bed.'

Selby had to think about that for a while.

As the meal progressed, Dick was intrigued to hear about James Villiers' royal connection. Villiers, who was now on his third bottle of wine, had shot up the royal ascendancy list to about eighth in line to the throne. Gina, who was sitting next to Fay, was intrigued by the way Dick was leering at the younger woman who pouted and flirted with him. Fay told everyone she had brought with her a selection of nightwear, so he was going to have to choose between a nurse or policewoman uniform or a stewardess outfit to wear, which would be a change from him wearing female attire. Gina thought *The Benny Hill Show* was about to start. Villiers decided that in his opinion the nurse's uniform was always the most erotic, and having decided the couple went off to their room in ardent spirits.

From Cardiff the group went over to Amsterdam, It was the first time Selby and Emery had visited the city. Selby recalled that while he loved the buildings and the canals, they spent most of the time trying to avoid dog turds, which were everywhere, dried, soggy with bicycle and pram tracks through them, then footprints and ironically dog paw prints, it was vile. Selby suggested that it was probably the only advantage of suffering from spondylitis; Emery agreed. It was a quick, business-like visit, and they didn't have time to visit Anne Frank House, the Van Gogh Museum or the Rijksmuseum. As they left the city, they broke into song,

'When it's Spring again, we'll sing again, dogshit in Amsterdam.'

When Selby did eventually re-visit the home of Amstel, it was far more fragrant, and the canine deposits had been cleared up.

From Amsterdam they returned to the UK then went straight up to Blackpool, and on the journey up there Tony mentioned about his stay in Stanley Matthews' house. Dick said, 'You know, he was the most boring man I have ever met.'

Then after a few moments' thought, Emery added, 'Perhaps the third most boring man after Gilbert Harding and Charlie Drake.'

On the first weekend off, Gina caught the train up to the Las Vegas of the North, Villiers shot back to London and Fay was not around which meant Emery had to decide if he was going to have a bit on the side or a hobby weekend. He was one of those people who had a remarkable energy and many interests, other than sexual intercourse. He had a private pilot's licence, a collection of vintage cars and motorbikes, and presumably a wardrobe full of an interesting collection of female uniforms. He found a motorbike showroom and spent the weekend playing around with high-powered motorcycles.

Tony and Gina, after sheltering from the cold, wild Irish Sea breeze, decided to pursue one of Emery's other fond pursuits.

He had found *Jack of Diamonds* a good production to work on and also good fun. Emery was not sure if there was to be a third series, but he was optimistic for other ideas he was working on. He promised Tony that he would keep him in mind for future roles. In one of their last scenes together they were aboard a boat, with Tony on the deck while below Emery was awaiting his cue to climb up through the cabin hatch. The director was still finalising his camera options when a woman walked by with her daughter. The girl looked at Tony then the film crew, 'Look mum, that's the star off the telly.'

As she said it, Dick's head popped up from the hatch to find out why there was a delay. Tony pointed at Emery and said,

'No sweetheart, he's the star.'

Dick smiled at her.

'You are quite right young lady, he is a star'

'Who are you then?'

'I'm the superstar.'

Emery was a little deflated when her mum said,

'That's whatsisname, Stanley Baxter'

At the flat in Fulham, Gina had been adding a few touches to the place, such as cushions and throws, interesting curios and a few of her paintings and drawings. In Cardiff she had found some peacock feathers which she had arranged as a fan in a container around the fireplace. Tony couldn't remember if they were supposed to be lucky or unlucky.

Although he had not been in touch with the RADAS for some time, James Villiers had still been in contact with Ronnie Fraser who was still knocking back the Fraser waters. Ronnie had met up with Richard Harris and also with Albert Finney; they were all asking after Selby.

Just before starting work on *Dick Emery Presents*, Peter O'Toole had called, Tony had not seen him for a while but had heard O'Toole had been through a life-threatening illness; his hell-for-leather lifestyle had caught up with him. O'Toole told Tony he had been experiencing severe stomach pains, but the doctors said this was down to his lifestyle and heavy alcohol consumption. It was a dreadful misdiagnosis: the cause was bowel cancer, so they removed the part of his stomach affected then part of his pancreas after he was diagnosed with exocrine pancreatic cancer.

'So other than that, you are feeling OK, Peter?' Tony said.

O'Toole laughed; he had just returned from Los Angeles after completing a film called *My Favourite Year* and he was bouncing back.

O'Toole had contacted his old friend because he was co-producing for ITV a television production of *Man and Superman*. He wanted Tony to play the part of Harry Straker to his Jack Tanner, but unfortunately Selby was under contract for the Emery series.

Now O'Toole planned to return to the stage with the play as producer and lead actor at the Cambridge Theatre. This would be his third involvement with George Bernard Shaw's comedy of manners. Selby had missed out twice, firstly when O'Toole produced the play in Dublin and then when he was already committed to another project. It was now third time lucky; they were due to go in rehearsal at the end of the year, but before they met with the rest of the company, O'Toole invited him up to his house in Hampstead where Selby recalled meeting his then partner, Karen Brown, heavily pregnant with their son Lorcan. They went into a lounge where a large coffee table had been arranged with two scripts, a jug of water and a bottle of whisky. O'Toole drank the water. They had a slow read-through, made notes then slight changes in pace then eventually they moved to a chaise longue which they used as a prop for the car, after which they sat back at the coffee table when O'Toole told him he was dropping the scene of Don Juan in Hell, and Tony agreed immediately. It was just too lengthy to include in what was, in his opinion, an already long play. It was just a diversion and the play could succeed without it. They met a few times more before the heavy rehearsal schedule began in the new year.

In between all this activity, Dick Emery, who had been talking to Selby about a new series, was taken seriously ill, and died of cardio-respiratory failure. Selby and Gina attended Emery's funeral at Mortlake Crematorium. Among the packed-in mourners along with his ex-wives and his children were a bevy of young blonde ladies and among them was Fay Hillier who waved over to Selby and Gina with a flutter of fingers. They were sitting next to the actor Victor Maddern and waited for the service to begin. Victor noticed first and gave Selby a nudge, he looked up to see the vicar arriving to begin the service and they tried to suppress a laugh, as did others around them. The vicar was the exact image of the character Dick had played in his television series, the buck-toothed Church of England clergyman. It was actually the vicar from his local church whom the family had asked to carry out the service. It must have been very difficult for his congregation to keep straight faces each Sunday. Selby thought of Don Juan in Hell, which reminded him he had to get back to work.

He arrived at the Cambridge Theatre to discover O'Toole and the director James Grant deep in conversation. Selby joined the rest of the cast until O'Toole and Grant eventually joined them. Grant told them they had decided because the play was so demanding of actors, there were to be no matinees. The actors gasped, but O'Toole explained the theatre would be guaranteed a sell-out for every performance and that he himself would underwrite losses. He also told them they would receive full wages despite the cutback in performances. It proved to be a successful run.

A few weeks later, O'Toole invited Selby to Hampstead again and told him he wanted to produce another Shaw play, this time *Pygmalion*, first for television then a stage run. He wanted Selby to play Alfred Doolittle which was fine by him, he would only be on stage for about 20 minutes overall. He left O'Toole to get on with the production.

Domestically things had been going well. Sam and Matt had adjusted to the changes, they liked Gina and the fact she also got along with Jacqui was helping. Gary, however, was proving to be of concern. He was by all accounts a bright and intelligent lad but academically his GCE results were awful, certainly not enough to take him on to University College London where he wanted to study. Study had given way to other interests; he was a gifted guitarist and had been playing successfully with a group of musicians from around the area, then he discovered something that kept him active on a less cerebral level, girlfriends. He realised fairly quickly he needed to get back on track so he enrolled again at the local college to re-sit his A-levels while Gina suggested he looked for a temporary job over the summer, which he did, working as a porter and general help at the local hospital.

In the meantime, Gina's employers Adventure went broke, but she was quickly snapped up by a public relations firm among whose clients were Guinness and Colman's Mustard whose products would have made an interesting flavour for crisps.

In the meantime, Sam had started at art college, Matt had been invited down to Brighton for trials with the football club while Tony had been offered a major part in a *Bergerac* episode, so all in all, life was optimistic and looking good.

The *Bergerac* series was set in Jersey, a tiny island which can be driven around in 30 minutes. The producers then had to look at other areas of the Channel Islands and even mainland France for locations, and when Tony joined up with the Bergerac team he actually arrived in Guernsey for the first week of filming then went back to Jersey. The episode was the last in that series so there was to be a wrap party when they were to finish. Tony decided to bring Gina over for the last few days. When he spoke to Gina, she seemed a little worried; Gary was unwell, it seemed he had developed a high temperature, had aches and pains, was lethargic and fatigued. Gina wasn't sure if she should go over, but she spoke to her mother who suggested it was probably flu, and she would look after him.

Gina arrived on the island, was given a tour and they prepared for the party at the Old Courthouse in Saint Aubin, the fictional Royal Barge in the series. The following day Gina received a call from her sister Linda, to say that Gary's condition had worsened, and the family were really concerned. Tony took Gina to the airport, but bad weather had caused delays and cancellations to flights to the mainland, and it was late evening when she boarded a flight back to London. When she arrived back at the flat most of the family were waiting. Gary was lying in his bed in a dreadful state, looking helpless while mumbling senselessly. Gina immediately called an ambulance, wondering why no one had done so already. She travelled with Gary to Charing Cross Hospital where he was immediately taken into a side room, and after a while, with no contact from anyone, she barged into the room to see her son, his eyes yellow, now hallucinating and sobbing. The medical staff seemed unsure of what to do, so Gina pleaded with them to help him, then in desperation she called Gary's father, her ex-husband Stanley Sellers, who in turn contacted a doctor he knew, and a transfer was organised to King's College Hospital where Gary was immediately placed into intensive care.

In the meantime Tony packed his bags quickly and returned home, and when he arrived at King's College the news was not good. He was shocked by Gary's appearance, he looked gaunt, his skin yellow from jaundice. Shortly afterwards the doctors confirmed that Gary had contracted a severe form of hepatitis, but were concerned on how he had become infected. Their original thoughts were that it must have been from the hospital where he had been working, he might have caught the tip of a syringe perhaps, but that was quickly discounted because they reasoned, the symptoms would not normally appear for several weeks, especially with this type of acute viral hepatitis. It was a chronic infection usually caused by eating or drinking something contaminated by faecal matter or from contaminated blood. It was going to be a battle.

Gary was drifting in and out of consciousness, antibiotics and saline slowly feeding from the tubes into his body, oxygen pumping gently into his lungs. Gina and Tony were given a room nearby, with friends and family toing and froing each day with fresh clothing, food, and drinks. They were with Gary for ten days, and on the tenth he couldn't fight things any more, then after a small sigh he was gone.

Tony would always remember Gina's wail of torment shuddering through her body when her son died. Tony held her closely but could not stem the searing gut-wrenching pain. He felt her sorrow and torment, the desolation and despair.

24
CANADA AND AUSTRALIA

Tony had no thoughts for work after Gary's death. He felt he needed to be there for Gina but eventually, despite the intense sense of grief, he persuaded her to return to her PR job as they attempted to get back to some normality.

Peter O'Toole called him once again; the plans for *Pygmalion* were ongoing but he had been offered part as a Cockney gangster and was debating whether or not to take it. Selby thought back to *Villain* and warned him to be careful after Richard Burton's performance. O'Toole sent over a script and a tape recorder and asked him to read through and use his accent as a basis for the character. Included in the package was a substantial fee. Selby taped the dialogue with a few notes including some advice, suggesting O'Toole did not accept the job.

Selby was suddenly inundated with work including several voiceovers. He had done a few for television and cinema ads over the years but since the growth of commercial radio, a whole new industry had grown with agents who concentrated solely in that medium.

Maurice Aza, in his own words, knew 'bugger all' about that part of the business and suggested that Selby signed up with one of the specialist agencies for any radio work. He had a choice of Hobsons, Lipsincs and Yakety Yak, and he liked Helen Roberts at Yakety so let her handle his work. As a result he had regular gigs at Silk Sounds in Dean Street where most of the radio commercials were recorded. The attractive nature of the radio work was the quick turnaround, Tony could be in the studio then on his way home within a couple of hours. More importantly, the cheque would be in the post within days.

In a few weeks he appeared in a BBC production of *Antigone*, which the cast eventually managed to pronounce correctly, and after two episodes of *Minder* with his old friend Dennis Waterman, he was offered a prolonged run of the Ray Cooney farce *Run for Your Wife* with an option for the production to tour Canada and then Australia, a period of about 18 months work.

Tony was told it would not be a problem if Gina joined him on the Australia tour, so he signed up, which was a pity because Peter O'Toole called him immediately afterwards to confirm that *Pygmalion* was going ahead and the part of Doolittle was his. He could not do Doolittle because he was doing *Run for Your Wife*.

The O'Toole production was opening at the Shaftesbury Theatre, and was then spending a few weeks in the Yvonne Arnaud Theatre in Guildford before transferring to Broadway. Tony was now facing a dilemma: the thought of working with O'Toole again and the prospect of finally making it on to the New York stage was overwhelming.

He talked to Aza. The contracts had been signed with Ray Cooney, it was a year and half's guaranteed work and as Maurice pointed out, receiving a more glamorous offer was not an option in breaking a contract.

Selby informed O'Toole of the situation and O'Toole sympathised and had to recast. [John Thaw was available to do Doolittle and did]. O'Toole then asked Selby to go over to Hampstead again, he explained that the English actress playing Eliza, Jackie Smith-Wood, would only be in the production at the Shaftesbury, and when it moved to Guildford, the show would have a new Eliza before moving on to New York. The replacement actor was Amanda Plummer, an American, the daughter of Christopher Plummer who many people assumed was British. Plummer was in fact a Canadian who moved to New York before moving to London where he had assumed many English character roles. When he arrived in London he was estranged from his wife and daughter. Amanda was brought up and educated in the USA.

O'Toole wanted Tony Selby to be her voice coach and as usual arranged a very generous fee for the job. Amanda was an actor who had already won a Tony Award for her role in *Agnes of God*, and she had appeared in the American production of *A Taste of Honey* but she had always wanted to play Eliza. Her main worry, however, was not to sound like a female version of Dick van Dyke's Australian Cockney. In her hotel room the three of them went through the script and then Amanda read Eliza for them, they both felt that she wasn't all that bad. Selby took her through the myths of the origins of Cockney and also the concept of rhyming slang, not that it featured much in Shaw's dialogue, but it would help with the rhythm. It proved good fun for Amanda, so it was apples and pears; trouble and strife; frog and toad, then some of the ruder ones, Hampton Wick and Jack and Danny. When Tony translated, Amanda roared with laughter, especially when she learned the separate meaning of fanny in English as opposed to American slang.

He took her to a few London pubs where she was facinated to hear a few more examples:- Gold Watch for Scotch, Vera Lynn for Gin and Pig's Ear for Beer. She became more fasinated when she heard an exchange between the barman and a customer.

'Ere, can you sausage and mash [cash] me a Gregory Peck [cheque]?'

The barman duly obliged, and Amanda sort of worked it out. On another visit to the pub she said to Tony that she would order. It was the same barman, so Amanda decided to order in her best Eliza voice,

'Two pig shits please.'

Her accent, though not necessarily her native wit, was perfect.

When *Pygmalion* opened at Guildford, Tony and Gina were invited; he remembered that O'Toole was wonderful, Amanda beguiling and John Thaw was not bad as well. Amanda was nominated for a Tony Award for the Broadway production, or a Selby Award as she wrote to him afterwards.

Selby started rehearsals for *Run for Your Wife*, a farce about a mild-mannered London taxi driver called John Smith who loves two women, so he marries them both, one installed in a flat in Streatham, the other in a flat in Wimbledon. He is operating on a very tight love life schedule, rather like Sam Selby but without the mild manners. John gets mugged which leaves him concussed and confused. He is unable to keep up his domestic timetable, the two wives call the police because they cant get in touch with him, then the neighbours get involved then just about everyone else.

Ray Cooney was a founder member of the Theatre of Comedy under whose banner they would be touring, and he was also the director. The rehearsal period consisted of long days followed by even longer days.

Selby always insisted that farce is not a theatrical technique many actors can muster; it needs faultless production, timing and a perfection in every feature, every facial expression and vocal inflexion, and lots of stamina.

They opened at the Theatre Royal, Norwich, used the week to become word and technically perfect, then from the City of mustard went straight to Toronto, the anchor of the Golden Horshoe by all accounts and the home of the Ed Mirvish Theatre.

They began to rehearse, Robin Nedwell was playing the main role of John Smith, Carol Hawkins and Anita Graham the two wives, while Selby and Eric Sykes were the two detectives.

After the first run through they noticed a distinguished looking man sitting with Ray Cooney in the stalls. When the actors were taking a break, Ray and the man joined them on stage, he was Ed Mirvish the theatre owner.

Mirvish owned several stores across Canada and had substansial interests in property and restaurants. His wealth enabled him to become a generous philanthropist, he supported numerous charities and good causes but above all he was a devoted theatregoer and benefactor.

As well as the Mirvish Theatre he also at the time owned the Old Vic in London.

After the initial introductions, Ed invited them all to dinner at one of his restaurants. He proved to be a charming and witty raconteur and asked Selby how long he had been in the business. Selby gave Ed a brief history, mentioning he had started doing impressions of Al Jolson, as a kid. Ed listened intently then raised his hand to interrupt,

'Excuse me Tony, did you know that I was circumcised by Al Jolson's father?'

Which Tony didn't, of course, he nodded and said,

'What a coincidence.'

Ed was a regular visitor to his theatre during the nine-week run. The audiences were good, and the reviews even better as were the apartments the cast had been allocated, roomy and comfortable, important for when their families visited. Gina arrived with some of the other relatives, and they soon found their way around. They quickly found the jazz and blues clubs along Yonge Street and managed the round trip to Niagra Falls. Overall the cast and families bonded quickly, it was a happy company.

Eric Sykes, whose son David was the show's technical manager, was perhaps the most enigmatic cast member. It was well known that Sykes was as deaf as a doorknob while his eyesight was on a par with a bat without a neuronal compass but he and David were nothing if not inventive.

David was something of an electronic wizard who had worked with several rock bands on their amplifier systems and had a good knowledge of oscillation. Eric had asked him to make some electronic spectacles to magnify his script, normally his scripts were recorded for him to learn. The specs also had a device on the temples which sent vibrations into his very complicated auditory system which apparently caused his eardrum and the tiny, attached bones to vibrate which in turn sent impulses to his brain. This technical wizardry was fine but for the fact this sophisticated ocular and auditory system meant Sykes was never sure what was going on unless he was looking straight at someone, and in an uncontrolled mode he was confused for most of the time.

In social situations, having a meal or a drink at the bar, a joke or an anecdote was being told and if he was not face-to-face, he would laugh in the wrong places or make an unrelated comment. He could also pick up conversations from tables yards away from where he was sitting. This unusual technology meant as the two police officers in the play, Sykes and Selby had to ensure they were always in each other's eye contact.

Tony and Gina were keen swimmers, and each day they took advantage of the swimming pool in their apartment block. He woke up one morning and could hardly hear a thing, so after seeing the company doctor he was told he had otitis external – in layman's terms, swimmer's earhole – and was given some ear drops and antibiotics. His ears popped slightly but his hearing was still impaired. Things had not improved much when Tony arrived at the theatre for the evening performance, but he knew his lines well enough and thought things would be fine, until he met Sykes in the dressing room.

'Hello, Tony.'

'What?'

'I said, hello Tony.'

While Selby was tempted to say,

'It's half past seven.'

he managed to explain he had an ear infection.

Sykes looked at him,

'Tony, this is going to be a very interesting performance.'

And so it proved. Instead of following stage directions, they carried out improvised and synchronised movements while the others, being utterly professional, quickly realised they now had two cast members with hearing difficulties. Not only that, but two who had an unerring ability to move in almost perfect symmetry. Even the Royal Ballet would have been envious. The other actors seemed to realise what was going on and compensated for Tony and Sykes having to ghost each other's footsteps by wandering off their own marks as well. It turned out it was one of the funniest, well-received shows they had performed.

Before they left Canada, Ed Mirvish invited them all to a farewell dinner. Tony had his ears syringed while Eric was regularly removing his side frames and tapping the plastic. He was also relieved that Ed did not mention his Brit Mila or his Mohel again.

Before they had left Canada, Ray Cooney told them that his plans to secure a long tour in Australia were proving to be a little optimistic, he wouldn't know until the New Year. Shortly after they arrived back in the U.K., Maurice Aza confirmed that the Australia tour was on, however, the play would have to be re-cast so it would mean a short run at the Criterion Theatre in London. Good news for Selby, a home fixture and home for Christmas.

Only Selby, Anita Graham and Carol Hawkins were available for the new production. The opportunity for the play to be performed in Australia was down to Ray Cooney's persistence. He had been in contact with the Australian Elizabethan Trust, whose patron was HM Queen Elizabeth II which might have given a clue to the nomenclature. Ray had worked hard to enable an exchange programme between the Trust and the Theatre of Comedy, and once Equity and the Australian Actors' Union agreed on a mutual exchange programme, they were on their way.

When they touched down in Perth in the early afternoon, they blinked at the sunshine as they walked across the tarmac, then they sailed through customs, clambered on to the transport, checking into the hotel and despite the jet lag and fatigue managed to pick up their expenses.

Selby, although he had been in a fairly good run of work, was still unsure how his career would pan out. The play, although paying well, was not really what he wanted for his future work. It had taken some time to shed the Corporal Marsh character; although it had served him well for summer shows and some pantomime runs, he felt he needed a good meaty television series or film.

The new cast for *Run for Your Wife* was full of actors from former TV sitcoms: James Bolam from *The Likely Lads* took over the part of John Smith, Bernard Cribbins as Stanley Gardiner was a stalwart of several series and Bryan Pringle, one of the RADAS who replaced Sykes who was also a sitcom veteran. He did however have the hearing of an owl and the sight of an eagle which would help Tony considerably.

In the meantime Selby had a tour to complete and a career rethink afterwards, he also arranged for Gina to join him. She had established a good relationship with the female actors when they were in Toronto, and she also quickly made friends with the other actors' wives after they arrived.

Perth, and Western Australia, as a whole was politically and economically a hugely interesting place to be in the mid-1980s; other than Perth and the Port of Freemantle, there were no cities or towns of any real size, so the city and port were the epicentre of growth while the mining companies operating in the north all had headquarters in Perth, and billions in investment flowed through the system. There were three major players, famous names, who had a great deal of influence then: Kerry Packer, the cricket and media tycoon; Rupert Murdoch, the sports and media mogul who would go on to own most of the sports and news media worldwide; and then a man called Alan Bond, an ex-thief and fraudster who had built up the Bond Corporation whose companies seemed to own most of Perth including the casinos and hotels. Perth was also a city full of British expats, a lot less cosmopolitan than the Eastern coast cities. The accents were predominently Scots, Scouse or Manc.

There were full houses when the play opened at the Royal Theatre in Subiaco. On time off, the cast were entertained lavishly by the wealthier citizens on yachts along the coast and in stunning villas along the river.

One day Selby was standing with an ice-cold tinny watching the activity along the Swan when he noticed two things. One was that the beer he was drinking was named after the river, then secondly, he was joined by a bloke holding his own tinny. He was the host of the party and possibly related to Alan Bond or worked for him, Selby was never sure. He told him that *Enemy* was one of his favourite plays having seen it in London, and when Dennis Waterman had been on a tour of Australia he told the star he wanted to make it into a film. Waterman told the man that when he had the film rights to let him know. The bloke told Tony he now had the film rights, and asked if he would be interested in appearing in the film with Waterman. Tony told the man he would be more than interested, and to let him know when the deal was set up. The man then took out a packet of salt and Selby took a pinch from it, he knew that he would hear no more about it. It was always the same, people always hung around with projects that went no further, a whimsical folly, a tax loss or something would be set up then would leave a trail of debt and mess from lack of finance.

They left Perth after a successful six-week run and then moved on to Sydney. When their flight landed, Selby's ears decided to malfunction again.

'Tony, what time is it?'

'No thanks, already had one.'

After they had returned from Toronto he and Eric Sykes had almost learned to sign. Sykes gave him the name of his hearing consultant in London. Selby arranged an appointment and after a thorough examination the specialist couldn't find any significant problem, so gave him some ear drops with advice not to swim or fly for a while, then a bill.

'What?!'

The first thing Selby did in Sydney was to see a doctor who told him he had a slight perforation in his left ear and blockage in the other, again not to swim for a while or to fly, particularly in an aircraft. The doctor then gave him a bill which was given to the production accountant. 'Fucking what?!'

Tony discussed his hearing problem with Bryan Pringle in case they might have to adjust on stage. He told Pringle what the doctor had said and that he had seen Sykes's hearing specialist in London before they had left to Australia. Pringle absorbed the information for a moment, 'You know Tony, that's almost on par with going to see Mr Magoo's optician.'

Then suddenly it was all over; Tony had really enjoyed working with the two Theatre of Comedy casts and Ray Cooney.

Tony and Gina had loved Australia. On the west coast they had visited Yanchep to see the exceptional marsupial and avian wildlife and the koalas, the lovable adorable creatures which were unfortunately stoned most of the time from the eucalyptus diet. When they are not sleeping they are rutting, they are torpid and smelly, spreading chlamydia through the torpor a little like the reflection of narcissists on *Love Island*. Gina was perhaps a little disillusioned after smelling the pee and generally unpleasant secretions, and the koalas weren't much better.

In Sydney they sailed around the harbour and its famous bridge, and visited the Opera House, the restaurants and the Rocks and the ferry trips to Manly. They arrived back in the UK on an early spring morning, but as soon as they arrived back at the flat, Gina's spirits wilted and the peacock feathers stared back at her accusingly. It was time to move home.

25
SABALOM GLITZ

Tony and Gina quickly found a new home in York Street, just off Baker Street. The property had been used as an office and accommodation by Cliff Richard's production company. It was complete luck; they were in the estate agent's office just when the flat's conversion back to become a fully residential home was being signed off. It was ideal for them, with a generous living space and patio, and they moved in very quickly.

Shortly after the move, Anita Graham called. She had become a close friend after the *Run for Your Wife* tour and was having a birthday meal at a restaurant owned by Nunzio Peluso, the husband of Linda Bellingham, who was also a mutual friend of Tony and Gina. Among the other guests was John Nathan-Turner, the producer of the science fiction show *Doctor Who*, and Chris Clough, one of the main series directors.

They talked about Australia, the flat move and then what everyone else was doing; the answer seemed to be *Doctor Who*. John, who was sitting with Gina, asked her if Tony could put on a few pounds in weight. She told him he could lose half a stone over a month then put it back on again in about four days. When Gina asked why, John mentioned he had a part in mind that he wanted Tony to play. It seemed that Nathan-Turner and Clough had already cast Linda and Anita in roles for the new *Doctor Who* series but had not made their minds up about who was to play a significant new character until Tony had arrived at the restaurant. Nathan-Turner asked him to meet him at his production office at Wood Lane and talk about the part in more detail. The more John talked the more Tony liked the idea, and he was to become Sabalom Glitz.

The reason they wanted Tony to put on a little more weight was the character was basically a lazy sod who had a partner to do all the running around for him while Glitz enjoyed his sedentary lifestyle. Tony still had a lot to think about. He didn't have any great knowledge about the series. He remembered when it began in the early 1960s; it had been a novelty then and the Daleks were the much-loved villains, but he had not seen any of the more modern episodes which meant a catch-up and then absorbing more of the *Doctor Who* history and style. While doing so he found out there was an awful lot of politics going on around the future of the Doctor. Michael Grade, the then BBC controller, was not an enthusiastic fan of *Doctor Who*. He had suspended the series because he felt it displayed too much violence and gravitas. Grade wanted more human stories with a lighter touch. He was also instigating large budget cuts for light entertainment, mainly because the BBC had commissioned *EastEnders* as a new soap opera to rival *Coronation Street* in the ratings.

Another problem for the programme was John Nathan-Taylor, who had been involved with *Doctor Who* since the late 1960s when he became the floor manager. He was very possessive and proved ruthless when it came to hiring and firing. When Tony decided to become Mr Glitz he found a belligerent BBC boss, a megalomaniac director, while he had still to meet the sixth Doctor, played by Colin Baker. In the meantime Tony was still trying to re-acquaint himself with the concept and history. His research reminded him that the Doctor is a Time Lord from the planet Gallifrey and travels through space and time in his Tardis. The Doctor is centuries old and when his body starts to wear out and he is about to expire one way or another, it then regenerates into another physical being through a process of cellular reconstruction resulting in a new appearance, rather like Joan Collins or Jess Conrad.

Tony further researched; he knew *Doctor Who* had a worldwide audience with dedicated fans with a wondrous knowledge. He found out that Gallifrey purchased a job lot of police boxes from the Metropolitan Police in 1959; the planet had some brilliant mechanics who knew all about dimensionally transcendental astrophysics which transformed the police boxes into KOBBS, an acronym for Knackered Old Bill Blue Structures. Unfortunately the name didn't really capture the imagination or match the capability.

The more catchy and apposite Time and Relative Dimension in Space, or TARDIS, was chosen, quite correctly in the opinion of most people. Things then became a little more complicated. The Time Lords who ruled the planet were the self-appointed guardians of time and space throughout the universe, but with a caveat they were not allowed to interfere in planning permissions, or arguments about a right of way or any boundary disputes.

Who grew up on Gallifrey as a lonely soul, in fact they had a lousy childhood all round. When Who was a little older, he went to technical college, only passing his exams by a whisker. His best mate then was called the Master, whom Who had known since they were kids, Many years earlier they had been on a school trip to have a look at the space and time vortex. Most of the kids were inspired and texted each other or went on to say they were all going to achieve good things in their lives, but some went a bit loopy and turned nasty, including the Master. Eventually Who became Doctor Who because no one knew his given name. He stole a KOBBS, realised it was an old model, so nicked a new TARDIS and set off on his adventures. The Master nicked another TARDIS, set off on his own career path and created the Daleks. Tony thought most of this was accurate although the police boxes might well have been purchased in the late 1940s. He also thought of another possibility as well, that in a parallel universe on the planet Equidae, the Time Lords there had purchased horse boxes. The inhabitants were known as Centaurs who travelled around in a Sidrat because they were a little backward. One of the Sidrats was manned by an equine veterinarian Who but that seemed a little far fetched.

Series 23 of *Doctor Who* began filming in the spring of 1986, with 14 episodes to be shown later in the year from late Autumn to Christmas so they had a lot of work to get on with.

Tony had thought long and hard of how to play Glitz, and together with Chris Clough it was decided he would be a lovable rascal. You wouldn't trust him as far as you could throw him, but he might well help you out in a jam, particularly if there was anything in it for him; conversely he was an evil git, not averse to a bit of duplicity or easing others out of the way when it suited.

Tony had worked on two *Minder* episodes and decided a galactic Arthur Daley might well be part of Glitz's character as well. He also knew this new series would be under great scrutiny, not only from the BBC hierarchy, but from fans and viewers generally. There were now many science fiction competitors on television: besides the longstanding *Star Trek* with huge budgets, *Buck Rogers* had materialised with wondrous SFX, while in cinemas Stephen Spielberg was taking things to another level of wonder with his films *Close Encounters* and *E.T.*.

The synopsis for this new *Doctor Who* series was complicated, even for the greatest aficionados. Normally each series had one continuous story, but 'Trial of the Time Lord' had at least four different storylines and some tangential links, all connected but obscurely so.

That was undoubtedly due to Robert Holmes, the main scriptwriter who liked to create a good villain or two. He had gone through it all with a fine-tooth comb with the script editor Eric Saward who loved Glitz and some of the other new characters being introduced. Then there was a tragedy, as halfway through the scripts Robert died, taking the rest of the stories with him. Nathan-Turner then brought in Pip and June Baker to re-write and finish the scripts.

Tony remembered Nathan-Turner's summary of the storylines with some bemusement. He was once sitting with Geoffrey Hughes, the actor who would always be cast as the perennial 'loveable rogue'.

He said to Geoff,

'Right the Doctor is on trial, he has allegedly broken several laws of Gallifrey then is accused of interfering in the affairs of planets, oh! and also genocide.'

'Correct, allegedly' replied adubious Hughes.

The two of them then had a go at understanding the trial, surreal in the real sense of the adjective because events were presented before they had happened, and characters the Doctor had not met before appeared, then re-appeared again after he had met them. Then his old school mate the Master appeared to tell everyone what a great man Who was, mainly because the Master would be implicated himself in a devious plot if he didn't.

The confusion continued.

Everything started when the TARDIS was hijacked by the Time Lords. The Doctor was then charged with fiddling about with the space/time continuum, but all the evidence was rigged against him. Suddenly the Earth was moved a million miles from its original position as the third planet from the Sun and the only survivors of that mean trick lived underneath Marble Arch Tube station. One of them was a robot called Dratho, the holder of secrets stolen from the Time Lords.

Tony then appeared as Glitz with his partner Dibber who was described as a man of deceptive intelligence, presumably because he was thicker than people first thought. Dibber did all the running about for Glitz. The actor playing him was Glen Murphy who got on with Tony immediately, mainly through their mutual interests. Murphy, as well as being a knowledgeable football fan, was also a martial arts expert, so Tony didn't really want to upset him. Instead they concentrated their roles on Glitz and Dibber who the Time Lords had hired to retrieve the secret files.

The hard part of the job meant they had to put out of action the black light system that powered Dratho. Dratho's real function was to protect the three sleepers, astronauts who were in suspended animation a lot when making long-distance space trips, and also to keep an eye on their air miles. The robot kept the place nice and tidy in its spare time.

Because he was an idiot, Dibber destroyed the external aerial that powered the black light system, meaning everything could become unstable and destroy everything around it. With its power source fading, Glitz and Dibber persuaded Dratho to come with them so they could hand over Dratho and his secrets to the Time Lords who presumably would have an alternative power provider. The automon, although pretty good at fixing the telly or the air conditioning, had not been programmed to repair the black light or anything else of universal importance, so followed the two humans to the surface. The machine was even more idiotic than Dibber, it trips over and explodes, taking the secrets with it. Then the Doctor arrived, fixed the errant power source and everyone was saved and happy. The whole series of events was then replayed at the Doctor's trial.

Tony decided rather than trying to understand the strange twists and turns, convoluted plots and eccentricities, he would concentrate on his lines and follow direction. He was, however, thoroughly enjoying his role as Glitz, and working with the other actors.

Geoffrey Hughes was playing one of the great characters created for the series, Mr Popplewick, an officious bureaucrat. Geoffrey was a professional Scouser in every way and hardly ever in his work stepped out of his accent. In the storyline Popplewick was part of the mysterious and evil Valeyard, a constant villain and threat to the Doctor throughout the series. Some suggested that the figure was part of the Doctor's darker side. When Hughes turned up on set with his long sideburns and blue frockcoat it was as if he had stepped out of a Charles Dickens novel. In the storyline, Popplewick had a powerful explosive quill tucked behind an ear so it was not advisable to be near him when he coughed, sneezed or farted, rather like Hughes himself really.

Despite the notorious wobbly internal sets, *Doctor Who* did a considerable amount of location filming which Mr Popplewick liked because Hughes collected things. Tony had once visited him at his home, a sort of smallholding with a museum of enamel signs, and train memorabilia. They were once on location in Stoke-on-Trent where they had been filming at a former pottery factory that had been converted into a pottery museum which had retained all the original buildings and artefacts. It was, however, about to lose one of them. Tony was on the bus with the other members of the cast and crew but there was no sign of Hughes; Tony was tasked with finding him, and as he walked back towards the museum entrance, Hughes appeared from around the side of the building with a manhole cover he had nicked from the cobbled courtyard at the back of the building. It must have weighed in at 100lb; he staggered to the luggage compartment at the side of the coach and dumped it in, and the whole vehicle sank to one side by several inches. The coach arrived at the hotel, the passengers got off, and stood around as Hughes removed the huge lump of metal, then staggered off towards his car shouting by way of an explanation,

'It's for my collection.'

Everyone nodded and exhaled 'oh' by way of acceptance. Hughes finished up having his face ripped off after the Doctor exposed him, as Popplewick, to be part of the Valeyard evil and went off to admire his manhole collection. Whether or not anyone fell down the hole he left in Stoke-on-Trent is unknown.

Tony had given up trying to understand the plots of the series; well he had a basic understanding which was enough to give a superb performance as Glitz, but the more intricate and worrying plots were starting to manifest dissatisfaction within the *Doctor Who* production.

Colin Baker, the Doctor, was an actor under pressure. He had not been a popular choice among Whovians who were great fans of the previous Doctor, Peter Davison. They were also unhappy that Davison had left the role because he didn't want to become typecast. Tony felt that was hardly Colin's fault; he found him an endearing man with a great sense of humour, as did the director Chris Clough.

If Clough's actors were having fun they were enjoying the job, but another of the actors was also under pressure from fans and critics, Bonnie Langford. Langford had been playing the Doctor's companion, Melanie Bush. She was a seasoned performer having been a child star, indeed she first appeared on television at 15 months old. She and Tony got on well. Langford was also a former pupil at Italia Conti, and he thought she was a very underrated actor, perhaps suffering from her status as a perceived precocious child star. He felt there was a little bit of unfounded resentment from other actors. Tony also thought that Bonnie was one of the most professional, prepared and genuine of people he had worked with but she was now facing a dilemma. She confided that because of the uncertainty of the next series she was unsure how far she wanted to go with her role as Melanie. That was soon to be resolved.

At the series denouement, the good Doctor was exonerated of all charges against him, the space/time continuum managed to realign, the Master went off to sulk, perhaps with Valeyard, to scheme and plan for further horrible incidents, and Glitz's mate Dibber disappeared, to become a very successful actor and mainstay of *London's Burning* for many years.

The end of the series also brought more artistic or egotistical eruptions. Script editor Eric Saward resigned after a magnificent blazing row with John Nathan-Taylor, then Michael Grade insisted that if Nathan-Taylor did not fire Colin Baker there would not be a new series. By way of explanation he thought Colin's Doctor was far too flippant.

Tony could only wonder at Grade's capricious opinions and his nature but that was not really his concern any more. Glitz's career had disappeared to another galaxy, or had it?

Baker was effectively sacked, so once he was off the books Grade gave the go-ahead for series 24. In the meantime Tony, who was meeting up with Chris Clough socially, was kept up to date with the series gossip. Chris told him they were bringing in Sylvester McCoy as Doctor number seven but because of the way Baker had been treated it was going to cause big problems with the all-important new format and the re-generation, they would need Baker to transform into McCoy's Doctor. Baker, with perhaps some justification, told them to 'fuck off' and absolutely refused to return for the scene.

A few months before the new series was to go into production, Clough called Tony. His team had worked hard on the new series, and they had concluded Glitz had proven such a popular character that they had developed a substantial storyline for him, so was Tony available? Tony really admired Clough and enjoyed working with him, but he had a few reservations, mainly financial. If he agreed he would be unable to pick up a possibly substantial role if he wanted, the BBC did not necessarily pay top wages, and his diary for the year was reasonably full. His voiceover work from Yakety Yak was proving lucrative, he had a run guesting in a few sitcoms and was contracted for some episodes of a new hospital soap called *Casualty*, then Peter O'Toole called him up just prior to opening up in the New York production of *Pygmalion*. O'Toole had brought Amanda Plummer back with him for some further 'Cockney' voice coaching. O'Toole told Tony he had still wanted him for the role of Alfred Doolittle but had been overruled by the American producers when Plummer and O'Toole returned to America. Tony went off to Marbella for a brief run in *Duty Free*.

Shortly afterwards, Tony received a message from Michael Jayston who played the real Valeyard in *Doctor Who*, and who was not a Merseysider who nicked manhole covers. He invited Tony to the Lords Cricket Ground for lunch and as he fancied a bit of cricket, he wore his best linen and met up with Michael.

Instead of wickets and lbw's, stumps and yorkers, they talked about knocking over cardboard controls, robots, or papier mâché palm trees. Shortly afterwards, Tony called up Clough and agreed to return as Glitz. Sabalom took Tony by the hand and introduced him to Sylvester McCoy, the seventh Doctor, in his first episode, 'Dragonfire'.

McCoy had the good-natured humour of Colin Baker which meant a good transition for the cast and crew although he was certainly eccentric. His real name was Percy James Patrick Kent-Smith from Dunoon. Tony's immediate reaction was the man from Argyll and Bute was born to play the Doctor, and he was further convinced when he learned McCoy had been part of Ken Campbell's manic theatre group, renowned for putting nails up each other's nostrils and live ferrets down their trousers among the more gentle routines.

McCoy's first scene was the regeneration, but because Colin Baker had told everyone to eff off, the new Doctor appeared face down on the floor wearing a wig and Baker's hat perched on the back of his head. The screen did its squiggly and wriggly distortion and McCoy appeared with his enigmatic smile. The production also had to bring in a new assistant to replace Langford's character Mel, and her replacement was called Ace played by Sophie Aldred. Ace was to be closely linked with Glitz, so Tony had to fully concentrate, and he blinked a little when he heard the storyline.

Ace was a 16-year-old waitress from Perivale in west London, who was propelled forward in time by a solar wind caused by a mysterious time storm that suddenly manifested itself in her bedroom while she was experimenting with an explosive she had invented … while singing into a hairbrush.

Once the rest of the cast had decided that was reasonable, the plot continued. Ace found herself on Ice World, not the one with skaters in short, sequinned skirts and tight-fitting trousers, but a sort of space trading colony where she met up with Sabalom Glitz who lasciviously suggested she join him on some adventures. There have been many interpretations or misinterpretations of the script suggesting Glitz asked Ace if she was a virgin, which she wasn't shortly after the question was posed.

The start of Dragonfire quickly introduced a newly regenerated Doctor to Mel and Glitz and the possibly just deflowered Ace, just the sort of story to appeal to peak-time early evening television.

Ice World was controlled by a nasty fellow called Kane with a body and heart so cold that just a touch from his finger would kill. Glitz owed Kane lots of money, and if it were not paid back he would have to forfeit his spaceship and his intergalactic football league programmes.

Once they all understood the scripts, vaguely, roughly, or just about, they started work. Sophie Aldred, who was 25 at the time, bonded immediately with Bonnie Langford who was just slightly older. They giggled a lot, mainly at McCoy who tried to make them laugh at every opportunity until they were given a gentle bollocking from Chris Clough or a more severe one from John Nathan-Turner.

Ice World was not a planet but a gigantic spaceship, and Kane was trapped there because he could not power the craft because the power system was within the cranium of a dragon. Dragons can basically live anywhere, the caves on a mountain, under the sea, castles in the air, but this particular dragon chose to live in the basement of a shopping centre. Kane could not bear any form of light, sunlight, or warmth, rather like Geordies, so going anywhere near a dragon and its Scotch Bonnet chilli breath was a no-no. Tony recalled,

'I won, or Glitz did, a map in a card game which was set up by Kane. The map revealed the location of the dragon's hidden treasure. The plot had me going off to find the treasure but from then on things got a little madder.

'The Doctor decided to accompany Glitz on his adventure to find the treasure but the girls were banned from going either because it was too dangerous or he fancied a bit of male company for a while. They set off, but, unbeknown to them the map contained a tracking device, and Kane knew their every step. In the meantime the girls were bonding back at the bedsit which Glitz had set up for Ace. Mel then discovered that Ace was a millennial, years before they became a species, but because Mel was also a polyglot she could quickly switch to her idiom. When she asked how Ace had become mixed up with Glitz, Aldred's character replied, 'So, well I was like doing stuff, like an experiment with like chemistry and stuff, then like a time storm hit me, it was like so unfair and finished up here with old Sabalom.'

The script changed slightly to cater for pre-millennial audiences.

Mel and Ace got bored with fashion tips and how strange men were so decided it would be good to venture down to the ice caves and sort the Kane problem out themselves. Tony remembered things became a little farcical, which was perhaps the intention, but they all became a little unsure about what was going on.

It was explained that Kane had sent men to follow Glitz and the Doctor, so Selby and McCoy nodded. Just as the men caught up with them, on the other side of the set Kane's other men found Ace and Mel. Langford and Aldred nodded, then they would all arrive together at the same time, and after a few takes to allow for trips, pile-ups and giggling the actors arrived at the dragon area on cue.

When the dragon appeared it showed them a hologram which if nothing else revealed why the creature had such an unusually shaped cranium. Kane's men then chopped the dragon's head off then to speed things up a little, they were then all killed.

The four heroes then took back the dragon's head to Kane but the power system was designed before Kane's old planet had become a black hole so it was completely useless. Kane then melted, peace and order was restored to spaceship and planet, Glitz had his own spaceship and football programmes back, the Doctor and he did a partner swap and Tony left the series with the lovely Bonnie on his arm.

In the re-telling of this story there may be some possible deviations or revision. Thanks to Glitz, Tony had great fun and considered the character one of his most satisfying roles. Over the years he attended many *Doctor Who* conventions and fairs, and found the Whovians amazingly loyal, good company and respectful, embracing the show's culture with great knowledge and humour.

26
IF I WERE A RICH MAN

After his galactic adventures had concluded, Tony asked Gina one morning in 1986 if she fancied getting married; she disappeared into the kitchen to make some toast, returned with a seductive look with butter and Marmite on her nose, and said, 'OK.'

So they did, at Marylebone Registry Office with a few Selbys, Brights and close friends for company, then flew out to Mombasa for a month's honeymoon, returning to London early in the new year to begin life in the new flat. The couple shared part of a large patio with their neighbour, Wendy Richard, who played the part of Pauline Fowler in the BBC soap *EastEnders*. She lived with her partner Paul.

The couples didn't know each other that well. Paul seemed friendly enough but they felt that Wendy was a little offhand. Tony had not come across her professionally but she had made a good career over the years in various sitcoms and had become a major character in *EastEnders*. One morning, a letter arrived from Richard's solicitor; Gina looked quizzically then passed it over to Tony. It was a request to move some patio furniture and plant pots she alleged were infringing on her property. The Selbys scratched their heads and laughed. They both wondered why Richard had not come around to see them to discuss the matter rather than the cost of instructing a solicitor. Gina went around to see her and told her how much they had been looking forward to moving in, especially after Gary's death. Wendy replied brusquely she really didn't 'care about all that'. Gina gave her short shrift after that and told her that as far as she was concerned the patio was shared. Tony was really annoyed with the pettiness of it all and wrote back to the solicitors with the reply given by *Private Eye* in the brief conflict of Arkell v Pressdram. They heard nothing more but relations with their neighbours were decidedly frosty.

One Sunday, the Selbys noticed a few of the cast of *EastEnders* passing by to Richard's flat. Their own back door was open when Leslie Grantham walked by, saw Tony in his kitchen and went in to say hello. They had worked on a couple of shows together but Grantham had become one of the biggest soap stars in his role as Dirty Den. They had a quick catch-up then Grantham said he would see Tony at the party; it became awkward when Tony told him they had not been invited. Shortly after Grantham left, Wendy banged on the door and asked if he would like to come over. Tony thanked her and said he would go and tell Gina, but Wendy replied,

'No, just you, I don't want Gina.'

When Tony told Wendy he wouldn't be there with his wife, with reluctance she told him,

'You had better both come then.'

They picked a couple of bottles of red from the wine rack and joined the fun. Richard kept her distance while the Selbys mixed freely with the other guests. Tony and Grantham began to get thoroughly pissed, and in an indiscreet moment Grantham told Tony that Richard's success in her role as Pauline Fowler was because she was just playing herself. The evening eventually ended with the two drunks being escorted home by their respective partners. When Tony woke up the following morning he could feel a Siberian wind blowing across the patio divide despite it being a fine summer. A while later the Selbys were entertaining friends around for drinks and a bite to eat, including a gay couple who had lived in the flats for a long time. It was a warm evening and the doors were open and it was normal for others in the flats to pop in for a drink and gossip, with two exceptions next door.

Richard's partner Paul suddenly appeared at the doorway. Paul was a big man, around six foot three and well built, fortunately he had a pleasant temperament. Apologetically he asked if they could keep the noise down as Wendy had an early call. It was just six thirty in the early evening. They closed the doors and windows; the gay couple Fraser and Richard were mortified but they had gone through many incidents with 'Ms Richard' as they called her, so much so they had built a dividing wall between their properties. It seemed she complained a lot, from the activities of their cat to some of their more flamboyant friends. The Selbys decided they would have to live with their neighbour's idiosyncrasies but not necessarily on her terms.

Gina's PR agency was looking after an Israeli company who were trying to attract investors for a golf resort and when they arranged for a flight out to Tel Aviv Tony went along for the ride. There were around 30 in the group including a couple of freelance journalists, one of whom Tony knew. His name was Derek Shuff, who was always on the periphery of the action, particularly writing about celebrities or sports stars. Tony always found him an affable, straightforward bloke.

During the trip, Tony told him the BBC were issuing some *Doctor Who* videos featuring Sabalom Glitz scheduled for release in a few weeks time. Shuff suggested that would be of interest to him and further suggested they do could a good retrospective piece about Tony's career generally. Tony cleared the interview with the *Doctor Who* office then arranged for Shuff to go over to the flat where they spent a few hours in interview then taking some external photographs. When Shuff left, he promised to let Tony know when the interview would be appearing.

Shortly afterwards the Selbys left for a show business golf jaunt to Tenerife. He pinged a ball around for a few days with some of his old mates like Johnny Briggs and the singer Tony Christie, who was still asking how to get to Amarillo.

On the flight home the comedian Stan Boardman, who had picked up a copy of the *News of the World* at the airport, suddenly stood up and called for hush, then read aloud,

'My soap star neighbour is a nightmare. *EastEnders* star branded a sour-faced meanie by TV star.'

Tony recalled that it sounded even harsher in Stan's Liverpool accent. When Stan eventually passed the newspaper over the article was by Derek Shuff. The photo was even more damaging. Shuff had set Tony up so in the background was a property For Sale board, and the caption read, 'Tony considering to sell up his property.'

Tony thought back to the interview. Shuff had asked him how he was getting on with Wendy Richard, and when Tony asked what he meant by that Shuff said he had heard

Wendy could be a bit feisty. Tony had in fact just been offered a part in *EastEnders* by the producer Julia Smith. Shuff had got wind of this and asked if it would mean a few scenes with Richard. Selby confirmed it would and said wearily, 'I've had a few scenes with her already.'

Shuff gave this prominence in the story. When they arrived back at York Street, Tony decided to write a conciliatory letter to Richard, and explained he had given the interview in good faith to someone he believed was a responsible journalist and it was to coincide with the *Doctor Who* videos. He offered apologies and hoped she would let bygones be bygones; she did not and never spoke to the couple again. However, that was not the reason Tony and Gina left York Street.

They discovered a fabulous basement flat at Marble Arch just across the road from Hyde Park, so promptly bought the lease. The flat had an exquisite courtyard which backed on to a convent inhabited by a cloister of nuns. The Selbys thought they had found their own spiritual home, and the rest of the family agreed. Sam, who was now a talented artist and designer, took one look at the convent wall and painted a stunning Italianate country scene along the whole length. Shortly afterwards, when Tony was working on a show at London Weekend, she showed up to meet him and was carrying some of her artwork. The art director and designer asked to look at them, and they were impressed. They were about to start on a series called *London's Burning* and Sam was about to begin her career as a set designer.

Matt liked the flat as well, particularly because it would provide an ideal crash pad. His football career proved short-lived so he decided to become a dancer and singer, a combination of the talents of his parents. He joined what was probably the first boy band, but unfortunately there were 12 of them which was a lot of testosterone and ego, and even worse they called themselves Rich Street. The band's first single was called 'Hitch Your Love'. Again unfortunately, it was also their last single and the dodgy dozen went their separate ways.

Tony also went a separate way, from his long standing agent Maurice Aza.

One weekend Tony and Gina had taken advantage of a freebie invitation to a health spa, and while in the sauna he met up with Derek Webster, an agent who looked after June Brown, Brian Blessed and Martin Kemp among others. Webster asked him how everything was going, he replied truthfully that things were a little flat. Webster offered to take him on. Tony called Maurice, telling him he was sorry but work had dropped considerably and he also felt the parts he was being offered were not really suitable. Aza stopped him in mid-flow,

'I'm sorry to hear that Tony, but if you are giving up the business, good luck to you.'

Tony Selby had always loved musical theatre and wished that he had been able to have performed more. A part that he had coveted for a very long time was the lead role of Tevye, the milkman in *Fiddler on the Roof*. He had first seen the show in 1967 when Chaim Topol played the role. Shortly after signing with Webster, his new agent secured him his dream role, for a three-month run at the Theatre Royal in Plymouth. The director was Roger Redfarn, who was also the artistic director of the Theatre Royal. Redfarn had a great reputation and had worked in many London and Broadway productions. Tony travelled down to Plymouth to meet up with Redfarn and the movement leader Irene Clair. Clair had worked not only on the first London production but also the film version of the show.

The first thing they explained to him was that the original director and choreographer, Jerome Robbins, would only give permission for new productions if the choreography was performed exactly as it was in the original New York and London productions with absolutely no deviation or changes. Irene Clair knew full well the consistency and discipline required, and her experience would also prove to be invaluable.

The cast of forty knew they were in good hands. Tony thought about the role, and having seen Topol, then later Alfie Bass play Tevye, he pitched somewhere in between. Redfarn liked it and they began intensive rehearsals. The songs are powerful, and after the opener, 'Tradition', the pace quickens, firstly with 'Matchmaker, Matchmaker' then, 'If I Were a Rich Man' which lifts the whole show and the song audiences recognise and connect to. It has to be just right. The director and leading man discussed this at great length.

Tony learned that 'If I Were a Rich Man' was based on a poem, 'If I were a Rothchild', referring to the banking family. The song includes many Jewish idioms in the first few lines, such as Hassidic folklore, a Klezmer style, and also includes the unforgettable 'bidi bidi bum' because the songwriter's instinct had been the words just fitted. More importantly, Tony felt the song introduced the audience to Tevye, the aspirations he had for his family, and the wealth that would enable him to study the Torah more assiduously. Tevye would share his wealth to enrich the lives of others. Redfarrn explained that the song had been sung in Finnish, French, Turkish and Hebrew (certainly apposite) then in various more unusual interpretations, it had been covered by an Israeli punk band called Yidcore (not necessarily apposite) and in two other versions entitled 'If I Were a Midget' and 'If I Were a Tishman' (a prominent Jewish American family).

After much consideration they decided to be loyal to the original! The director and lead were happy with Tevye's character, his posture, his nuances and the voice.

When the cast turned up for their costume fittings, they discovered that the workshops had faithfully reproduced the original costumes from the first Broadway production in 1964. They then discovered after the run in Plymouth that all the sets and costumes were to be placed in containers and shipped out to New York for a Broadway revival then a subsequent tour of the USA, with an all-American cast.

On opening night the Plymouth 40 said 'good luck' to each other, got 'If I Were a Rich Man' out of the way to huge audience approval then enjoyed its warm ripple for the rest of the show. The encores were genuine and the reviews warm and generous. *Fiddler on the Roof* became an exhilarating experience for the whole company, they had filled the theatre with an increasingly enthusiastic audience response after each performance. The whole cast bonded, and Tony felt he had not worked with so large a group of performers where there was such a consistent and genuine level of warmth and respect.

From a professional point of view, he had achieved one of his great ambitions, and after the final performance there were tears and fond farewells. He had loved that early winter in Plymouth.

The glow was diminishing when Derek Webster called Tony. Bob Larbey wanted to meet up with him as he had written a new series specifically for him to star in. It would be Larbey's first script without John Esmonde. At first he was a little concerned, he didn't want Percy Marsh lurking about in the storyline. He was grateful for the character and the prominence Percy had provided, but once *Get Some In!* finished he had had a fairly tough time afterwards and he did not want any further roles playing military types, indeed anything connected to the wearing of uniforms. He told Webster no.

In reality Tony needed a change of direction, and he also needed more varied and interesting work. He could have made some form of career parodying Percy on a regular basis but it would have been short-term.

Tony then looked at his future career more positively. Perhaps Derek Webster, who after all had provided him with his personal dream job, would be the catalyst for more varied and challenging jobs. He agreed to meet up with Bob Larbey, who explained that John Esmonde and he were having a break from each other for a while, to develop some solo ideas. Larbey took him through the synopsis.

The main character was called conveniently Tony, a self-made millionaire after turning his minicab firm into a hugely successful chauffeur-driven car service (Sam Selby could be detected spinning in his grave). Larbey outlined the progression: Tony moves from London to Esher in Surrey, where he lives in a large detached house with his snooty wife, a troublesome daughter sent to an expensive school, an opinionated mother and quirky domestic staff including a driver who was a mate from schooldays and a cordon bleu cook who likes a sherry or several. Tony loved the pilot script and went down to Dorset to shoot it. Dora Bryan agreed to play the mum, Sam Kelly the driver and Joan Sims the imbibing cook. The shoot went well, there was a good vibe, a fun cast then, and they waited for the BBC to confirm the series.

They did but without Selby in the role of Tony. They wanted Dennis Waterman.

Tony naturally was furious, not with Waterman particularly as it was the BBC who wanted him, but with Larbey for not fighting his corner. He had a strong position as a long-time successful writer with the BBC and his opinion should have mattered. Waterman later told Tony that he had no inkling of the role having been written for him originally, and had he done so he would have bowed out.

C'est la vie. It would be a long time before Tony and Bob Larbey kissed and made up.

27
LOVE HURTS AND HEART ACHE

The first day of January 1990 was a Monday, which was nice because it gave everyone a long weekend. Tony Selby could look forward to in the new decade, the development of cable television, a thing called the internet, the dissolution of the Soviet Union and wars in the Balkans, Somalia and the Gulf.

Unfortunately, the start of the decade brought some sad news. His mother, who had been suffering poor health for a while passed away quietly and without
fuss. Unlike Sam's more populist funeral, Anne's was dignified and respectful, just close family and friends.

Later that year he would have the personal satisfaction of seeing Margaret Thatcher crying as she left Downing Street as even her own party spat and threw rhetorical excrement after her.

Tony was not a great fan; his argument was that Thatcher had dismantled the mining and manufacturing industries but without attracting any further investment. She had sold off the country's assets cheaply to her Tory base and the land surrounding the gas, water and utilities companies for quick profit and good dividends to investors. Forget further investment. In her own words Thatcher did not believe in society, and she watched as the social system more or less crumbled.

Tony had not been that active in politics over the years. He had attended a few rallies and supported a few worthy causes, but his last real effort was to support the miners and their families when Thatcher announced 20 pits and thousands of mining workers' jobs were to go. She knew the National Union of Miners would call for strikes, but she also knew coal had been stockpiled to see the country through the winter. The battle between her government and the NUM began.

The Welsh coalfields had by far the staunchest support for the strike and they and the Yorkshire coalfields were suffering more than most. Vanessa Redgrave organised a bus to transport a group of supporters to travel down to Wales with cash and food donations for the families. Some of the supporters were from the Socialist Workers Party, most of them earnest but dour. Tony, with a couple of other actors, travelled down with them. Tony was wearing a suit and tie, while most of the SWP were wearing boiler suits or denim jeans and jackets.

They arrived in the Rhondda Valley around noon and descended on one of the local collieries. The SWP thrust their placards and flags towards the nearest pickets and were told to fuck off by both the pickets and the police, because they were illegally increasing the picket line numbers.

The capital elite then returned to their coach, retrieved all the gifts and marched on towards the local miners' institute and social club. Rather sadly, other than Tony and two others, they were denied entry because they were not wearing suits! Selby knew the social etiquette of the miners: every Sunday after chapel they would have a few pints in their club in their best suit and tie, which is why it was known as 'Sunday Best'. While the rest were outside chanting 'Thatcher out', Tony sat with the miners and families supping pints of Brains (it's a beer). He felt miserable when the strike ended; the miners returned to work defeated and fragmented until the coal industry closed down. After a rather deflated journey back to London, with a few toilet stops for Tony, Redgrave and her SWP colleagues agreed to meet up to decide their next solidarity meeting, after they had signed on at the benefits office. Tony Selby didn't need to sign on, he was approached to appear in an interesting new series entitled *Love Hurts*.

It was written by Laurence Marks and Maurice Gran, who had a good comedy track record including *The New Statesman Goodnight Sweetheart* and, er, *Birds of a Feather*. Rather like Bob Larbey and John Esmonde they had been friends since their schooldays, similarly writing for radio before progressing to television.

When Tony read the synopsis he was a little unsure. The basic premise of *Love Hurts* is the main character, Frank Craver, a self-made millionaire former plumber and city wheeler dealer whose best mate, Max Taplow, his oldest friend, becomes his driver. Tony's initial reaction was that it seemed to have a similar storyline to *On the Up* but it became more interesting for him when he found the main love interest, Tessa Piggott, was to be played by Zoë Wanamaker.

Wanamaker's character had left her high-flying City career after being dumped by her ex-boss and lover. She took over as the head of a charity run by her best friend and confidante, Rabbi Diane Warburg, with Jane Lapotaire in the role. Derek Webster went through the part and offer with Tony, telling him,

'Basically it's good money, at least a couple of years' work.'

The producers wanted two mainstream stars to buttress the series and an acting stalwart. Zoe Wanamaker and Jane Lapotaire were the stars, Tony was the stalwart. Tony asked who would be playing the main character, Frank Carver. Derek coughed slightly, 'Er, Adam Faith.' Tony did a silent 'fucking hell'.

The casting of Adam Faith was perhaps unusual. Although he had acted in a few roles over the years, he was essentially a former pop singer and then the manager of Roger Daltrey after he had left The Who. Faith was a wheeler and dealer, and when Tony met up with Marks and Gran they explained they had Faith in mind because they were both fans of Budgie, the role that Faith had played in the 1970's.

When *Love Hurts* finally started, Tony and Faith got along well, but he noticed that Faith had a pronounced limp. Faith told him that he had been involved in a car crash a few years back and medics had put him back together with metal pins and braces. Tony made a note not to stand near him going through airports or any strong magnets.

Faith was also one of the first people to have a GSM mobile phone, but the big problem for the rest was that he was always on the damn thing: in between takes, on breaks, during meals and in the hotel bar. He told the crew that the phone could hold 100 numbers, all of which he seemed to contact during a day, and it finally got to the point he went missing or was late for scenes. The others finally had enough and one of the assistants confiscated it.

Love Hurt was a success, getting good ratings and a new series to come.

Meanwhile, he had become friends again with

Bob Larbey who in turn was back with John Esmonde. They had just written a new series, *Mulberry*, in which Selby would be partnering an old friend of his, Karl Howman. They had worked together on *Get Some In!* and met each other socially.

Karl was to play a mysterious stranger, Mulberry, who turns up at the home of Miss Farnaby, a cantankerous old bat played by Geraldine McEwan. Mulberry was an apprentice of the 'Grim Reaper', Miss Farnaby was his first assignment. Mulberry becomes her housekeeper while Tony was Bert, the odd job man; they all thought the series odd anyway. Mulberry was not a very good 'Grim Reaper', certainly not as good as his dad, but his mum was Springtime and he had inherited more of her genes so in effect, he is sentimental with a love of life which rather cancelled his raison d'être. Howman thought the writers had nicked the storyline of Hades and Persephone from Greek mythology with both parents trying to influence their son, one into killing the old crone and one into allowing her to live.

The two friends enjoyed the trips down to Dorset even though they felt that the story line was disappearing up its own arse. They managed to complete two series with another in the pipeline. Tony then went straight into the second series of *Love Hurts*, some of which was to be filmed in Russia which was to be a first for most of the cast and crew. Russia was by then changing rapidly; the old Soviet Union was dismantling but stories were still circulating about how grey and sinister Moscow could be and how awful the food was. Tony was surprised when they arrived, as the stores and buildings were displaying garish advertisements for Hershey's chocolate, Panasonic Electronic goods or Opel Cars although the products were not necessarily for the population as a whole, mainly for the emerging oligarchs and their cohorts. Tony thought if Sam was alive he would have been dumbfounded. The food was still vile though; in the hotel on the first morning for breakfast they had a choice of beetroot, boiled eggs and very stale bread, but fortunately, the production team hired a local caterer who managed to procure some more edible feasts which meant they could all avoid the first McDonald's restaurant that had just opened.

The storyline is that Carver is setting up a freezer plant in St Petersburg with a local beauty who is assisting him in the project. Tessa arrives to help him with the project and discovers the liaison, which was interesting because Adam Faith was already having a liaison with a local blonde beauty he had met in the hotel when they had arrived. He was also fortunate to discover the hotel had GSM reception.

The work schedule was heavy though. They had very short-term visas and location permissions and really did not have time to see much of Moscow. The cast returned home after a few days but with some caviar and vodka bought on the cheap and some colourful Russian dolls.

The end of *Love Hurts* left the show open ended but there had been no decision of a third series. Tony, with nothing on the horizon, was suddenly asked to be a guest on *Pebble Mill*, a lunchtime magazine programme. Judi Spiers, the main presenter, took him through some questions about his career and past roles when, out of the blue, she asked if he was looking forward to the new series of *Love Hurts* to which he replied, 'That's odd, I didn't know there was one!'

He found out from Spiers that her researchers had discovered from the production company that the new series was to start later that year. It did.

Unfortunately, or perhaps not, a third series of *Mulberry* was not taken up so nobody, not Tony, Howman nor probably the writers, would know the ending. Maybe others were thankful.

Tony completed the third series of *Love Hurts* and it went well, and again the ending was fairly open but most felt it had probably run its course. After the last shoot, Tony was determined to get Adam Faith to pay for a round of drinks. For a man who was vertically challenged, his short arms should have reached his pockets but they were very long indeed. He asked Faith to meet him in the bar for a farewell drink, and arrived a little late to find the former pop star nursing a glass of white wine, so he said,

'Hello mate, I'd love a beer.'

Faith bought him one.

Suddenly, the rest of the crew arrived, Selby had tipped them off about his ruse,

'Good timing everyone, Adam is in the chair.'

Tony later learned that Faith had billed the production company for his bar bill then claimed it was expenses on a tax return.

Faith, as well as being a car crash victim, also had a history of heart problems, and once told Tony,

'Ere, Tone, if you ever get a pain in your chest don't fuck about, go straight to casualty and get yourself an angiogram.'

Tony promised he would remember that advice, then didn't for a while at least.

The rest of the 1990s was good fun in terms of of work, he started a series of *The Detectives* with Jasper Carrott and Robert Powell and along with having a few guest TV roles he was then offered a part in the Regent's Park Open Air Theatre production of *Paint Your Wagon*, playing Ben Rumson.

The show had not been performed in London since 1953 so many people associated it with the film with Lee Marvin, rather than Loewe and Lerners stage version.

When he met up with the show's director, Ian Talbot, they discussed how they would interpret the standout song 'Wand'rin Star.' Talbot called Marvin's version a seismic rumble. The song was pivotal, as much as 'If I Were a Rich Man' is to *Fiddler on the Roof*. They decided on a light baritone. They also thought that Talbot had a lot more to think about, an open-air theatre production susceptible to London's variable weather, then recreating a crummy, indeed squalid, run-down town in the beautiful setting of Regent's Park.

The story itself is remarkably squalid: a gold-mining town inhabited by hundreds of men without female company who quite frankly all want to have it away with Ben Rumson's little girl, Jennifer, who for some reason is happily washing the skidmarks from a Mormon bloke's underwear who just happens to be passing by and then sells one of his wives to Ben in exchange for Jennifer whose true love is a Mexican who lives several miles from Regent's Park, probably Isleworth or somewhere near Heathrow.

The group of actors were committed, however, to reflecting the show's dreams of achievement, aspirations, finding in each character goodness and soul rather than the greed and avarice of the gold prospectors. In reality of course, to achieve anything like that within the confines of a small stage area rather than a huge theatre or widescreen required several clever manoeuvres for Talbot, he did so brilliantly.

Talbot had to reduce the big orchestrated arrangements for a much smaller group of musicians who in turn had to adjust to the more momentous numbers such as 'They Call the Wind Maria', or when there was a mini gale blowing

'they call the fucking wind gonorrhoea'.

The musical director Catherine Jayes was fairly lenient with them.

Overall the reviews were favourable except for the *Financial Times*, which was not necessarily on the productions regular newspaper delivery.

Later that year Tony Selby was nominated for a Laurence Olivier Award for best supporting performance in a musical but lost out to Clive Rowe. It was rather unfortunate considering his large body of work as it was the only time he was nominated for an award. After Regents Park, musicals became a bit of a curse. One website erroneously credited Tony as having made appearances in over 100 different plays at the Royal National Theatre, something he would have really wished. In fact he had only been on stage at the Royal National once, or once and a bit.

His debut was in a production of Bertolt Brecht's play, *Mother Courage*, in which an impressive Diana Rigg played the lead. The play opened in late November and continued over the Christmas period. He and Rigg told everyone they were in pantomime in *Mother Goose*.

They had to look at the play with a degree of levity, David Hare had worked hard at rejigging what many considered a difficult, even boring work, into a much clearer, more easily understood version which helped the cast considerably, including two younger actors, Leslie Sharp and Martin Freeman. It helped that the *Observer*'s critic reviewed the play, 'A highly polished production, bursting with intelligence.'

Tony Selby's next engagement with the National Theatre was a complete disaster, not for the production but for him personally. Trevor Nunn had cast him to play Andrew Carnes in *Oklahoma* with Maureen Lipman as Aunt Ella and Hugh Jackman as Curly McLain. The rehearsals were progressing well until the dance captain decided to make some adjustments to the movement. Susan Stroment, the choreographer, was not on the stage and it was probable that her assistant was a little distracted when he asked Tony to step forward a little just as another cast member was making a spectacular leap straight into him.

Tony broke two ribs and was out of the production; he was compensated but was depressed and distressed about missing out on what became a great critical success. His Royal National Theatre record, to set things straight, was one and a bit.

After his ribs knitted back together, Tony was offered some voiceover work. He was hurrying to catch a bus to Dean Street when he felt a sharp pain in his chest and his ears popped while his heart began pounding away like a Japanese Taiko drum beat. He felt short of breath and quite panicky. He arrived at the studio a little calmer and finished the voiceover quickly and then remembered the words of experience from Adam Faith. When he arrived at the hospital they immediately attached him to an electrocardiograph.

He was booked in for an angiogram after which he found himself wearing a hospital gown lying on a medical bed in the Trendelenburg position. The doctors stuck a long, thin tube into his groin and then up towards his heart, and he was eventually seen by cardiologist Rodney Foal. Foal told him he had some good news for him, then some bad; the patient went straight for the bad news. He was told that the coronary arteries were blocked, and a heart bypass operation was needed urgently. Tony tensed as he listened, then he asked how long the procedure would take. Foal explained that it was difficult to be precise, surgeons could only be sure about how many coronary arteries were bypassed during the surgery itself. In other words, a double bypass would mean two arteries are bypassed and then so on. He also explained that the operation would involve taking a saphenous vein from his leg, which was fine by him because he didn't know he had one.

The operation was to take place in three days, and when Tony was leaving Foal's office he asked him,

'By the way, what's the good news?'

'Oh, yes. One of the nurses is a great fan of yours, could you give her a signed photo?'

The operation was carried out at St Mary's Hospital in Paddington and when he eventually came round the surgeon who had carried out the procedure, Rex Stanbridge, went to see him. Tony asked how the bypass had gone.

'It was more than one bypass.'

'What, two?'

'No'

'Three?,'

The surgeon held up his hand.

'You had a quintuple bypass, we all managed to get some overtime.'

While Tony was pleased for the medical team to have a few pounds extra at the end of the month, he really felt awful. He was drained, drugged and exhausted so went back to sleep. A few days later he began to feel a little stronger then noticed as well as his leg being bandaged, so was his left arm. He was told they had run out of saphenous vein so they had nicked some more from his arm. Things seemed to be going well when he suddenly had a relapse, which he had been warned could happen, as there was always a chance of complications after such a major operation. In his case, it was around the sternum which had been cracked open to get at his heart. It was called a non-union of the sternum which means in layman's terms a sternum devascularisation risk. Tony also had abnormal blood pressure, irregular heart rhythms and was under critical care. Nurses were assigned to his bedside 24 hours a day, one of them possibly clutching a signed photo.

Tony slowly started to recover and after a few weeks he was allowed home with a bag containing an enormous amount of medication including heart-specific, penicillin, aspirin and painkillers. He met up with Rodney Foal for his first post-operation consultation, and the specialist was more than pleased with the way his recovery was progressing but gave him strict instructions to take things easy.

He returned to work, gently with a few voiceovers, then remarkably it was suddenly another New Year's Eve, and everyone thought the world was going to explode because of the millennium bug. The Selbys toasted in the new year with friends, and 2000 started with everything still functioning in the world, except perhaps at the Millennium Dome. There were no aircraft or computer crashes and all was well in the work, or so he thought.

28
ZOMBIES AND HOSPITAL FOOD

When the Selbys woke up on the new millennium morning – though it was probably more like lunchtime – they took a peek through the curtains to make sure the millennium bug hadn't taken everyone by surprise and crept in later.
Hyde Park was still there being cleared of revellers and detritus, while the nuns in the convent were confirming that God had looked after them.

Her Majesty Queen Elizabeth II and Philip, the Duke of Edinburgh, were perhaps less than happy about their night out with the Blairs and other politicians, then someone had nicked a Picasso from the Ashmolean Museum. It wasn't Johnny Wade because he had been with the Selbys the night before. Then Cherie Blair was nicked for not having a valid train ticket, her excuse being she only had Portuguese money on her at the time and her credit card transaction would not process, so there was at least some proof that the bug might have affected some computer functions, albeit retrospectively.

Realistically, Tony had slowed down considerably after the operation but he was upping his time in the swimming pool most days, showing off his scars and his reduced-veined arm and leg. He stopped smoking after over 50 years and his diet improved, no more English breakfasts or chips. He returned to work firstly on the detective series *Burnside* and then various interesting but very weird jobs. *Dream Team* was one of Sky's first drama productions, and it had been going for a while when he first joined the cast. It was about a fictional football team but the plots were getting very silly indeed: one of the players was shot by a sniper, then a supporter was brought on from the crowd to play in a game. Tony did point out that he would have been ineligible to play, but no one was really concerned. It became even more ludicrous when the goalkeeper held the whole squad hostage with a gun until the police arrived and shot him.

Tony's own participation in football was a lot less harrowing. He had not played for a long time but he was a regular visitor to Loftus Road where Gina's PR firm had a contract with Guinness who at that time had a sponsorship deal with Queens Park Rangers. He was asked to present the man of the match award a few times without getting shot or kidnapped!

Tony was also no longer performing at the jazz venues, some of the Tones had passed away or retired but he still visited the Bull's Head and went over to Ronnie Scott's when he could. Tony remembered the last time he saw Ronnie Scott before he ascended into the great Jazz Couriers in the sky, Scott had made one of his best one liners.

'I love this place, it's just like home, it's filthy, smells and full of people I don't know.'

Tony had changed his agent again prior to his heart operation and was being represented by Barry Burnett, whose main client was Barbara Windsor. The weird job run continued when Burnett secured him a part in another Sky series entitled *Is Harry on the Boat?*. The title was Cockney rhyming slang, Harry Monk on the boat race. The series was all about a group of tour reps in Ibiza who looked after holiday-makers in the 18-to-30 age range. The main content was sex, drugs then more sex, which might help to explain the title, monk meaning spunk and boat race meaning face.

Although the series was set in Ibiza, it was actually filmed around Malaga. Tony's part was not particularly demanding, but it did give him the opportunity to work with some younger actors just starting their careers, Danny Dyer, Will Mellor, Davinia Taylor and Ralf Little among them. Dyer and Little were particularly respectful; they were both fans of Tony's work and asked for advice or help with the scripts. On their time off Tony was pleased to see the cast putting in lots of extracurricular research.

He stayed on for a few days after filming; the sun and sea gave him a boost and he really felt quite fit. On his return shortly afterwards he and Gina met up for dinner with his old friend Johnny Wade and his partner Julie Samuel. Johnny had more or less retired, he was still acting in a sitcom or two, but Julie – besides managing some pop groups – also ran a theatre production company. Over dinner Julie told them she had met up with David Martin, a successful songwriter among whose hits included 'Can't Smile Without You.' They had come up with the concept of a musical based on *Great Expectations* and wanted Tony to play the part of the mysterious convict and benefactor, Magwitch.

He met up with them again at Martin's studio and went through the book and score. It looked really promising and he agreed to play Magwitch. Rehearsals began for a showcase to be held at the Shaw Theatre.

Things were going well as rehearsal times increased, then suddenly Tony started to feel a little feeble, so he decided to have a check-up. He returned to St Mary's Hospital where they kept him in overnight, and after scans and heart tests he was told he had suffered a mini stroke. He could not continue in *Great Expectations* and had to cancel some other work that he had in pipeline. Tony was worried. He was making regular visits to see Rodney Foal, yet despite the stroke, the feedback from his check-ups was very positive. Foal encouraged him to keep up his regular swimming and walking schedule while Gina offered further encouragement and helped him with the disciplined exercise regime.

Now into his seventies, Tony Selby needed a good rational think about how things could progress, he had to be philosophical; he was no longer a stalwart but a veteran stalwart who would be playing old man roles. One of his friends had been sent to an audition to play a corpse but didn't get the job! As his generation of actors grew older they all agreed part of their pension plan was a role in one of the soaps.

The problem was that most of them had been in the major ones, some in three or four different roles over the years. Soaps were also becoming more vibrant, aimed at a younger audience, particularly the newer ones such as *Hollyoaks*.

Tony went over to see Barry Burnett to talk things over. Barry himself was now getting on a bit and slowing down, while he was there, Barbara Windsor arrived and they finished up having a coffee together. Windsor was just winding up her career in *EastEnders*, and her career generally. She had just been diagnosed with Alzheimer's although it had not started its awful debilitating progress. She told Tony she didn't really have the stamina any more to do anything, never mind the demands of a soap schedule, and suggested for him to be a little wary about any future roles, particularly long-term ones. With her characteristic laugh she advised,

'Well, longer than six months Tone!'

Burnett agreed that Tony was now looking at a sort of semi-retirement and available for more gentle, avuncular roles.

Tony and Gina were also determined to keep going with a sensible lifestyle, but they both had an extensive network of family and close friends. It was once said kindly of the Selbys that they would attend the opening of an envelope, but they really did have a vibrant and varied social life. They loved the theatre, which was no surprise – they were always at the Royal National or the Tricycle and the fringe theatres like the Orange Tree or the Battersea Arts Centre – and they were also members of the Tate galleries and the Royal Academy.

Gina's love of the art world meant she would always find the more obscure shows to visit, although they didn't find the proverbial opening of an envelope because Yoko Ono had not done a London exhibition for many years!

They were also visiting Tony's sister Kathy regularly. Jimmy had died a few years back and Kathy had not been taking good care of herself, finding solace in alcohol over the years then personal neglect; her customary energy and humour eroded rapidly.

Kathy had been such a big part of Tony's life since they were children: the original song and dance partnership, the records, her support and encouragement when he started his younger career, her steadfastness when their parents separated, later years the roast duck special Sunday lunches and the sing-songs. On their last visit, Kathy was desperately ill and was taken to hospital and was not expected to survive the night; she didn't. After her funeral, Tony was the last of the Tachbrook gang.

In a more positive and effervescent turn of events, Tony had a call from Barry Burnett: would he be interested in a role with his old mate Dennis Waterman? A few years before, Waterman had been performing as Doolittle in Trevor Nunn's National Theatre production of *My Fair Lady* (a role perhaps Tony was born to play). It had transferred from the National to the Drury Lane Theatre and Waterman invited Tony and Gina to the show and then for them to meet up in his dressing room after the performance, which they did. Typically, Dennis had converted the space into a pub called the Waterman's Arms complete with optics and a barrel of draft beer and a dartboard.

Waterman then told Tony that when the musical finished, he would be working on a series about an ex-copper who together with other ex-coppers would be looking to solve cold-case crimes, he was going to push for Selby for one of the main roles. It didn't work out; the producers went for James Bolam.

It would have been just the role Selby needed to catch up with some old mates, not a huge cheque but a welcome one and a little confidence boost to show that maybe there really was life in the old dog yet. The dog barked for a while but not too loudly, then it became more subdued when he was approached to play a part in what would prove to be his last film as it would indeed be for most of the actors in it.

The film was called *Cockneys vs Zombies*, not just Cockneys but old ones. Tony looked at the script, but while it was utter garbage, he liked the fee and the other old farts he would be working with. The zombie genre as they were perhaps saying in cinematic circles was gaining legions of fans worldwide, but not necessarily those over fifty years of age. There were Zombie enthusiasts everywhere mainly young people dragging their feet along the street, covered in blood and slime, pasty faced, rather like a Young Conservatives Summer Ball.

Tony's role was as one of a group of old fogies living in a retirement home in the East End of London who were about to be evicted by a property company who had bought out the owners.

The producers described the film as a mad rollicking mash-up of *Shaun of the Dead* and *Lock, Stock and Two Smoking Barrels*. The opening scene starts with two builders unearthing an old burial site, two zombies who had been fasting for a couple of centuries had their first meal since George III was on the throne, then an epidemic of zombies take over the East End, all mumbling,

'Cor, 'ows yer father?'

'Bite off yer Bristols luv?'

'Snap yer knees orf Mother Brown?'

Two young men whose grandad is one of the retirement home residents are unaware of the undead schlepping all around. They have just robbed a bank to pay for the freehold of the building and secure the future of younger old farts to come in later. Tony played Daryl, a former thug who spent most of his time selling his prescribed drugs to the local kids. Dudley Sutton and Richard Briers were all contemporary pensioners, in character and in real life, then they were joined by the legendary Honor Blackman – Cathy Gale from *The Avengers* and Pussy Galore of Bond legend, the sex interest, or as she commented,

'Rather dry in so many ways.'

Selby had worked with Briers in *The Good Life* a few decades before. Briers was not in the best of health – he used to smoke more cigarettes in a year than the population of Shanghai – and had by then had an advanced case of emphysema and used a zimmer frame for most of the shoot.

Tony loved Dudley Sutton, who had been expelled from RADA for bad behaviour, which considering the other RADAS around at that time was quite an achievement. Despite the stigma, he had forged a prolific if often eccentric career.

The other old codger was played by an actor called Alan Ford, who none of the others had met or heard of before. He played the grandad of the two lads and their mates who had robbed the bank of £2m, which would have been fine if they were not being pursued by thousands of zombies who eventually surround the old codgers' home. Tony thought that while Ford was not necessarily gifted with social skills, he was certainly suited to his hard man role. He had been cast in several hard man gangster roles and was good at it in a predictable way.

In between breaks from firing machine guns and chopping heads off the zombies, Honor Blackman would pour them tea and explain the concept of zombie culture, if that is not a contradiction in terms, telling them it went back to voodoo in the Caribbean and earlier in Africa. They were all indeed impressed by her knowledge, then the team went back on set to shoot and decapitate the hordes of corporeal revenants before escaping in a boat but without Harry Monk.

Tony really enjoyed the film, but all of the older actors were completely knackered at the completion. They had coughed and spluttered after each action sequence. At the wrap party, Honor said to Tony,

'Do you know darling, that's it, I think we are all absolutely fucked.'

Briers must have agreed, as he sadly went to the good afterlife just after the film was complete. The film did not garner any good reviews or cinema release, then went straight to DVD. Shocker!

Cockneys vs Zombies was to be Tony's last film, and shortly after completion he began to feel unwell again. He was experiencing excruciating stomach pain and volatile bowel movements, but despite that, instead of having it checked out, he and Gina went on holiday to Turkey. His condition worsened and he went straight to hospital when they returned. He went back to St Mary's where by now he had a permanent parking space, and after blood tests the doctor had a chat about when the condition had started and about his bowel habits. Tony told him he had a bowel movement around half past seven each morning, and the doctor thought that was encouraging until he explained that it wasn't really, he didn't wake up until eight. The doctor roared with laughter then arranged for a CT scan and then a colonoscopy. It proved less funny when it revealed he had a large cancerous tumour.

The medics told him it could be removed but he would need to be fitted with a colostomy bag, then there could possibly be a reversal operation where the surgeons would re-connect the bowel. He came out of surgery the day before Gina's birthday. He told the family that he had given her a new record by The Police,

it was called,

'Dont Stand So Colostomy'

Tony was desperate to get some form of normality to his life as soon as possible but had to cope with using the bag and the other unsavoury functions which he, and particularly Gina, had to cope with. He began to start walking again and consuming a very strict prescribed diet.

When he returned to the hospital the doctors were minded to prescribe a form of chemotherapy but decided the best way forward would be the reversal procedure which proved to be the best option, however, it woud mean a considerable period of recovery.

Tony had now come through considerable and complicated heart surgery, a mini stroke and bowel cancer, so it was probably a good time to consider retirement from his profession after nearly eight decades.

Medical care was now a priority, he then received another kick up the arse when his heart function began misbehaving again. The surgeons this time decided he needed a TAVI, which he thought was a Lebanese sweet, but it was his aortic valve that had decided to narrow which required another operation called Transcatheter Aortic Valve Implementation. After that operation, Tony started to show signs of confusion and forgetfulness and was also a little short-tempered. Gina originally thought it was probably the result of the tremendous amount of surgery and medication over the past couple of years. Some days he was fine, then others unpredictable and angry. Incredibly he had another offer of work, this time in another soap filmed in Birmingham. It seemed that the writers and director specifically wanted him for the role. He travelled up to the second city alone, gave a faultless performance and returned home to London and Gina.

Rather appropriately, his last role was in *Doctors*.

EPILOGUE

On Tony's 80th birthday he was surrounded by his family and friends. Two years earlier he had been diagnosed with vascular dementia, meaning he had a memory impairment which affected his hippocampus, which both Sam Selby and Stanley Holloway would have been distressed to hear!

The party was fun and loud; he sat quietly on his favourite chair, his eyes twinkling, his guests mingled and chatted, someone brought a guitar and accompanied Tony through a medley of songs which he sang with gusto and was word-perfect. Many of the guests had a few tears.

Tony now had to use a wheelchair but still liked to visit Hyde Park, or his front garden as he called it, going around the Serpentine then stopping off at the gallery for a coffee and a snack.

Such was the insidious and progressive nature of his condition that he soon became housebound. Gina, who had been selfless and exceptional in helping him to overcome his various setbacks, eventually had to engage full time carers to help her through. Tony was in and out of hospital on a regular basis until one final blow, when he became infected with Covid-19.

Tony Selby died on 5 September 2021, aged 83.

His legacy? Anthony, Tony, Tone, Selby had been a very good actor, he did not reach the fame or notoriety of his contemporaries, Albert Finney, Peter O'Toole or Richard Harris, but he was respected and admired particularly by O'Toole for his ability to quickly understand a role, then his disciplined approach to work.

He was also respected by producers, directors and writers. Tony's early work with Ken Loach and Tony Garnett was a testimony of their faith in his acting ability. His fellow actors loved him for his sensitivity and humour: he could play for laughs, deliver pathos and gravitas and reach the high notes with an orchestra.

Tony's versatility gave him the opportunity for many different roles.

Sir Henry Irving would have been proud of the boy from Pimlico.

Alan Rowlands
Twickenham 2024

ACKNOWLEDGEMENTS

As history joggers, online information was accessed from Google, BBC Genome, IMDB and Wikipedia. Books consulted were *Reminder* by Dennis Waterman (Random House) and *The Day the Music Died* by Tony Garnett (Constable).

ABOUT THE AUTHOR

Alan Rowlands was born in Barton-on-Irwell, Manchester. He has been a contributor to numerous football magazines and radio broadcasts, and has worked with the Footballers' Football Channel.

He is the author of the acclaimed book *Trautmann – The Biography*, the story of which was made into the film *The Keeper*.

He has appeared in the documentary *Hello Fritz, Fancy a Cup of Tea?*, and has also worked with ESPN.